Christina Rossetti

Ad Feminam: Women and Literature
Edited by Sandra M. Gilbert

Lunacy of Light: Emily Dickinson and a
Female Tradition of Metaphor
By Wendy Barker

Christina Rossetti
The Poetry of Endurance

Dolores Rosenblum

Southern Illinois University Press
Carbondale and Edwardsville

For David Ryback, Becky Rosenblum, and Isaac Rosenblum
and in memory of Mary Ryback

Copyright © 1986 by the Board of Trustees,
Southern Illinois University

All rights reserved

Printed in the United States of America

Designed by Joyce Kachergis

Library of Congress Cataloging-in-Publication Data

Rosenblum, Dolores.
    Christina Rossetti : the poetry of endurance.
    (Ad Feminam)
    Bibliography: p.
    Includes index.
    1. Rossetti, Christina Georgina, 1830–94—
Criticism and interpretation. 2. Women in literature.
3. Sex role in literature. 4. Feminism and literature.
I. Title.
PR5238.R67   1986   821'.8   85-30739
ISBN 0-8093-1269-7

Contents

Ad Feminam: Women and Literature

Ad Hominem: to the man; appealing to personal interests, prejudices, or emotions rather than to reason; *an argument ad hominem.*
—*American Heritage Dictionary*

Until quite recently, much literary criticism, like most humanistic studies, has been in some sense constituted out of arguments *ad hominem.* Not only have examinations of literary history tended to address themselves "to the man"—that is, to the identity of what was presumed to be the *man* of letters who created our culture's monuments of unaging intellect—but many aesthetic analyses and evaluations have consciously or unconsciously appealed to the "personal interests, prejudices, or emotions" of male critics and readers. As the title of this series is meant to indicate, the intellectual project called "feminist criticism" has sought to counter the limitations of *ad hominem* thinking about literature by asking a series of questions addressed *ad feminam:* "to the woman"—to the woman as both writer and reader of texts.

First, and most crucially, feminist critics ask What is the relationship between gender and genre, between sexuality and textuality? But in meditating on these issues they raise a number of more specific questions. Does a woman of letters have a literature—a language, a history, a tradition—of her own? Have conventional methods of canon-formation tended to exclude or marginalize female achievements? More generally, do men and women have different modes of literary representation, different definitions of literary production? Do such differences mean that distinctive male- (or female-) authored images of women (or men), as well as distinctly male and female genres, are part of our intellectual heritage? Perhaps most important, are literary differences between men and women essential or accidental, biologically determined or culturally constructed?

Feminist critics have addressed themselves to these problems with increasing sophistication during the last two decades, as they sought to revise, or at times replace, *ad hominem* arguments with *ad feminam* speculations. Whether explicating individual texts, studying the *oeuvre* of a single author, examining the permutations of a major theme, or charting the contours of a tradition, these theorists and scholars have consistently sought to define literary manifestations of difference and to understand the dynamics that have shaped the accomplishments of literary women.

As a consequence of such work, feminist critics, often employing new modes of analysis, have begun to uncover a neglected female tradition along with a heretofore hidden history of the literary dialogue between men and women. This series is dedicated to publishing books that will use innovative as well as traditional interpretive methods in order to help readers of both sexes achieve a better understanding of that hidden history, a clearer consciousness of that neglected but powerful tradition. Reason tells us, after all, that if, transcending prejudice and special pleading, we speak to, and focus on, the woman as well as the man—if we think *ad feminam* as well as *ad hominem*—we will have a better chance of understanding what constitutes the human.

Sandra M. Gilbert

Foreword
Dorothy Mermin

The major tradition of women's poetry in English begins for all practical purposes in the nineteenth century. Women had written good and very interesting poetry before—the Matchless Orinda and Aphra Behn in England, for instance, and Anne Bradstreet in America, as well as others who are even less well known to the academic curriculum—and the literary scene of the earlier nineteenth century was marked by the emergence of such prolific and popular poetesses (that is the right word for them) as Felicia Hemans and Letitia Landon (L. E. L.). Women poets seem always to have read other women poets, and the influence of minor precursors should not be underestimated. But apart from the lone figure of Sappho offering ambiguous encouragement from the dim mythic background in a language that almost no Englishwoman could read, the women who first wrote poetry that claims a major place in English literature and established the female tradition that has come to rich fruition in this century were Elizabeth Barrett Browning, born in 1806, and in the next generation Christina Rossetti and Emily Dickinson, both born in 1830.

The poetry of these women was read and written about in their century and ours, and yet much of it has been almost invisible to criticism for a very long time: sometimes because it was hidden, more often because it could not be seen. Dickinson allowed only a handful of her poems to go out into the world during her lifetime, and her caution was justified both by the incomprehension that those poems met and by the way her works were tidied up after she died and made into simple, conventional, harmless things, their subversive violence tamed to suit the world of gift books for girls or drugstore greeting cards. Her poems were not published as she wrote them until 1955. The poetry of Emily Brontë, the other important female poet of the time, who was six years younger than Barrett Browning, not only was unread in the nineteenth century but receives remarkably little attention even now. Barrett Browning and Rossetti were widely published and well reviewed in their lifetimes, but praise was almost always diluted by condescension; their works were segregated into the women's corner and poems which did not fit conventional notions of women's work and nature were vilified, ignored, or misread. Serious study of Dickinson began in the mid-twentieth century, but neither modernism nor New Criticism could do much with Barrett Browning and Rossetti, and despite some solid studies in the past three decades they have just begun to be reinterpreted and revalued by critics who are trying first of all to find the appropriate terms in which to read them. There has not even been a serious edition of Barrett Browning's works since the turn of the century; Rossetti's, however, are at last being properly edited.

Rossetti's poetry has been in some ways the least vulnerable to the tides of critical fashion and neglect. In the nineteenth century she was regarded as Barrett Browning's only rival for the position of leading woman poet in English—she was considered less dangerous, less daring, and more accomplished in her craft—and at the worst of times she never quite lost her standing as a distinguished minor poet or her (usually rather small, however) place in anthologies. The purity of her music and her ability to express (or appear to express) in their purest plangency the feelings that we expect to find in amatory or religious lyrics have warded off both hostility and scrutiny—her poems seemed to belong to a special, if limited, class of female sensitivity and musicality, artful in a way but nonetheless spontaneous and sincere, not to be taken too seriously, of course, but excellent stuff in its kind. Poems that did not fit this pattern were either ignored or, like *Goblin Market*, read in the guise of simple moral tales for children under which their author with wise artfulness presented them. It was for her songs of frustrated affection and her moral and devotional works—the poems that are apparently the most conventional, least subversive, most expressive (at any rate on the surface) of the feelings that were thought to be appropriate for Victorian women, and least distinctively female in method—that Rossetti was most admired in her day. And it is her love lyrics—the poems that express (again, on the surface at least) the feelings that young women are expected to have about men—that have been most widely read and anthologized in this century. Her poetry has been valued, that is, for its affirmations of female piety, passivity, and submission, while her strength and independence of thought and art have hardly been recognized at all.

Feminist criticism has set itself the task of learning how to read women writers, which in the first instance has meant a radical rereading of women's lives. The domestication of women's writing by nineteenth-century readers depended on an ideal notion of women's characters and circumstances; but of course most individuals, and especially the unusual ones who become major poets, find some difficulty in being precisely what society expects, and recent scholarship has demonstrated the particular stresses and discomforts of conforming to Victorian ideals of womanhood—ideals both embodied and parodied by Emily Dickinson, both accepted and resisted by Elizabeth Barrett Browning and Christina Rossetti. The new biographical attentiveness builds, however, on a long-standing critical tradition that has first to be displaced or undone, since the lives of women poets have always received relatively much more attention than the lives of men (with the exception, perhaps, of those like Byron and Swinburne whose sexuality is flamboyant and masculinity not above suspicion). Criticism of their works has been cursed by a biographical curiosity that more often than not has pushed the works themselves out of view, and until very recently real or phantom lovers have not only haunted but often relentlessly dominated critical discussion. The presumed sexual frustration of unmarried women, for instance, has been solemnly regarded as both essential and debilitating to the tone and content of their verse, although nothing similar is ever said about the male poets of their time—Tennyson, for instance, who was unmarried and very likely celibate until the age of forty. Feminist criticism is just now learning how to go beyond this sort of thing and to discover the various subtle ways in which the circumstances of women's lives affected not just their themes but, more interestingly, their basic poetic attitudes and strategies.

Christina Rossetti's place in respect to male poetry (that is, to almost all the poetry she knew) was enacted with unusual clarity in her life. Unlike Barrett Browning, Brontë, and Dickinson, she lived when she was a young woman in close proximity to a group of artists, so that her isolation cannot be ascribed simply to the unavailability of like-minded companions for a brilliant young poet. Not only did she, like the other three women poets, have a brother whose education, desires, and opportunities were fostered while hers were stinted and repressed; Dante Gabriel Rossetti was an immensely talented and dramatically original poet and painter, the center of a lively artistic world. Both her brothers were members of the Pre-Raphaelite Brotherhood, a group of young men, mostly painters, who came together in 1848, when she was seventeen, and drifted apart a few years later. They very much enjoyed the fun of being a secret society, shocking the public with unconventional paintings and developing theories that were soon to make a great impression on British art. Her brother William Michael fondly recalled many years later:

> We were really like brothers, continually together, and confiding to one another all experiences bearing upon questions of art and literature, and many affecting us as individuals. We dropped using the term "Esquire" on letters, and substituted "P.R.B.".... We had our thoughts, our unrestrained converse, our studies, aspirations, efforts, and actual doings. ... Those were the days of youth; and each man in the company, even if he did not project great things of his own, revelled in poetry or sunned himself in art.

This was the kind of shared artistic life and ambition, jokingly codified in mock-serious ritual and secrecy, that nourished the lives of young male poets in the nineteenth century—but not the women's. Christina Rossetti gave the brotherhood poems for their magazine, the *Germ*; she achieved the first literary success of the movement with the publication of *Goblin Market* in 1862; she was, said Swinburne, "the Jael who led their host to victory"; but she was not one of them. Dante Gabriel proposed her as an honorary member, but the brethren would admit no woman, and he withdrew the suggestion:

When I proposed that my sister should join, I never meant that she should attend the meetings, to which I know it would be impossible to persuade her, as it would bring her to a pitch of nervousness. . . . I merely intended that she could entrust her productions to my reading; but must give up the idea, as I find she objects to this also, under the impression that it would seem like display, I believe,—a sort of thing she abhors.

Exclusion is explained away, in an entirely typical interpretation of Rossetti's life, as withdrawal.

And if she was excluded from the brotherhood, she was not part of what might be called the Pre-Raphaelite Sisterhood either. She was the model for the first painting that Dante Gabriel exhibited with the initials P.R.B., *The Girlhood of Mary Virgin*, and during the period of the brotherhood's existence she was engaged to one of the brothers, the painter James Collinson (the engagement ended about the same time that the brotherhood did); but she could not ally herself (although she could sympathize) with the women, mostly lower class, poorly educated, and of doubtful virtue, whom Dante Gabriel and his friends were soon to take as models, mistresses, and wives. Not only was she too unlike them in education, habits of life, and social and religious values; more important, to be one of them would have meant not being one of the artists. The serious, devout female world of her mother and sister in which she mostly lived, however, contained no artists but herself, and her short novel *Maude* makes it clear that wanting to be a poet felt to her like a betrayal and disruption of that world. Thematically, much of her poetry deals with the sense of having no place to live and write from: belonging nowhere, neither with the artists nor with the women. In deeper and more complicated ways, her poems attempt to deal with the fact that a woman artist finds herself to be both artist and model, both subject and object, both male and female—both, or perhaps neither, and therefore nothing at all.

Her doubled identification—with the poet who sings, and the women (usually dead) that he sings about—appears with delicate and ambiguous poignancy in one of her earliest and most famous lyrics:

> When I am dead, my dearest,
>   Sing no sad songs for me;
> Plant thou no roses at my head,

> Nor shady cypress tree:
> Be the green grass above me
>   With showers and dewdrops wet;
> And if thou wilt, remember,
> And if thou wilt, forget.
>
> I shall not see the shadows,
>   I shall not feel the rain;
> I shall not hear the nightingale
>   Sing on, as if in pain:
> And dreaming through the twilight
>   That doth not rise nor set,
> Haply I may remember,
> And haply may forget.

The trappings of sweet poetic sorrow hardly matter to the dead woman for and about whom male poets have written, as she points out even while, in effect, singing both the male lover's song and the woman's response. Her poems, like this one, often describe double or transitional states of being and are typically built on paradox, including the central paradox of her career: that she became famous for speaking of silence and oblivion. In what is apparently the last poem she ever wrote her voice comes, with brilliantly elaborate and living artistry, as if from the grave:

> Sleeping at last, the trouble and tumult over,
>   Sleeping at last, the struggle and horror past,
> Cold and white, out of sight of friend and of lover,
>   Sleeping at last.
>
> No more a tired heart downcast or overcast,
> No more pangs that wring or shifting fears that hover,
> Sleeping at last in a dreamless sleep locked fast.
>
> Fast asleep. Singing birds in their leafy cover
>   Cannot wake her, nor shake her the gusty blast.
> Under the purple thyme and the purple clover
>   Sleeping at last.

She had many notes, but this is her most characteristic one, articulating with a rich and haunting music not only an emotion and an attitude but, more generally, the situation in which she found herself as a woman writing in the male poetic tradition. It is this situation that Dolores Rosenblum's study discovers and defines.

Preface

This book is a textual analysis of Christina Rossetti's poetry, and an apologia. I aim to rescue Rossetti from such critical commonplaces as the claims that hers is a limited, "one-note" talent, that her devotional poetry is impelled by religious hysteria, that her themes of loss reflect unrequited love. My textual reading depends on a reading of her life that is both broader and more limited than has been attempted by previous critics. I believe that she was a deliberate poet, in her poetry making stylized gestures of renunciation that both protest her predicament and articulate an adaptive myth of self. Crucial to this myth is a woman's experience of herself as "other," specifically as an object that is *seen*. I argue that Christina Rossetti mythologizes this experience in the images and in the formal design of her poetry, creating the figure of the enduring stone-woman who is both spectacle and witness. In doing so, she draws on the particular life situation of posing as a model, primarily for her brother Dante Gabriel Rossetti, and of observing Dante Gabriel's conversion of his models into art. This relatively localized but yet pervasive situation becomes a paradigm for the poet's experience of herself, and for her transmutation of that experience into art. Throughout, I raise issues concerning the source of Rossetti's poetic language. I suggest that rather than overtly challenge the patriarchal literary tradition which makes it difficult for the female poet to assert the lyric "I," Rossetti deploys strategies used by other women poets of the nineteenth century. These strategies engage patriarchal tradition in ways that make it usable for female experience, and that provide a critique of male objectification of women in art.

The Introduction traces the sources of Rossetti's female aesthetic and suggests how the aesthetic of renunciation generates the poetry of endurance. Chapter 1, "An Exemplary Life," provides a biographical summary which aims to show how Rossetti chose to make an example out of her life, and how the exemplary mode characterizes her poetry. Chapter 2, "*Goblin Market*: Dearth and Sufficiency," contains an analysis of *Goblin Market*, followed by a series of exegetical commentary relating certain key passages in *Goblin Market* to the devotional poems. With the religious poetry as context, *Goblin Market*'s particular variation on the garden myth becomes clear, as does its dependence on the religious and literary metaphor of oral appetite (hunger and fullness, dearth and plenitude) for the soul's infinite desire for God, and for the female self's alienation from knowledge and power. Chapter 3, "The Female Pose: Model and Artist: Spectacle and Witness," examines Rossetti's central metaphor, the visual metaphor for possession and knowledge, and her chief persona, the fixed watcher who sees herself being seen. As well as conveying alienation, "watching" makes possible an inward pose that strengthens and liberates the lyric speaker and subject. Chapter 4, "Self-Sisters: The Rhetorical Crisis," explores the company of female personae who surround the watcher. Mothers, daughters, brides, nuns, corpses and ghosts, they are all the sister-descendants of the prototypical Laura and Lizzie of *Goblin Market*. By giving these women voices, Rossetti often mounts a criticism of language conventions that mark the fall of the female self into "natural" womanhood. By exhorting, lamenting, and commemorating these figures, Rossetti creates a sisterhood of self, even if the sisters cannot directly acknowledge each other. Chapter 5, "From Renunciation to Valediction: The Ongoing Crisis," takes up the figure of the nun in her passion of renunciation and moves through the *Monna Innominata* sonnet sequence to a consideration of how Rossetti turns renunciation into valediction, the poetic mode that allows the lyric speaker to relinquish the self who both suffers and turns to stone. In the Conclusion I suggest how Rossetti's poetic strategies are similar to, and different from, those of her contemporary, Algernon Swinburne, how her aesthetic does and does not extend to her female contemporaries, and how her aesthetic is brought to its logical conclusion in the poetry of Alice Meynell.

Because it was not yet available, I was unable to use Rebecca Crump's definitive *Complete Poems of Christina Rossetti: A Variorum Edition*, the second volume of which appeared this year. Instead, it was necessary for me to rely on the William Michael Rossetti edition of 1904. Along with the page numbers of that edition, my citations include dates that will help the reader to locate poems in the Crump edition.

I wish to express my gratitude to the Andrew Mellon Foundation for the Post-Doctoral Fellowship, whith allowed me to get my work underway. Among those who helped me bring the manuscript to completion, I wish to thank especially Linda David, Sandra Gilbert, Donald Gray, Susan Gubar, Michael Rosenblum, and Anthony Schipps. I owe special thanks also to Pat Johnson and Jennifer Beam, who typed the manuscript, and to Andrew McGarrell, who translated the Italian poems.

Christina Rossetti

Introduction

Some months after Christina Rossetti's death in 1894, Andrew Lang wrote: "There can be little doubt that we are now deprived of the greatest English poet of her sex, which is made to inspire poetry rather than to create it."[1] Writing twenty years later, in 1915, Arthur Waugh summed up her achievement as typifying the best work of a woman, because "it accepts the burden of womanhood," and succeeds where Elizabeth Barrett Browning's poetry fails, "because she is trying to make a woman's voice thunder like a man's."[2] Although other male critics in the decades between Rossetti's death and the centenary of her birth may have made gender-free evaluations of Rossetti's work, Lang's and Waugh's views offer pointed commentary on the "burden of womanhood" which has weighed so heavily on most woman poets. For Christina Rossetti, this means that at worst, the fact that she wrote poetry at all was considered a transgression of cultural rules for gender-appropriate behavior, while at best, the quality of her work was almost always assessed in terms of gender. Her poetry was judged womanly in its avoidance of the hysterical prolixity of other woman writers, womanly in its concern with love and religion, and womanly in its limited range.

While no longer faced with the task of clearing away this kind of sexist debris, the feminist critic who aims to see Rossetti at least as clearly as Virginia Woolf saw her cannot—unlike Woolf—afford to ignore gender,[3] for the devaluation of female writing cannot be redressed without taking into account the inescapable conditions of its creation. This devaluation shapes the careers of Rossetti's female predecessors, contemporaries, and descendants, those poets, for instance, housed in two equal but separate volumes of Alfred Miles'

1907 edition, *The Poets and the Poetry of the Nineteenth Century*: Baillie to Ingelow (vol. 8) and Rossetti to Tynan (vol. 9).

In the face of this literary segregation, the task of the feminist critic is to locate the woman poet in relation to the masculine tradition while neither assimilating her work to male models nor degendering what may be a distinctly female tradition. This introduction will define Rossetti's uniqueness as a woman poet by exploring the preconditions for her work—not so much the larger cultural milieu as the play of various traditions in the gendering of literary works—and by sketching in a female poetic tradition. In response to certain gender constraints, Rossetti, like other woman poets, mimics male reification of women in poetry in order to parody and transcend it, but she also participates in a general feminization of poetry in the nineteenth century. Finally she deals with the problem of poetic creativity by a collectivization of voice involving both the female sentimental tradition and the religious tradition in English poetry.

Comparing Rossetti to the most famous British women poets of her time, Elizabeth Barrett Browning and Emily Brontë, we find that like Barrett Browning and unlike Brontë, her output is very large, some one thousand poems, most of which were published in her lifetime. Unlike Barrett Browning, whose talent is largely narrative and discursive, Rossetti and Brontë are both lyric poets. But while Brontë invents a fictive Byronic world as context for her lyric outbursts and Barrett Browning confronts the "real" world, her aim being to write an epic for her age, Rossetti deliberately sets her sights on another world, the reverse image of this one, where death equals life, "all" replaces "nothing," and insatiable desire is endlessly fulfilled. All three poets engage the Romantic literary tradition, each struggling to assert a voice that is characteristically denied them as female symbols within that tradition.

Less overtly engaged with monolithic Romantic precursors than either Brontë or Barrett Browning, Rossetti does not seem as concerned with originality: her poems are deliberately echoic, reflecting each other and other texts. To the extent that she is chameleonlike in appropriating established forms and themes, the issue of female creativity in her case is an especially vexed one. Ostensibly varied in subject matter and verse forms, Rossetti's output is repetitive at deeper levels of theme and structure. Her work is characterized by repeated themes of loss and deprivation; by a limited lexicon tending toward strong binary oppositions—between life and death, fullness and depletion, now and then, earth and heaven—by the extensive use of scripture, both in allusions and in phrases quoted verbatim; by echoing repetitions within poems and from poem to poem; and, with a few notable exceptions, by little metaphorical complexity or variety of imagery. The themes and the limpidity of style she shares with some of the Pre-Raphaelite brothers, but in comparison with the often feverish colorations and dark turns of her brother's poetry, for instance, her style seems transparent, both "pure" and "pallid." This austerity can look like creative impoverishment, an inability or an unwillingness to confront issues of poetic creativity. At times her poetry seems both overly self-effacing and overly self-concerned, and the lyric voice asserts a self that is largely passive and reactive.

This "problem" with Rossetti's poetry has certain obvious sources in the particular circumstances of its composition and publication. Like her transatlantic contemporary, Emily Dickinson, Rossetti was extremely reticent, both in her presentation of self and in her habits of composition. Most of our information about her habits comes from her brother William, the family historian. He tells us, for instance, that she usually wrote standing up at the corner of a washstand in her small bedroom at the back of their house.[4] Here we see the author as amateur, diffident and casual in her habits of composition. And yet, like Emily Dickinson's hand-sewn packets, these scribblings were meticulously transcribed in notebooks, and—here the similarity with Dickinson ends—handed around the family. In general, William represents her as an "inspired" writer; apparently she wrote what came into her head, when it did, and wrote easily, without much need for revision. He also remarks on her unwillingness to submit her work for editing: "and still had she, in the course of her work, invited any hint, counsel, or cooperation."[5] And although Dante Gabriel would attempt to edit her work in progress at certain stages, Rossetti did not usually allow her intentions to be interfered with. In her social role as author William tells us that she was extremely self-effacing, never presuming on her poetic reputation: "in a roomful of mediocrities she consented to seem the most mediocre."[6] The impression that emerges from these accounts is of a writer who, without being artificial, carefully and deliberately chooses self-protective poses. Rossetti herself confirms this impression, telling Katherine Hinkson in later years how she was "tenacious of [her] obscurity."[7] The tenacity and obscurity recall Emily Dickinson—Dickinson the bride of death in white, Rossetti the mourner and vigil keeper in black.

Tenacious of her obscurity, she was "acquainted," as William tells us, with Coventry Patmore, Sir Eduard Burne-Jones, William Morris, Robert Browning, Jean Ingelow, and Dora Greenwell, among others, and must have been at least an observer at the literary evenings sponsored by the Rossetti household. Excluded officially from the Pre-Raphaelite Brotherhood, unofficially she was one of its earliest successes, the "Jael" who would lead them on to victory, as Swinburne put it. Further, she was fully aware of writing for an audience: not only for a literary elite but also for the wider bourgeois audience who read journals like the *Atheneum* and the various Literary Annuals, and ultimately for the least literary of her followers, the readership of the Society for Promoting Christian Knowledge, which published her devotional prose and much of her devotional poetry.

In all, Rossetti wrote one thousand and fifty-seven poems, including the longer narratives, *Goblin Market, Repining, The Prince's Progress, The Iniquity of the Fathers upon the Children, Three Nuns, The Lowest Room,* and *From House to Home*; two sonnet sequences, *Monna Innominata* and *Later Life*; some one hundred forty poems for children; twenty-three Italian poems under the title *Il Rossegiar dell'Oriente*; and sixty-one poems unpublished at the time of William's edition of the collected works. This edition was arranged by William according to "type," secular or religious, and roughly chronologically. Originally, her work was issued in three volumes by Macmillan, *"Goblin Market" and Other Poems* (1862), *"The Prince's Progress" and Other Poems* (1866), and *"A Pageant" and Other Poems* (1881). These volumes were reissued in a collected form, with the inclusion of some new poems. Routledge published her children's volume, *Sing-Song,* in 1872, and the Society for Promoting Christian Knowledge issued *Verses* in 1893, a collection from three works in prose and verse, *Time Flies, Seek and Find*, and *The Face of The Deep*. In *New Poems* (1896), William collected and edited previously published work along with some previously unpublished poems, which he lists in his preface to the collected works, first published by Macmillan in 1904.

What we learn from this enumeration, and from Rossetti's correspondence with her publishers, is that she was a deliberate and persevering artist, aware of her readers, and that she was quite prolific. On the one hand, then, we have the picture of the inspired, retiring writer who could never write to demand; on the other, there is the evidence, in print, that Rossetti assiduously cultivated a public literary career. In addition, there are complaints that she wrote too much, that she was not scrupulous enough in exercising her aesthetic judgment, and driven by extraliterary concerns. These contradictions, the critics' feeling of unease in the face of the whole corpus, can best be understood if we take a look at Rossetti's situation as a woman poet in nineteenth-century England, and a woman poet with an accessible, if devalued, female tradition.

Sandra Gilbert has shown us how women poets have found it difficult, if not impossible, to assert the lyric "I" that speaks for the male poet, especially in the Romantic tradition. She finds Rossetti and Barrett Browning both motivated by what she calls the "aesthetic of renunciation."[8] I would argue that this aesthetic generates—or adequately describes—what I shall call the "poetry of endurance." The poet of endurance—in most, but not all, cases identical with the female sentimental poet—does not invent new worlds of vision but, rather, complains repetitively and endlessly, reinscribing the same discontinuities over and over again. But although her themes and forms may be as codified as any Petrarchan sonneteer's, her repetitions and stylizations are survival strategies. Her writing is almost literally inexhaustible, her unadmitted aim being to outlast her inscription as a symbol of both her mutability and her inorganic permanence within the masculine tradition.

The nineteenth-century woman poet's endurance—both her persistence in writing poems and her creation of female figures who enact endurance or female voices which assert endurance—can also be seen as constituting what French feminist critic Luce Irigaray has called "mimetism."⁹ Her experience of her own otherness in the seeming inescapability of her social and literary roles as Nature, as door and gateway, as mandala or mirror for the male poet's visionary quest, confers upon her a special immobility. Often transfixed in art, the female as symbolic figure or icon has the power to transfix.¹⁰ Through the poetry of endurance, nineteenth-century women poets, Rossetti and Barrett Browning and many of their contemporaries and predecessors, capitalize on this reification of women in art. They "freeze," taking on the protective coloration of their surroundings, mimicking male visions of women. In doing so, they create art that is revisionary in much the same way as that of Pierre Menard, Borges' often cited hero, who reinvents *Don Quixote* by rewriting it word for word. They take on their assigned poses in order to show and hide; they write *exemplary* poetry in which, more often than not, a female figure displays, or a female voice announces, both alienation and the means by which she overcomes alienation. In Rossetti's work the most exemplary figure is the "witness." The witness who endures suffering is both a "gazing-stock," an alienated spectacle, and God's "all-amazing monument," the conversion of that spectacle into an astonishing vision. In Rossetti's lexicon endurance comes to mean not only bearing the "burden of womanhood" but outlasting mortal change.

What lies behind these kinds of reversals is the Christian tradition, of course, which transforms the stoicism of Ecclesiastes in the face of last things into consolation for the oppressed. The Christian stoic endures until the end, when the last shall be first, and all losses made good. That these themes and attitudes should be foregrounded in the Victorian period, in a time of radical material and ideological change, that is, is not surprising. What is less apparent is the way in which Christian ideology becomes feminized. Myra Jehlen has suggested that the interior life, the conscious self, in the English novel is female, and that a female inability to act is a basic structure of the novel. I would argue that this feminization is even more apparent in the poetry of the Victorian period.¹¹ But the emotional life which is figured as female and passive is not as a result muted; rather it is always at a pitch of extremity, always on the borders of dissolution, always at the penultimate moment. There is always much to be borne in isolation, and to will to endure through suffering is at times the only action possible. Paralysis of the will, often symbolized by the dreamy immobilization of a "repining" female figure, can be countered by allowing that figure the will to endure, to undergo what has been foreordained.

For the nineteenth-century women poets, however, the passively enduring female figure is not simply a symbol for shared inner experience. It also stands for female experience within patriarchal culture. What the male poet may feel and symbolize as female in his art, the female poet enacts—or endures—both in life and in art. In the culture she suffers various kinds of confinement and immobiliza- tion. In the patriarchal literary tradition she is most often the station- ary—or fleeting—symbol of the poet's quest for self-transcendence. Whether she is the cold, or merely absent, beloved or the terrifying Medusa or the wanly repining virgin, she is a mirror for the poet, a gateway to life and death, heaven and hell, changeful and unchang- ing, always something that means, never the originator of meaning. The female poet, weighed down by these monolithic projections, vampirized by *his* dream, enters into the spirit of his project, and at once displays her vulnerability and masks her power. This power derives at least in part from her adaptation to the literary roles available to her, using the symbolic female for her own meanings. Yes, she says, this is how women live and write, masking secret lives, turning a face to the world, turning their "true" faces to the wall, like L. E. L. in Rossetti's tribute to her. Highly visible, even exhibi- tionistic, the female subject remains elusive in the sense that de Beauvoir means: "They did invent her. But she exists also apart from their inventiveness."[12] In its elusiveness, its duplicity, even, the poetry of endurance is the poetry of the divided self with a vengeance, another mimicry of the male tradition, from Byronic alienation to Tennysonian dialogue of selves. For the nineteenth- century woman poet, the poetry of endurance becomes a strategy for dealing with the most extreme kind of self-division, a division forced, rather than reinforced, by a particular symbolic system and by particular cultural attitudes. Yet in composing her masks and poses of destitution endured by a terrible effort of will, Rossetti is not only drawing from and reacting to the patriarchal literary establishment. The female sentimental tradition, a tradition which is from the male perspective "weak," becomes for the female poet the source of essential strengths. In this tradition Rossetti discovers various models for the poetry of endurance.

Ever elusive in its strategies, the female tradition takes power from female powerlessness. Out of their powerlessness to act—or to assert the creative "I"—the women poets of the nineteenth century take on the powers of exhibitionistic and masochistic self-display. Frozen in the pose of death, for instance, they will strike the viewer, compelling a kind of recognition they did not receive in life: they are types of the Lady of Shalott who floats down in funeral display to Camelot, at last eliciting recognition of her powers as artifact, if not as creative artist. If in their culture they are, as de Beauvoir tells us, object and other, they will refine upon that objectification, stylizing it to the point of parodic subversion—again mimetism. Suffering and the pose of death serve primarily, then, as strategies to distinguish female projects from male projects. These literary strategies become a way of asserting a self which can compete in intensity and purposiveness with the masculine creative "I" that depends so heavily on female reification and female silence. The end of suffering—death—is no longer, as in the male tradition, a symbol for the unattainability of the quest object, but rather for female immunity from reification as quest object. The female figure becomes elusive and unapproachable on her own terms, an awe-inspiring representative of Persephone's kingdom, a Medusa who might turn the gazer to stone, a witness not so much to the impossibility of male enterprises as to the power of female endurance. The stony corpse or the mortuary statue speaks without words, in her meaning-laden silence parodying female reification in life and art. As an iconic version of the live woman, who often endures a living death, the dead woman not only compels pity but also mocks the lover who scorns or fails to understand, who always comes "too late," as in Rossetti's *The Prince's Progress*. She proves that a picture, or a tableau, or an effigy, or a dumb show, is worth a thousand words, especially when the subject has been denied speech and the capacity to originate meaning.

Yet it would be misleading to claim that the women poets of

the nineteenth century lack words. A torrent pours forth: voices lamenting, regretting, recriminating, beseeching, renouncing, hoping against hope—all declaring their wounded helplessness and perseverance in their suffering. At the very least, Rossetti does not lack examples of women writing poetry, and writing and publishing prolifically. Although Barrett Browning complains of the lack of poetic "grandmothers,"[13] there are a host of godmothers and maiden aunts, women whose writing is greatly uneven, no better—but no worse—than that of numerous minor male poets of the period. Foremost among these women poets are Felicia Hemans (1793–1835) and Letitia Elizabeth Landon (1802–38), known as L. E. L., both of whom achieved great popular success in their day.[14]

Hemans and L. E. L. share an approach to poetry that is more visibly the legacy of such contemporaries of Rossetti's as Jean Ingelow and Adelaide Procter, than of Rossetti herself. Unlike Rossetti, these poets are in no way constrained in their choice of poetic subject. Undaunted by their lack of experience, they canvass geography and history for their heroic types. Hemans' *Records of Women: With Other Poems* (1828) is a clearly defined female project, containing titles such as "Properzia Rossi" and "The American Forest-Girl," while the added *Miscellaneous Pieces* is a catchall, ranging from "The Homes of England" to "Tasso and his Sister" to "The Landing of the Pilgrim Fathers in New England." Although her work includes "Songs of the Affections," Hemans is not especially interested in exploring psychological states; rather she focuses on types and typifying occasions; the virtue and pathos of "The Indian Maid" and "The Italian Girl's Hymn to the Virgin Day," or the revelatory moments of the "Bridal Day" and "The Storm Painter in His Dungeon," for instance. Although this kind of focus marks Hemans as an eighteenth-century poet, her preoccupation with the exemplary—and highly visible—heroine suggests that Hemans is more interested in establishing her own models than in following an eighteenth-century aesthetic. Her "affections" are both exemplary and relentless, even tasteless—in a word, excessive. It has been suggested that all the nineteenth-century women poets—Hemans, Landon, Greenwell, Procter, Webster, Ingelow, as well as Brontë, Barrett Browning, and even the austere Rossetti—share a kind of flamboyance.[15] Constrained by conventional morality, they are un-restrained when it comes to criteria of "taste" in literature. But while, on the one hand, their poetry exhibits bathos and melodrama along with didacticism, on the other, their claim to make everything exemplary goes beyond didactic and figural readings of experience. In the guise of creating exemplary types they display their shameless stylistic excesses, but in the bravura performances of their heroines they show how when very little is possible almost anything is allow-able. The poet of endurance, treating herself and all women as sensational exemplars, writes exemplary poems that go a little too far. The poems themselves are like the women themselves, witness-ing the excesses of female suffering, which always goes too far.

This tendency to yoke excess and exemplariness may be character-istic of a female aesthetic which includes displays not only of suffer-ing but also of fantastic power, as when Landon's Erinna receives the laurel from Olympus and "thousands" acclaim her. Not only is suffering a component of Landon's aesthetic, but it is also something that she calls "enthusiasm," something that looks or sounds like excess: again the poet goes too far, in her raptures, in her passionate displays. In their sensationalism the female poets of the nineteenth century are the counterpart of one line of female novelists, the writers of Gothic romance and domestic melodrama. But this paral-lel underscores the difference between Rossetti and the others. Put simply, Hemans' poetry and the line that runs through Barrett Browning and Ingelow have little to do with the concerns of lyric poetry. Although Hemans writes of the "affections," her assertions are distanced, predictable generalizations, often in the form of odes or occasional pieces. While Rossetti is above all a poet of the feeling life which has its purely internal occasions, in their extremity her lyrics are in their own way as flamboyant as Hemans' narratives and odes. Looked at from this perspective, Rossetti's ascesis takes on a double and parodic aspect. On the one hand, the poet renounces and negates everything, vanity of vanities; on the other, she makes everything out of herself and her sorrow in a transfixing display of her stigmata.

In her preemptive sorrow and in her lyric "enthusiasm," Rossetti owes more to Landon than to Hemans. Although it is difficult to make a case for direct influence, we know that Rossetti was much taken in early life with the works of the eighteenth-century librettist, Metastasio.[16] The operatic mode is at work in such poems of Rossetti's as "The Convent Threshold," a lurid recitative in which the speaker details the pain of renunciation, or "Look on This Picture and on This," which presents a florid triangle of passion. Much of Landon's poetry has this operatic character. But what attracted Rossetti to Landon was, as much as the operatic stance, the aesthetic that was enunciated in her poetry and played out in her life. This aesthetic, as delivered by the Improvisatrice, the woman troubador, is as applicable to Rossetti's work as to Landon's:

> I touch'd my lute,—it would not waken,
> Save to old songs of sorrowing—
> Of hope betrayed—of hearts forsaken—
> Each lay of lighter feeling slept,
> I sang, but as I sang, I wept.[17]

Even more explicit is L. E. L.'s tribute to Felicia Hemans:

> Yet what is mind in women, but revealing
> In sweet clear light the hidden world below,
> . . . .
> The fable of Prometheus and the vulture
> Reveals the poet's and the woman's art.[18]

This aesthetic of sorrow and renunciation can be related to the persistent situation of giving up what you cannot will or act to have anyway. Some women poets seem to have been undaunted by their lack of "experience," like Ingelow and Hemans, and plunged into enthusiastic imaginings; others, like Rossetti and to a certain extent Landon, wrote precisely about their lack of experience, about the feeling life that goes on independent of experience or becomes experience itself: desire that feeds on loss and absence.

To an extent "experience" was inaccessible to Landon and Rossetti because, like most nineteenth-century women, they were randomly educated. But while Rossetti only implicitly rejects female education, Landon is frank in her scorn. Of a visit to her uncle's family she writes: "When I first arrived, Julia and Isabel began to cross-question me. 'Can you play?' 'No.'—'Can you draw?' 'No.'

'Can you speak Italian?' 'No.' At last they came down to 'Can you read and write?' Here I was able to answer, to their great relief, 'Yes, a little.' I believe Julia, in the first warmth of cousinly affection, was going to offer to teach me the alphabet.'[19] Landon in life, then, takes up the stance of Rossetti's prose heroine, Maude, who disdains similar female accomplishments, and cultivates her wits and her writing. The difference between the fictional Maude, as well as her creator, and Landon, is that Landon was literally forced to live by her wits and her writing. At an early age Landon was discovered by the editor of the *Literary Gazette*, in which she established her reputation. She became a regular contributor to the Annuals, from which she derived considerable sums, and can be said to be one of the first women to make her living by writing poetry.

What made Landon such a popular success was probably her talent for flamboyant narrative, her predilection for sentimentalized Byronic themes, and, above all, her acceptance of the female mask, her eagerness to convey that she was not intruding upon masculine territory. The heroine of *The Improvisatrice*, for instance, is a female artist who attains to great art, with the qualification that "her power was but a woman's power." Among her sketches of unhappy loves, the poet's aesthetic of renunciation surfaces in her depiction of Sappho's sorrow, which leads her to renounce her art. Although Landon's depiction can be seen as deriving from pastoral models, it is significant that Sappho, the model for all women poets, is the exemplary model of renunciation. Sappho's poetic gesture can be considered as a model for Rossetti's gestures of renunciation as in the figure of the singer who weeps while she sings ("Song," "She sat and sang alway") and in the figure who hangs her "silenced harp" upon "a weeping willow" in a lake ("Mirage"). In Rossetti's unpublished poems about Sappho, especially in "What Sappho Would Have Said Had Her Leap Cured Instead of Killing Her," Sappho is made to return to a pastoral setting in order for the poet to invoke the landscape of destitution—a blighted rose, a cankered lily, a violet withering in spring—and to work out the terms of an aesthetic of deprivation, or pain that fills the lack: "O come again, thou pain divine-/ Fill me and make me wholly thine."[20] Another model for this aesthetic is Landon's Erinna, an ancient poet who describes her role as a female artist thus: "I do not hope for a sunshine burst of flame, / My lyre asks but a wreath of fragile flowers" (p. 43). As a female artist, her special province is "Sketches . . . from that most passionate page / A woman's heart . . ." (p. 45). Finally, in her tribute to Hemans cited above, Landon defines woman's special province as the "hidden world below."

While the sufferings of Prometheus suggest the Christian myth of suffering for its own sake which, as I shall point out later, serves as an important link between women's poetry and religious poetry in general, the "hidden world below" suggests Persephone's descent into the underworld, in order to pass again into the upper world renewed. This myth has important implications for a female aesthetic. Renunciation of fulfillment instigates a fruitful renewal, made possible by an acknowledgment of truths of female nature that would shatter—or at least be at odds with—the masks of decorum; for most of these nineteenth-century women poets have something to say about the woman within or below, and the suffering that the containment of this self entails. Even the pious Dora Greenwell wishes to be "anywhere, anywhere out of this room,"[21] while Elizabeth Barrett Browning represents herself as trapped behind a smiling mask ("The Mask") and Rossetti claims that stiff and masklike Englishwomen are "deep at their deepest, strong and free."[22]

But the reality of women's inner lives has low status as a writer's qualifications. In a Hogarth Press book of 1928, entitled *L. E. L.: A Mystery of the Thirties,* D. E. Enfield complains that L. E. L. had no "contact with life" and in her work "no sign of progress or maturity."[23] He stresses the Byronic influences on her work, while denigrating her skills: "Her phantasies remain to the end those of a schoolgirl, and her disillusionment Byronic."[24] The charge that the poet lacks experience in "life" and does not "mature" in her writing could be laid against Rossetti herself. Women poets, deprived of "life" or, rather, excluded from certain topics in literature, retreat to a narrower ground, to their inner life, their own "sensuality," as Enfield puts it. What is important here is the denigration of the female Byronic mode, the denigration of what is essentially a literary, intertextual process, by an appeal to "life," implicitly life in the world as it is lived by men. But despite his low opinion of L. E. L. as a poet, Enfield remains fascinated by her as a female enigma and attempts a kind of psychobiography. He probes the source of her talent and finds it hopelessly contaminated by female—that is, debased—Romanticism: "By what magic does a little girl who has never been a hundred miles from her birthplace, create from the blank words of the printed page the splendors of the East and the glories of a dozen past and varied ages? Hundreds of them do it. Little girls who pass our doors every morning on their way to school, with ugly hats and not very good manners. May life be kinder to them than it was to Laetitia Landon."[25]

More than her art, what interests Enfield—and other generations of women poets—is the pattern of her life. Enright sees Landon's literary aspirations as compensation for her lack of physical beauty: "When in the dawn of self-consciousness she had seen that she was considered plain and unattractive, her intense vitality had been driven inwards from the real world to one of her own creation."[26] What would seem to be normal literary practice is seen here as a typical female "lack," an unhealthy turning away from her life as a woman. But what is remarkable about L. E. L.'s life is that it did involve great risk taking. After her father's death in 1822, when she was twenty, she lived alone in a single room in a boardinghouse run by a genteel spinster. By writing and publishing prolifically, including three three-volume novels, she was able to support her mother and contribute to her brother's support. From 1830 onward, however, she paid the penalty for her independence: anonymous enemies accused her of immoral conduct in general, and of an affair with a married man. This, along with what her biographer describes as her "intimate" manner with the literary men of her acquaintance, apparently ruined her reputation. In her late thirties, however, she maneuvered a Captain Maclean, a saturnine colonial officer, into marriage. She sailed with him for the Gold Coast, to his "Cape Castle," where she lived miserably, greatly isolated and overburdened with housekeeping duties. She died suddenly in 1838 of what was reported to be an overdose of prussic acid which she had been using for hysterical "spasms." Despite the indications of suicide, there were suspicions among her friends in England that Maclean himself had poisoned her.

Rossetti, in her tribute to L. E. L., says nothing about L. E. L.'s life as a poet, except, perhaps, by way of treating her as one of her own poetic creations or by assimilating her life to Rossetti's own conception of the role of the poet. In the poem she is represented as a woman whose show of gaiety "downstairs," presumably at a social gathering, perhaps one of L. E. L.'s literary salons, belies her inner life: "But in my solitary room above / I turn my face in silence to the wall; / My heart is breaking for a little love" (*Works*, p. 344). Arming herself for this world, flinging herself once more into the mating game, she decks herself out in mating plumage, parodying the stirrings of springtime nature from which she is as totally excluded as from the social world of pairing couples. Like so many of Rossetti's female figures, she is defined in terms of absolute lack and absolute fulfillment. Rossetti predicts for her, as for her other heroines and personae, a total reversal whereby she will be translated into another realm, and another realm of language, where "death" is "life" and the void will be annulled, for "love" will "fill" her and make her "fat." For Rossetti, then, L. E. L.'s life is significant as a figure for pure desire. In Rossetti's poem about Sappho, pain would fill the lack, and generate poetry. In her poem about L. E. L., the aesthetic of renunciation is fulfilled, and L. E. L. is ready for a more apocalyptic transformation in which the unfulfilled desire that generates poems is no longer necessary, and the "all" rushes in to fill the void. Rossetti thus makes L. E. L. her paradigmatic woman and poet.

What links Rossetti, then, to Hemans and L. E. L., and to contemporaneous women poets, is the aesthetic of renunciation and the poetry of endurance. Nineteenth-century women poets typically write about unfulfilled desire, loss, and self-sacrifice, and also about the persistence of desire through pain, sometimes leading to an apocalyptic reversal of terms, life into death and death into life. What they also share is their "flamboyance": their female figures, no matter how mobile and intense their inner life, are always illustrations, exemplary models caught forever in some penultimate moment, their faces turned either toward the wall or toward the transcendent light. In Rossetti, this exemplariness is strongly linked to the visual metaphor that pervades the Western literary tradition, and becomes a way of registering both female alienation and female transcendence, often signaled by the same figures and the same structures of imagery. The woman in her pose resists her exposure by enduring and remaining ultimately opaque, by turning to stone while maintaining her secret inner life. Occasionally she may vanish from sight altogether, blazing into an apocalyptic spectacle that blinds the gazer.

As well as the specific heritage of the female sentimental poets, Rossetti's art is fueled by two broader formal traditions: the secular love lyric, which includes the song and the complaint, and the devotional lyric, which includes the prayer and the hymn. While the religious tradition is not a female tradition, it contributes strongly to Rossetti's female myth in that it provides her with a collective voice for what may come to appear an excessively personal and hermetic experience; religious poetry enlarges the context of the female experience of renunciation and endurance and offers legitimized ways of imagining recognition and restitution. The particular religious tradition that Rossetti adopts is not so much the visionary and idiosyncratic (the line from Donne to Blake) as sacramental and communal. This poetry is properly called "devotional" because it is a linguistic performance that enacts belief. Rossetti's forebears in this tradition are the eighteenth-century hymnists and poets, such as Isaac Watts and Reginald Heber, who also influence such contemporaries of Rossetti's as Sarah Flower Adams and Isaac Williams.

Reginald Heber (1783–1826), for instance, "the bishop of Calcutta" and author of "Hark! the Herald Angels Sing," has a vision as austere and apocalyptic as Rossetti's: "The world is grown old, and trembles for fear; / For sorrows abound, and judgment is near."[27] Laconically, Hebert writes of nature's *memento mori*: "Death rides on every passing breeze, / He lurks in every flower; / Each season has its own disease, / Its peril every hour."[28] This kind of simplicity of diction and containment of form, as well as the "morbid" theme, is found time and time again in Rossetti's poetry. Taking this tradition as ground, she writes poems about death, the vanity of human wishes, and the reality of the life to come:

> The youngest blossoms die.
> They die and fall and nourish the rich earth
> From which they lately had their birth;

Sweet life, but sweeter death that passeth by
And is as though it had not been:—
All colours turn to green;
The bright hues vanish, and the odours fly,
The grass hath lasting worth. ("Sweet Death," *Works*, p. 116)

It is the scriptural context that gives her poetry the voice of authority, the voice of a community in which all flesh is grass, and women and men, as "souls," equal in the eyes of God. In her intense colloquies with her God there are intonations from Psalms and the Anglican liturgy, and her voice is part of a collectivity of voices, all, in a sense, raised in praise of the kingdom of death. Against the backdrop of Ecclesiastes, the fading of a woman's "bright hues" are as nothing, while in the light of the Beatitudes, female renunciation is a bold strategy.

The other tradition that feeds Rossetti's poetry, the secular line, is interbred in the seventeenth-century with the religious line: the poetry of love is shaped by a worshipful stance, and the poetry of religious devotion is fueled by the language of erotic love. While Rossetti might in a general way make the bridge between the poetry of love and the poetry of religion, she is not interested in the dynamics of metaphysical conceits. She is more interested in the highly stylized and musical forms of the cavalier lyric and the pastoral complaint. In these, poetry more closely approaches song, which calls for simplicity of diction, rhyme and repetition, short lines, metrical regularity, and a fairly narrow thematic range—all of which are characteristic of Rossetti in both her secular and devotional modes. This tradition is only a useful framing device, and it is obviously absorbed by the female sentimental poets as well. The distinction I mean to make here involves women poets, like Rossetti, in whom the lyric voice is especially strong, and for whom formal considerations seem especially important.

One such female forebear is Carolina Oliphant, Lady Nairne (1766–1845), who wrote not only the well-known and sprightly "Charlie is my Darling," but also the grimly decisive "Would be young again? / So would not I," and "What's the vain world to me?—Rest is not here."[29] What is particularly striking about Oliphant's declarations is their starkness and their control. This is the poetry of endurance being forced out at great pressure. The control is even more evident in the poetry of Caroline Southey—who nursed Robert Southey in his madness—and of whom Alfred H. Miles writes: "One can scarcely read her general poems without feeling that they came from a true, loving heart, nor peruse the poems which with an almost morbid recurrence she wrote upon the subject of death, without feeling that she had a true sense of the sublime."[30] Morbid or sublime, there is a seductive power in her "To Death" that parallels that of Rossetti's lyrics. Southey begins:

> Come not in terrors clad, to claim
>   An unresisting prey:
> Come like an evening shadow, Death!
>   So stealthily, so silently!
> And shut mine eyes, and steal my breath;
>   Then willingly—oh! willingly,
> With thee I'll go away.[31]

This dreamy courtship of oblivion appears in an early poem of Rossetti's, "Looking Forward" (1849), which echoes Southey's poem not only in its indebtedness to the Miltonic ode in its formal elements but also in its mediation between control and abandonment:

> Sleep, let me sleep, for I am sick of care;
>   Sleep, let me sleep, for my pain wearies me.
> Shut out the light; thicken the heavy air
>   With drowsy incense; let a distant stream
> Of music lull me, languid as a dream,
>   Soft as the whisper of a summer sea.   (*Works*, p. 293)

What is striking about both excerpts is not the morbidity—or sublimity—of the subject matter and tone but the degree of technical control. Neither poem is particularly personal; both exert impersonal control over themes which might appear to exemplify powerlessness and lack of control: a woman's morbid withdrawal from life, a woman's headlong emotionalism, a woman's will-less participation in the natural cycle of fruition and decay. The formalization tends to dissolve "sense," and to heighten "sensation" in an intense concentration of mood, as in these lines from Rossetti's poem: "But bring me poppies brimmed with sleepy death, / And ivy choking what it garlandeth, / And primroses that open to the moon." This is surely the Pre-Raphaelite Rossetti that Swinburne so admired, not only for her aesthetic of pain but also for her evocations of the garden of Proserpine, her incantations which suggest that, for the purposes of poetry, desire and death are the same, as we discover when we place "Looking Forward" alongside "Echo":

> Come to me in the silence of the night;
>> Come to me in the speaking silence of a dream;
> Come with soft rounded cheeks and eyes as bright
>> As sunlight on a stream;
>
> ....
>
> Yet come to me in dreams, that I may live
>> My very life again though cold in death:
> Come back to me in dreams, that I may give
>> Pulse for pulse, breath for breath:
>> Speak low, lean low,
> As long ago, my love, how long ago.   (*Works*, p. 314)

If there is a female sensibility in operation here, it is not in the nature of the theme nor in the lotus-land atmospherics but, rather, in the tension between control and abandonment—giving in, giving up— or between individuation and oceanic merging, or between formal concentration and incantatory diffusion.

The aesthetic of renunciation, then, appears first to involve poetic themes, the representation of the self as impoverished and obsessed. It also proves to operate on the level of form: denial, or the embracing of self-canceling states of being, is not so much self-denial as a poetic strategy for asserting control over diffusion, even dissolution of self. In Southey's and Rossetti's poems cited above, the speakers assert and sustain both will and desire: the self is not split, nor is it overwhelmed by external forces, as Margaret Homans suggests is the case with Emily Brontë and Dorothy Wordsworth.[32] Rather, the subject confronts and tolerates the possible dissolution of the self in a merging with death, or, as in "Echo," at the extreme edge of separation commands its fullest imaginative resources to establish a kind of eternal return: "Yet come to me in dreams that I may live / My very life again though cold in death." The dreamer fears neither separation nor invasion; the dream visitant will not take away her powers. Though rooted in particular female experience, these poems are not personal effusions, and though sharing their formal concerns with the poetry of aestheticism, they are not exercises in mood and tone coloration, involving the emptying out of meaning. Rather, they are poems about power—the power to will that which has been foreordained and to overturn that which has been enforced.

To shed further light on the sources of Rossetti's power to generate a consistent and authentic female myth involves bringing before the reader a sizable body of work which is remarkably consistent in its concerns. Justified by Rossetti's own procedure of carefully selecting and arranging her work according to nonchronological principles, and by the obvious formal and thematic recurrences which dominate her work, I have devised a synchronic model for understanding the female myth that informs her poetry. This model is fashioned as a "model," or series of "models," the exemplary female figure who, in various guises, testifies both to her alienation and to her transfiguration. While Rossetti's female myth is generated by a dialectic between renunciation and fulfillment, she achieves something like mediation in writing out of a collectivity of voices. The collective voice includes not only the language of the Christian church but also the language of an enduring female tradition which survives by mimicking and revising the language of patriarchal tradition.

1   *An Exemplary Life*

In 1849, when she was nineteen, Christina Rossetti wrote "Symbols," a poem which, underneath its prim didacticism, seems remarkably self-revealing. The poem unfolds succeeding states of expectation, disappointment, violent anger, and grotesque retribution:

> I watched a rosebud very long
>   Brought on by dew and sun and shower,
>   Waiting to see the perfect flower:
> Then, when I thought it should be strong,
>   It opened at the matin hour
> And fell at evensong.
>
> I watched a nest from day to day,
>   A green nest full of pleasant shade,
>   Wherein three speckled eggs were laid:
> But when they should have hatched in May,
>   The two old birds had grown afraid
> Or tired, and flew away.
>
> Then in my wrath I broke the bough
>   That I had tended so with care,
>   Hoping its scent should fill the air;
> I crushed the eggs, not heeding how
>   Their ancient promise had been fair:
> I would have vengeance now.
>
> But the dead branch spoke from the sod,
>   And the eggs answered me again:
>   Because we failed dost thou complain?
> Is thy wrath just? And what if God,
>   Who waiteth for thy fruits in vain,
> Should also take rod?   (*Works*, p. 116)

Ostensibly a miniature sermon in verse, "Symbols" reads like a strange ritual exorcism, performed in a child's private world. A naïve speaker links meaningless incidents—incidents that mean both nothing and the uselessness of human endeavor—in a narrative that unfolds their total signification. In this world, everything, it turns out, means, and in a terrible, monitory way. What the poem offers, then, is not so much a set of moral apothegms as a mythic formulation of childhood conflict. Looking more closely at the details of the poem, what kind of myth of childhood can the modern reader reconstruct?

The most obvious feature of this mythic childhood is that the child does not even come close to getting what she wants, and she is completely powerless. She can do nothing but watch and wait, transfixed, while a process runs its natural course. But the process is shockingly aborted: the blown rose withers unnaturally; the two old birds desert their offspring before they are hatched. Maturity seems attended by terrible perils: either a speeded-up aging leads to death, as in the case of the rose, or the maturation is aborted through a lack of nurturing, as in the case of the eggs. These unnatural natural occurrences are narrated matter-of-factly; only in the third stanza are we made aware that the watcher was not neutral, that she had reasonable expectations which were unreasonably thwarted. Her vengeful rage is shocking but not inappropriate. Not surprisingly, the criminal child is pursued by the specter of her victims. The branch and eggs that were expected to give pleasure return as ghostly voices invoking a retributive justice and enforcing passive acquiescence.

The voice throughout the poem sounds like that of a Victorian female child who has been moralizing her experience from an early age, administering her own eerie punishments. From several childhood anecdotes that Rossetti elaborated in later life, we get an idea of how the processes of repression were put into motion, how that moralizing child developed. Writing for the readers of the Society for Promoting Christian Knowledge in 1885, when she was fifty-five, Rossetti relates her childhood experiences of little horrors in nature, a Victorian garden-Gothic variation of Wordsworthian tutelage by fear. Once, like the rose in the poem, the experience is that of premature decay. On this occasion she and her sister watched a wild strawberry ripen, but "as it turned out we watched in vain: for a snail or some marauder must have forestalled us at a happy moment. One fatal day we found it half-eaten, and good for nothing."[1] Another time it is grotesque generation, life out of death. This time, returning to inspect a mouse she had buried a day or two before, she "removed the moss coverlet, and looked . . . a black insect emerged. [She] fled in horror, and for long years ensuing [she] never mentioned this ghastly adventure to anyone."[2] All this is quite vivid and familiar-sounding, unsurprising encounters between the pleasure principle and the reality principle, predictable falls from innocence. Predictable, too, is the "femaleness" of the response: a little girl's fastidiousness, a little girl's tenderness, a little girl's surprise and disgust at what seems to be the assaultive nature of reality. Since she cannot actively pursue what she wants, she thinks she may at least wait and watch for what she wants, the perfect strawberry, the full-blown rose, the hatched fledgling. What she gets, as if in punishment for the desire itself, as if thoughts were acts, is corruption, the cup of bitterness, the vanity of vanities. It is just this kind of lost innocence that pervades Rossetti's poetry: not the fall into fleshly wisdom, but a terribly premature yet somehow inevitable withering. Why is this Rossetti's version of the garden of self? What can be the failure that has disillusioned the child in "Symbols," and why are the consequences of her rage so catastrophic?

Given that the rose and the egg are archetypal symbols of female sexuality, and that in this poem they are both unfulfilled and mutilated, an orthodox Freudian reading offers one possibility for interpretation. The child in the poem seems to have made the classic discovery of female "castration"; she knows she must give up her vain hopes, but she is not reconciled. In Freud's view, the female child, subsequent to her discovery, turns in wrath on her mother, who she feels has deprived her of the phallus.[3] A more plausible, feminist view of this process is presented by Clara Thompson, who interprets the daughter's rejection of the mother as a rationally based rejection of the mother's actual cultural powerlessness ("Penis Envy in Women," *Psychoanalysis and Women*, ed. Jean B. Miller [New York: Brunner, Mazel, 1973], pp. 42–47). What the speaker of the poem recollects is possibly that moment of shocked discovery, followed by rage—masochistically turned against the self. Patient waiting and watching have been fruitless; she is outraged not only at the betrayal of her expectations but also, implicitly, at the worthlessness of her lessons in self-restraint. All at once she is transformed from the watchful "female" into the active "male" child who plunders nests and tramples roses. But this activity gets her nowhere either, of course. Even though the eggs were already aborted and the rose already mutilated, she feels like a murderer: the ghostly voices represent not only the agents but the effects of patriarchal retribution; they speak for lost selves, unrealized potential. If she is to escape with her life, she must renounce not only the "egg" and the "rose" but her anger, or at least turn it inward. If she cannot control her destiny, she can set herself the task of controlling her "self." The speaker of "Symbols" is split, then, between a self who watches, suffers, and acts and a self who frames her experience as exemplary and chides her action.

This strategy is evident in yet another moralized anecdote that shows Rossetti controlling a painful experience while revealing it. Her niece Helen Rossetti Angeli recounts how when she herself had burst out in anger as a small child, her aunt told her, as an exhortation to self-control, of her own childhood rage: on one occasion, in response to her mother's reprimand, the young Christina ripped up her own arm with a pair of scissors.[4] The experience, in the telling, like the little parables of the strawberry and the mouse, shows Rossetti constructing her personal myth. As a spinster aunt, Rossetti tells a small female child of her own rage and masochistic violence, the violence carefully moralized: the woman is exemplary, and everything that has happened to her has a lesson. As a girl of nineteen, Rossetti writes a poem that tells of frustrated desire, rage, and masochistic violence: as in the anecdote, a profound psychic experience is transformed into a cautionary tale, and the power and authenticity of the experience is preserved unmitigated.

This moralizing strategy is one aspect of the doubleness that pervades Rossetti's poetry and shapes her personal myth. Doubleness may be manifested thematically, in the oppositions between presence and absence, fulfillment and loss, joy and sorrow, life and

death; or structurally, as here, in the division between experience—
or the self who experiences—and meaning—or the self who gives
meaning. This framework of doubleness allows Rossetti not only to
moralize but to mythologize her experience for the sake of her art.
Within this context she enacts and reenacts her original "fall," the
ensuing suffering, the inevitable apotheosis. If there is no chance of
actively seizing the fruits of life, the "rose" and the "eggs," then she
will transform the deprivation and the passivity into an artistic
choice: she chooses the suffering that she did not choose; she
mythologizes her alienation.

With "Symbols" in mind as a model of Rossetti's own mythmak-
ing, I want to turn now to her personal history as recorded in diaries,
memoirs, and standard biographies, with a view to sifting out the
motifs that seem to coincide with the personal myth that emerges in
her poetry. Although a poem like "Symbols" to some extent invites a
psychoanalytic reading, there is no evidence or need for such a
reading of the life. More clearly observable are certain patterns of
family interaction and certain family ways of framing experience.
These patterns are then manifested as particular strategies in Rosset-
ti's life as a professional writer. Rossetti's poetic vision was strongly
shaped by how she was *seen*—as a woman in her family, as a woman
in her culture—and her poetic strategies can be usefully interpreted
as responses to and defenses against this "modeling" situation.
Section I will be concerned primarily with Rossetti's early life, when
the family interaction is most intense, when certain lifelong patterns
are first established. Section II will focus more directly on Rossetti's
literary career, which involved an often difficult negotiation between
what had been laid down, essentially by patriarchal culture, and her
freedom as a deliberate artist, choosing the economies and strategies
that would preserve her art—the poetry of endurance.

I

She was the youngest of four children, born in London on De-
cember 5, 1830, to Frances Polidori and her husband Gabriele Ros-
setti. Frances Polidori, one of a family of eight, was the product of a
match between an adventuring and aristocratic Italian, Gaetano

Polidori, who had finally settled in London as a teacher of Italian, and Anna Louise Pierce, an English governess and a strict adherent of the Church of England. A lively and successful man, with literary and artistic interests, Gaetano Polidori also played an important role in his granddaughter's life. His move to a house in Buckingham-shire, Holmer Green, gave the city-bred child some experience of the country; his admiration of her talent led him to publish her verses privately when she was only seventeen. In contrast, Anna Polidori was literally distant and disengaged. After giving birth to four sons and four daughters, she took to her bed as an invalid and directed her household from the room from which she never emerged. The four daughters were all trained as governesses; Eliza, the oldest, became the housekeeper for the family; Frances, the youngest, was the only one to marry, and her sisters Margaret and Charlotte, as well as Eliza, eventually exchanged their mother's household for hers. One of the brothers, John Polidori, won notoriety as Byron's companion and physician, and as the author of the sensational *Vampyre*; he committed suicide at the age of twenty-six. Despite the scandal, Frances hung his portrait on the parlor wall in the Rossetti home, where it might have served as a family totem of Byronic doom and Byronic glamour.

Like her father, Frances' husband, Gabriele, was a foreign trans-plant in Anglo-Saxon culture, a literary man, and something of an adventurer as well. He was a political exile who had left Italy during the early nineteenth-century upheavals in the kingdom of Naples. The gifted son of an Abruzzi blacksmith, he had made his way by patronage to a post first as librettist to the San Carlo opera company, then as assistant curator of ancient statuary at the Museum of Naples. His facility at improvisation, along with his talent for inspi-rational rhetoric, made him a popular political versifier. Having blown with the political winds for several changes of regime, he ultimately found himself on the wrong side. As a member of the republican Carbonari he had written particularly inflammatory verses denouncing the "tyrant" King Ferdinand of Naples, who had first proclaimed and then abolished a constitution. When Ferdinand put Gabriele on a list of dangerous enemies, Gabriele managed to escape from Naples, making his way first to Malta, then ultimately to

London where he became part of the large Italian refugee colony. In 1826, when he was forty-three, he married Frances Polidori, who was then almost twenty-six. After two wedding ceremonies, Roman Catholic for Gabriele, Anglican for Frances, who had been raised as a Protestant, the couple moved into a modest house at 38 Charlotte Street (now Hallam Street), an address that was just barely respectable. There the four children were born in rapid succession: Maria Francesca in February 1827; Gabriel Charles Dante in May 1828, William Michael in December 1829, and Christina in December 1830.

Like the match between Frances' parents, the match between Gabriele and Frances would seem to have been a romantic alliance between a poetic Latin refugee and a sedate and pious English governess, for Frances, as it turned out, was almost completely Anglicized in her opinions and habits. More significant than the romantic polarization, perhaps, are the pragmatic goals of upward mobility evident in both matches. Both families, that is, solved the problem of maintaining Italian identity while acquiring British middle-class respectability in similar ways. As foreigners in an insular and rigid class society, the Polidori and Rossetti families stood a better chance of assimilation into English life through the roles of artists or intellectuals. This is not to say that their claims to learning and artistic talent were not genuine but, rather, that the style of life of the artist or the scholar would allow them to present whatever might seem alien to English culture—whether their looks or their deportment—as an acceptable form of exoticism, artistic eccentricity. This role also provided them with a means of dealing with their very real economic impoverishment. If they could afford neither elegant dress nor a fashionable address, they could invoke other criteria; their minds were on higher things, whether artistic or religious. As foreigners, also, Gaetano Polidori and Gabriele Rossetti had as economic assets only their language and their cultural heritage: they could make a living only by teaching or translating. In a sense, then, although they wanted to settle into English society, their economic viability depended on their maintaining their Italian identity intact. Both men, however, could move toward assimilation through their wives: as governesses both Anna Pierce and Frances Polidori were primarily teachers, not only of academic subjects but of manners and morals, more especially, English manners and morals. Mother and daughter were models of respectability, well-educated, pious, and conventional Englishwomen who would raise English children.

The reasons for the women's choices are less easily defined. Obviously both were attracted by the dramatic color of their husbands' lives, and perhaps Frances sought, consciously or unconsciously, to imitate her mother's marriage. Perhaps she thought that she would rescue Gabriele from his rather desperate circumstances; perhaps she sensed that he would, like her father, make a good family man; perhaps, knowing that her next role in life would have to be that of matron, she thought she might achieve other roles vicariously, through a husband who obviously needed her assistance and through her children. The only evidence we have of Frances' attitude toward her marriage is a statement she made in her seventies: "I always had a passion for intellect, and my wish was that my husband should be distinguished for intellect and my children too. I have had my wish; and I now wish that there were a little less intellect in the family, so as to allow for a little more common sense."[5] In the latter part of this statement, Frances was no doubt referring not only to the wreck of her son's life but also to Gabriele Rossetti's obsessive and quixotic Dante studies.

As well as duplications of the roles of the wives in the two marriages there are striking reversals. Unlike Frances' successful and energetic father, Gabriele Rossetti was a proletarian dreamer who became increasingly immersed in his esoteric commentaries which set out to prove that Dante was secretly a Freemason and that his work was a complicated antipapal allegory. Although he did publish some of his writings, the cost was underwritten by subscribers and friends, and publication did not bring in any income. The year after Christina's birth, he obtained the professorship of Italian at King's College, but since the post paid no salary, only a percentage of the students' fees, he was still forced to augment the family income by private teaching and translating. On the one hand, then, Gabriele worked very hard to do the best he could for his family while keeping his identity—as poet, patriot, and man of letters—and his self-esteem intact. On the other, he retreated into what almost amounts to a delusional system, weaving strands of reality with pure fantasy: he had once been part of an actual conspiracy and now his writing concerned an elaborate literary conspiracy; he once had had deadly enemies, and now he believed that he had been done out of a more lucrative post by enemies. Dante Gabriel Rossetti's recent biographers, Brian and Judy Dobbs, describe Gabriele as "an extraordinary mixture composed of operatic Italian braggadocio, of Parson Adams-like simplicity, of an infinite capacity for self-delusion, and of aspirations quite contrary to those of his wife."[6] The Dobbses believe there were unarticulated tensions between husband and wife which inevitably affected the children, and that theirs was a "divided" household.[7] Although this conjecture seems plausible, there is no evidence of overt friction during their life together. It seems clear, however, that there was a strong polarization of roles which extended to all the family members.

Like the Polidori family, the Rossetti family was effectively half-English and half-Italian (although the Rossettis were only one-quarter English), and inevitably the Italian half would have to be suppressed if the family were to be assimilated successfully into English life. The cultural division was expressed in terms of gender. In the Polidori household, the girls were the mother's, raised as Anglicans and trained to be as much like their mother as possible; the boys, raised to be Roman Catholics like their father, seem to have had greater difficulties in making a successful identification with him. Very little is said of one brother, thought to be retarded; one anglicized his name to Polydore and became an unsuccessful barrister, having little to do with his sisters; the other was the infamous and desperate physician. For the boys, no doubt, the task of assimilation occasioned inner conflict, as well as practical difficulties. In the Rossetti household, however, all the children were baptized as Anglicans, and thus from the beginning were marked as their mother's. In this household a significant reversal of roles took place; unlike her own mother, who ruled from the bedroom, Frances had no opportunity to retreat into invalidism, for it was her husband who in later years became house bound as an invalid, while she took on the responsibilities of breadwinner and family counselor. It is she, then, who became their link with the "real" world, as she must have been from the beginning, in contrast with the labyrinthine fantasies that preoccupied their father. Ironically, as R. D. Waller astutely points out, we know very little of what this woman who *did* a great deal, working both inside and outside the home, actually thought and felt, whereas Gabriele's "endless lucubrations" fill volumes.[8] But whether because of Gabriele's abstraction or Frances' own personal force, it was her code of piety and propriety that prevailed.

Although the Rossetti children were being brought up as English children, they did not have much contact with other English children. In fact, the family's social contacts were almost exclusively confined to Frances' family, or to members of the Italian refugee community to whom Gabriele Rossetti generously offered his hospitality. At the end of Gabriele's teaching day they would gather round the fire to talk of their country's causes and their own and to hear Gabriele declaim, while family life went on as usual. Holman Hunt gives a vivid description of the Rossetti household and its guests at the time of the P. R. B.'s meetings; it must have been much the same when the children were young:

The tragic passions of the group around the fire did not in the slightest degree involve either the mother, the daughters or the sons. . . . The hearth guests took it in turn to discourse and not one had delivered many phrases ere the excitement of speaking made him rise from his chair, advance to the centre of the group, and there gesticulate as I had never seen people do except upon the stage. . . . Our circle conversed in English; the father talked with his friends from the hearth, and at the end of each course he got up and joined them, until he was once more called to the head of the table by the appearance of a new dish.[9]

The anecdote reveals a typical English reaction to foreign culture. Holman Hunt deliberately distances himself from the scene, representing the refugees as slightly absurd, their feelings and their style comprehensible only as theater. It also reveals the dynamics of the Rossetti family, showing how a group functions within a group. Mother and children form an island of English culture, with Gabriele ferrying between them and the "larger" or "outside" mass of Italian culture, which itself is surrounded by the totality of English culture. With this view of the total family configuration in mind, it is now possible to consider what the individual family members' roles were.

With the birth of Christina, it is as if the family achieved a perfect symmetry, a tidy polarization of roles: two girls and two boys, two stolid children and two volatile ones. In childhood, at least, the character types cut across gender. Maria and William were the stolid children, Gabriel and Christina the volatile ones. If it was the mother's character and acts that chiefly molded the children, it was perhaps the father's *words* that shaped their sense of themselves as role players in the family drama. It is Gabriele the improvisor, the phrasemaker, who sums up character in a line: as small children Maria and William are his "two calms," Gabriel and Christina his "two storms";[10] later they are *carissima Maria, ingegnose Gabriele, saggio Guglielmo, vivace Christina* (dearest, clever, wise, vivacious), and his wife is *ottima moglie* (excellent wife).[11] Soon the children themselves must have learned the knack of handing out roles. In the course of playing cards with their mother they assigned themselves suits. Maria was clubs, Gabriel hearts, William spades, and Christina diamonds.[12] What is interesting about these designations is not so much the destiny or even the character type they might have portended as the children's impulse to differentiate themselves according to fixed roles. This probably continued to be an absorbing family game: later in life Maria would characterize herself as having "good sense," William "good nature," Gabriel "good heart," and Christina the "bad temper of both father and mother."[13]

Whatever the role Christina was to play as time went on, we know that quite early a role was defined for her, possibly in response to the family's overall needs, certainly in response to her very definite temperament. Her mother was already very busy with the care of three small children. William says that she must have had a nurse-maid when the children were small, but that he does not remember such a person, and that later there was only one servant. Christina has been described as an irritable and difficult child, often in tears or in a temper. Perhaps there was a certain physiological predisposition which, in conjunction with outside stimuli and stresses, made her a nervous infant. But whatever the actuality there was an early and well-formulated mythology of Christina's infant nature, varying according to her age, sometimes according to the demands of the rhetorical situation. Gabriele Rossetti, with typical insouciance, wrote to his sister-in-law of her birth: "You have now another niece, born at the due time, last Sunday night, at ten minutes past three. Her mother suffered little, and now lies nursing the dear pledge who, to judge by her appetite, could not be doing better. She is considered to be the very picture of Maria, but more beautiful. She is fairer, and looks, with that round face of hers, like a little moon risen to the full."[14] Years later Christina herself penciled in the margin: "How could my dear Father give such a report? Dearest Mamma had a fearful time with me." This last piece of information must have been conveyed to Christina at a later date, as part of the changeling mythology that gets passed on to some children—you were such a funny, ugly baby, we wanted a girl/boy, you didn't really look like either of us, etc.—partly as a way of identifying the child, partly as a penalty for taking something from the parent. Christina Rossetti must have felt some guilt, then, for causing her mother "pain," and, of all the members of the family, chose—or was tacitly delegated—to take on the suffering, to ritualize it, in effect.

But in the early years of her life Christina seemed to be developing normally. As is appropriate to the pre-Oedipal phase, that is, she had not yet made the transition to female passivity. The infant who has had a difficult birth, but nurses vigorously, develops into what seems to be a fairly aggressive and confident child. Gabriele describes her at a year and a half as "our skittish little Christina with those rosy cheeks and sparkling eyes."[15] And in one of the most significant comments of all, writing of the opposition to the 1832 Reform Bill, he says: "They will make all the outcry and all the resistance that Christina is wont to make when you force her teeth, medicine glass in hand; but what is the end of the performance? Christina gulps the medicine."[16] The angel-demon child is made to swallow the bitter medicine in a kind of force-feeding which is bound to enrage the infant and stir up fantasies of poisoning. Lona Mosk Packer points out that futile resistance, followed by swallowing the bitter cup in the end, becomes a pattern of her life.[17] Whereas Gabriele, who shows a mixture of pride and disapproval in his comments on Christina's spirited nature, could play the role of the indulgent father, bringing home lollipops for the children, presumably Frances, who thought the lollipops "trash,"[18] administered the bitter medicine. She must also have administered other disciplines as part of the process of educating and civilizing her children. With her female children, however, her task was to teach passivity, self-abnegation, endurance: in other words, suffering. It has been one fashion in Rossetti criticism to consider Christina a passionate "Italian" nature curbed by English piety and propriety;[19] another, to offer the counterclaim that she was temperamentally morbid, low-keyed.[20] Her early history suggests, rather, that she was a high-spirited child of whom a great deal was expected, and for whom the transition to female passivity was especially difficult. The "bitter medicine" may have been the medicine of necessity—the necessity of exchanging the pleasure principle for a reality principle which would not allow the "angel" to integrate with the "demon" but, rather, required the suppression of demonic greed, demonic assertiveness. The child who has caused her mother "pain," who is "difficult," becomes the woman who takes the pain and difficulty back inside of her, herself her own affliction.

The early lessons are reinforced by later ones, in the actual process of schooling. Her brother Dante Gabriel was indisputably first: in looks, talent, and intelligence. Christina, as her first modern biographer puts it, "came next." The division according to gender within the Rossetti family, an exaggeration of the division between the sexes within the culture (and also a parody, in the sense that Mrs. Rossetti was "strong," Gabriele relatively "weak"), inevitably polarized the sister and brother who were most alike in temperament and gifts. If he was self-indulgent, she was self-denying; if he was extroverted, she became introverted; if he was color, she was black and white. This polarization was a result of their socialization, and beyond the deepest levels of personality formation, this socialization was accomplished by two different forms of education, the first at the hands of the mother within the family, the second outside of the family within a formal system. Put simply, all the children seem to have been treated with equal respect for their gifts and personalities, although there was tacit and overt differentiation and hierarchical sifting, until 1837, when the two boys were sent to school, while Maria and Christina remained at home to continue their education with their mother.

Until 1837 Frances Rossetti who, we must remember, had been trained as a governess, undertook the education of all four children, teaching them to read and write and providing them with religious instructions. Before they could read and write Frances read to them from the Bible, Augustine's *Confessions*, and *Pilgrim's Progress*, along with such edifying works as Maria Edgeworth's stories for children. For entertainment the children were allowed *The Arabian Knights* and Keightley's *Fairy Mythology*. When their grandfather moved back to London from Holmer Green, they had access to a much wider library. Their interests ranged from an illustrated Ariosto to the Waverly novels, to the Gothic treats they found on their Uncle Philip's bookshelves: William tells us that they "battened on *The Newgate Calendar*, Hone's *Everyday Book*, and a collection of stories, verse and prose, of ghosts, demons, and the like, called *Legends of Terror*."[21] All of this was nourishing food for the imagination, and all the children had equal access to it.

Gabriel and William, however, would go on to a literary feast, both to Byron, Shelley, Goethe, Schiller; William to Whitman and Dante, Gabriel to the pre-Petrarchan Italian poets as well as Dante. Although in later life Christina and Maria chose deliberately not to listen and not to look, their direction was set by the earlier distinction made between themselves and their brothers in the handling of their education. When Gabriel was nine and William seven, the boys began attending day school, first a small clergyman's school, and then the day school of King's College. Although the brothers found school confining and demeaning, a poor substitute for the kind of reading they had been doing on their own and, as William points out, a "descent from the tone of feeling and standard of conduct"[22] they had experienced at home, their schooling formally socialized their intellectual life.

Even if William and Gabriel did not exactly fit in, even if they looked down on their training and their schoolmates, they were still making contact with the surrounding culture, and learning the skills which would give them a place in the masculine world. At King's College School they associated with the sons of professional people, and studied primarily Latin, Greek, and French, with classes for writing, arithmetic, drawing, German, algebra, singing, some scripture, history, and geography. William is at pains to point out that he was not a diligent scholar, but that the instruction itself was rather perfunctory. He makes clear that family bonds prevailed over the calls of the outside, for when Gabriel eventually left school to attend art school and pursue his own eclectic intellectual pursuits, William found himself even less interested in the school regimen and followed his brother's example of reading what pleased him. Both William and Dante Gabriel, then, chose a mode of intellectual life that emphasized, in contrast to their sisters' self-imposed constraints, an eclecticism and breadth of choice.

And what of the girls' education? Mrs. Rossetti was proficient in Italian and French, and so along with readings in the Bible and religious literature, the girls were must have studied these languages. We know also that the girls were given German lessons at home, along with the boys, by a friend of their father's. But Latin and Greek—a traditional classical eduction, in other words—were to be learned only in a formal setting and were not considered as appropriate or necessary studies for females. Like Elizabeth Barrett Browning, however, who had determined not to be outdone by her brother when he was sent to school and followed up her study of Greek under the tutorship of the scholar Hugh Boyd, Maria insisted upon being taught Greek at home, and apparently outdistanced the boys: by the age of twelve she was reading Euripides in Italian and Hesiod's *Theogony* and Homer's epics in Greek.[23] Maria, it would seem, was a more diligent scholar than her brothers. Yet it is clear that within the family there was a premium on originality and creativity, or at least so it comes down to us through William's eyes, for Maria comes across as rather plodding and tenacious. It seems entirely possible, however, that William felt hostile toward Maria's "unwomanly" aggressiveness, and that Maria retreated from the arena of dangerous competition into a severely female sphere. Although we have no reason to doubt Frances' competence as a teacher, neither do we know what she instructed her daughters in, whether they knew more or less than the young women who did go to school. All that can be deduced is that there were different standards within the Rossetti family, as within the culture, concerning what was useful knowledge for females and males, once beyond childhood. William tells us that Christina was not much of a reader. Perhaps she was indeed intellectually lazy; perhaps she knew that she could not hope to emulate Maria and the boys in their enthusiasms; she would in any event know by now that certain avenues were inevitably closed to her, and so it was futile to pursue dead ends.

Except for the difference in the boys' education, all the children seem to have been treated as if they had equal intellectual gifts, and all seemed to have a sense of themselves as budding authors. They were encouraged to write, as well as read, partly as education, no doubt, but also as entertainment, as a family game. Books and writing were essential training for the business of life as cultivated adults. To some extent like the Brontës in their gifts, or rather, inclinations, and in their isolation—despite the difference between the Yorkshire wilds and central London—the Rossettis wrote romantic tales and poems, inspired by their reading and spurred on by their grandfather's acquisition of a printing press. But the young Rossettis were neither as original nor as intense as the young Brontës; no Angrian myth issued from their collaborations, only a family journal, first the *Hodge Podge*, then *The Illustrated Scrapbook*, to which Dante Gabriel contributed a first version of "The Blessed Damozel." Besides the journal, each wrote independent pieces: William started but never finished several romances with titles such as "Raimond and Matilda" and "Ulfred the Saxon, a Tale of the Conquest"; Dante Gabriel over the course of two years wrote "Sir Hugh the Heron," which his grandfather printed in 1841; Maria produced a blank-verse elegy on the death of the Princesse Borghese.

Christina began writing down her verses in 1842, copied into a small black notebook by her sister Maria; in 1847 her grandfather Polidori published these as *Verses by Christina G. Rossetti*, to be given away to friends and relatives. What these verses show is that Christina was "studying" to be a poet; imitating Dante, Tasso, Metastasio, as well as Herbert, Crabbe, Blake, Coleridge, Shelley, Keats, and Tennyson. Also evident is her Gothic reading: Ann Radcliffe, Monk Lewis, and Maturin. Packer notes that at fourteen Rossetti was studying a book of religious poetry called *The Sacred Harp*, using it as a "textbook" of models for her own religious verse.[24] Meanwhile, Dante Gabriel was making his own explorations of models. In 1847, when Christina's derivative verses were printed, Dante Gabriel was ostensibly attending the Antique School of the Royal Academy, copying statuary and casts but actually spending much of his time at the British Museum, translating the Italian poets, reading Shelley and Browning. There he came upon a manuscript notebook of Blake's, which a museum attendant sold him for ten shillings. In this notebook Dante Gabriel found a poetic model that would support his rejection of conventional notions of art. No such liberating discovery was forthcoming for Christina. She had to study whatever texts were available *at home*, in some ways—but not all—equivalent to Gabriel's detested plaster casts. She would discover her own voice by "copying," not only worn-out conventions but the timeless conventions of the Bible and the resonant myths of fairy tale and romance.

The voice of the seventeen-year-old poet has been found to be "melancholy," even to the point of morbidity. Lona Mosk Packer suggests that the morbidity derives in part from her Romantic heritage and eighteenth-century graveyard pieces, but even more significantly, from the crisis in the family that began in 1843 with the breakdown in her father's health.[25] The illness, diagnosed as bronchitis, was likely tuberculosis. At the same time his eyesight began to fail, and he was forced to resign his position at King's College. William says that the alarm over the possibility of his father's blindness "cast a thick mantle of gloom for months and years, not only over my father's own feelings, but over those of the entire family."[26] The worst years, he says, were 1846 and 1847. The crisis was, of course, an economic one as well. In order to make ends meet, the family had to disperse suddenly and take on new roles. William, at fifteen and a half, was found a job by a family friend in the Excise Office, and Maria at seventeen, in 1844, obtained a position as governess through her aunt Charlotte Polidori. Frances became the chief wage-earner, giving French and Italian lessons outside the home and later opening day schools, one in London and one in Somerset, in which Christina was expected to assist her. Apparently by family consensus, Gabriel was the one to be "saved," and so he went on taking the steps that would make possible his career as an artist, becoming a student of art under F. S. Cary at "Sass'

Academy." As William succinctly puts it: "He therefore cost some-thing and earned nothing."[27] What seemed to be happening, then, was a dispersal of the close-knit family, an end to childhood, really, and the taking-up of life roles, lifework. Gabriel was to be the artist, William the respectable bureaucrat, and Maria and Christina the governesses and schoolteachers. The lot of the governess, we know, was not a happy one, and Maria, like the Brontë sisters, longed to return home to the "bel nido natio."[28] As Packer points out, the prospects must have seemed dim to Christina. It would seem that she had no option but to leave the family nest to pursue an occupa-tion that she despised, and that would not leave her time to write poetry.

In 1845, however, Christina seems to have taken, if unconsciously, another option. She became seriously, but vaguely, ill with com-plaints that remained undiagnosed. Her physician provided her nineteenth-century biographer, Mackenzie Bell, with this brief but interesting description: "Fully the middle stature; appears older than she really is—15; hair brown; complexion brunette; but she is now pale (anaemic). Conformation good."[29] What this description makes clear is that Christina did not especially look like an invalid and that she was fully developed sexually—a young woman, not a child, in other words. As invalid, Rossetti could perhaps retreat from both the psychosexual demands of puberty and also from the kind of work that would jeopardize her life as a poet. It is striking, however, that Rossetti chose at this point in her life to ally herself with her stricken father: the wounded poet, the blind scholar. With their respective illnesses, it is as though this were her last chance, before her fall into womanhood, before his decline into death, for her to consolidate the gifts she, after all, inherited from him. If Dante Gabriel had inherited her father's poet's mantle officially, Christina would confirm her unofficial gifts by remaining at home, nurturing the ruminative mental life that was the source of her poetry.

In a lasting sense, however, Christina's identification was to be with her mother and sister. It is at this point also that religion, under the aegis of Frances Rossetti, came to dominate her daughters' lives. Although raised in an evangelical atmosphere, Frances had by the 1840s shifted to High Church services, attending the Albany St.

Church where the fiery Puseyite, William Dodsworth, gave his
millenarian sermons. In their attitudes toward religious belief and
practice the Rossetti family was, as usual, polarized as male/female,
for the religion of the fathers—Gaetano and Gabriele—was nomi-
nally Roman Catholicism, although as a freemason, Gabriele was
fiercely antipapist, if not irreligious. As Italian men, both Gabriele
and Gaetano must have considered churchgoing an essentially
female activity. It is not surprising, then, that although all the
children when young attended church with their mother, only the
girls continued to do so into adulthood. In addition to encountering
new intellectual horizons in their reading—Shelley, for instance—
the boys as adolescents were impelled to identify with their father's
masculine scepticism and, at least in his earlier life, relative worldli-
ness. The Rossetti women, on the other hand, were pointedly
unworldly in their indifference to elegance of dress and to such social
pretensions as morning calls. Their genteel poverty, their position as
"foreigners" striving for assimilation and perfect respectability,
combined with their situation as women in Victorian culture, left
them very little room to maneuver. For Frances and her two daugh-
ters, the Anglican church offered—in addition to the general Chris-
tian consolation that suffering is the common lot, to be rewarded in
the life to come—the pleasures of formal beauty along with intellec-
tual seriousness, a solidly middle-class ambience, and a sense of
spiritual exclusivity that made up for their exclusion from other
spheres. As Georgina Battiscombe, Rossetti's most recent biog-
rapher, is careful to point out, this aspect of the Oxford movement
was more concerned with matters of doctrine than with ritual
practices.[30] Still what formal ritual there was, as well as simply the
dignity of the institution, put a seal on the other constraints on their
lives; lacking power in the world, they could deliberately choose to
be otherworldly, to ritualize their lives, in effect, via the narrow,
circular path from family life to governessing and schoolteaching as a
distracting but necessary divagation, to church and the church's
charitable works, and back home again. Maria's taking of formal
vows is in one sense a large step in that she moves out of the confines
of the family; in other ways it is a small step, since the three Rossetti
women had already set themselves apart in a kind of lay sisterhood.

Christina went so far as to attach herself to Maria's convent as an *Outer Sister*; she also ministered to "fallen women" at the St. Mary Magdalene Home, even wearing the habit at times. But she was never tempted to follow her sister into the convent, just as she never followed other female callings: governessing, for instance, or the chance to go with her aunt Eliza to the Crimea as a nurse. She must have known that she could not throw herself energetically into the practical and managerial concerns of her mother and sister, whether to direct households or schools. Again her choice, her refusal, seems calculated to preserve her art.

Two more overtly dramatic refusals color Rossetti's life, or at least the biographical myth. These involve the two official suitors, James Collinson, who comes upon the scene when she is about seventeen, and Charles Cayley, whom she knew for most of her life. Almost all of the biographers agree that Collinson, short, rotund, and given to falling sleep on his feet, was an unlikely suitor. He did have, however, at least token plausibility on both aesthetic and religious grounds. Taken up by Dante Gabriel into the Pre-Raphaelite Brotherhood, he was a genre painter of some promise, who had already exhibited his work at the Academy. He was a devotional poet of sorts as well and had attended services at Christ Church, although he had joined the Roman Catholic church a short time before meeting the Rossettis. Some time in 1848, upon his return to the Church of England, he and Christina were officially engaged. The engagement persisted, though conducted with a marked lack of intensity, through 1850, when Collinson once again seceded to the Church of Rome. Christina immediately, of course, broke off the engagement and was sent off to Brighton to recover from a state of collapse. Some months after the severance, she seems to have been affected enough to fall into a faint upon catching sight of him in the street. The questions remain: Why she would have accepted such a faint suitor in the first place? Are the religious reasons for her refusal a cover for the impoverishment of the relation? The most sensible line of reasoning is offered by Georgina Battiscombe, who points out both the plausibility of Collinson's appeal as a first suitor and the seriousness of the religious objections. According to Battiscombe, Collinson did pursue Christina with some vigor, and he had the additional appeal of being an official Pre-Raphaelite brother. His defection to the Church of Rome, however, would be perceived as an especial threat by an adherent of the Oxford movement, constituting a denial of the catholicity of the Church of England.[31] But Battiscombe's partition of Christina's "nature" into the sensuous-Italian and the rational-religious, with Collinson—and marriage—representing the pull of the sensuous-Italian, does not satisfy.[32] Looking again at "Symbols" we can see that although the situation in the poem has no biographical referent, a situation like the broken engagement has some kind of formal appropriateness to the structure of feeling in the poem. The split is not so much between two "natures" as between the self who acts, is thwarted, for whatever reason, and suffers, and the self who withdraws to watch, ruminate, exemplify, and make poetry.

For what is going on during these years is the making of the poet, of course. It is perfectly natural that Collinson was associated in her mind with the vocation of poetry, particularly with the "brotherhood." Never seriously considered even for token membership in the Pre-Raphaelite Brotherhood, through her brother she came close to "brotherhood" in one way, through her fiancé in yet another way. It is also perfectly natural that she would find the actual prospect of marriage, like governessing and teaching, inimical to her art. More important, however, is the pattern of renunciation, in and of itself, as a mode of feeling that reflected her sense of exile from the country of the self and even, as Sandra Gilbert suggests, the country of poetry. The heroine of Rossetti's short novel *Maude*, written at about the same time as her break with Collinson, has nothing to do with suitors, but a great deal to do with the vanity of writing poetry. The novel ends with the "overturning" of the heroine in a carriage accident, her lingering death, and the interment of her works with her, all punishment for, as Gilbert would have it, the act of poetic assertion.[33] In one sense, then, her rejection of Collinson preserves her poetic self; in another, it stands for all the renunciations that indicate she can never be completely at home with that self.

With Charles Cayley the relationship appears both more serious and less problematic. Cayley was a skilled linguist who had translated the Hebrew Psalms as well as Dante and Homer and had even overseen the translation of the Bible into Iroquois. Rossetti had first met him when he had come to study Italian with Gabriele. With the passing years the impecunious scholar's fortunes did not improve, while his behavior became increasingly eccentric. As Battiscombe puts it, he was "the perfect example of the abstracted scholar,"[34] socially maladroit and unprepossessing. Battiscombe further points out that a man of this type might have appealed to Christina precisely because of his unworldliness. He, too, however, was an inappropriate suitor from the perspective of religion: nominally an Anglican, he appears to have been firmly agnostic in his views.

In 1862, at any rate, Cayley had resumed his earlier acquaintance with the Rossetti family. Sometime in the years between 1864 and 1866 Cayley proposed and Rossetti in 1866 refused him. The friendship persisted over the years, however: before his death Cayley wrote to Rossetti asking her to be his literary executor. Although it is evident that she had a great deal of affectionate regard for Cayley, there is no need to debate whether or not Rossetti was "in love" with him. On the one hand, the marriage was economically unfeasible. Cayley had no consistent source of income, and there is a good chance that the couple would have had to depend on William's generosity to maintain themselves: William did in fact offer the couple a home with him in his own house. On the other, Rossetti had deeper reasons, whether having to do with the religion question, which is the official story, or with her emotional and literary commitments. In September of 1866, at any rate, she wrote in response to William's offer:

> I can't tell you what I feel at your most more than brotherly letter. Of course I am not *merely* the happier for what has occurred, but I gain much in knowing how much I am loved, beyond my deserts. As to money, I might be selfish enough to wish that were the only bar, but you see from my point of view it is not. Now I am at least unselfish enough altogether to deprecate seeing C. B. C. [Cayley] continually (with nothing but mere feeling to offer) to his hamper and discomfort: but, if he likes to see me, God knows I like to see him, and any kindness you will show him will only be additional kindness loaded on me.[35]

What is evident in this letter is the firmness of Rossetti's decision, as well as her abiding affection for Cayley and her deep commitment to her family, here William in particular. Although Rossetti would seem to have refused a suitor at a time when the chances to marry were diminishing, it seems entirely plausible that she would prefer to maintain the family life that permitted the kind of independence and leisure conducive to a poet's routines. Here there is no ritual renunciation but, rather, a quietly firm assertion of her most essential needs.

In addition to Collinson and Cayley, there is a phantom suitor, a twentieth-century creation concocted by Rossetti's first modern biographer, Lona Mosk Packer. In all other ways an exemplary scholar, Packer seems driven by the need to account for Rossetti's poetic subject matter and tone as derived from a thwarted love affair. Since Collinson and Cayley are so pallid, Packer fashions a more glamorous and passionate suitor out of the family friend, William Bell Scott, using as evidence chiefly the poems themselves and speculating about the meetings and partings that must have occasioned them. Scott, born in Edinburgh, but residing at this time in Newcastle-upon-Tyne, became acquainted with the Rossetti family in 1848, when Rossetti was seventeen. All the family seemed taken with him, and Scott later wrote that "Dante Gabriel Rossetti, Christina and Maria his sisters and William his brother, from that day to this have all been very near and dear to me."[36] With no documentable evidence, Packer chronicles a romance that began in the winter of 1848–49 and lasted until 1857. The outlines of Packer's story are that Rossetti fell in love with Scott during a subsequent visit he made to London that winter, although she was already engaged to Collinson. Packer traces thematic variations in Rossetti's love poetry of 1848–57 and attributes them to the vicissitudes of the love affair. When in 1850 Rossetti broke off her engagement, her guilt over this secret betrayal gave way to fantasies of fulfilled love between herself and Scott. It was not until later in 1850, supposedly, when William visited Scott in Newcastle-upon-Tyne, that the family discovered that Scott was married. By this time, according to Packer, Scott was also in love with Christina, but Christina, according to the dictates of her conscience, was compelled to go through a private agony of renunciation over a period extending until 1857, until Scott broke off the relationship. As Georgina Battiscombe points out, there is simply no evidence that this romance existed.

But if Rossetti's own romantic life was lackluster, she lived in an ambience of high romance. Eighteen fifty was the year Dante Gabriel Rossetti met and fell in love with the beautiful milliner's apprentice, Elizabeth Siddal, and installed her as his muse and his beloved. Theirs was an intense and tortured relationship in which life and art were tightly interwoven. Much has been written about the influence on his art of the three significant women in his life, Elizabeth Siddal, Fanny Cornforth, and Jane Morris,[37] and it is clear that these women were in a sense invented and mythologized by his art. They live on in different guises in his poetry and painting, as Beata Beatrix, as Lilith, as Prosperpine. It is this "cannibalizing" of his women that, I will argue later, enabled Christina Rossetti to propose a countermyth, that of the woman who suffers and lives although embalmed in and for art, in and for male projects in general. Instead of the graceful muse or the fatal beauty Rossetti saw the suffering woman, worn down by her illnesses and miscarriages. Further, she saw Dante Gabriel himself being destroyed by his own demons, as if what he fed on returned, Eumenides fashion, to feed on him.

II

So far this biographical outline does not give any sense of Rossetti's literary life. She was writing poems all this time, however, especially prolifically during the fifties and sixties, when little else was going on in her life. What we know about her habits of composition is that she wrote in the solitude of her bedroom, that she was a spontaneous or "inspired" poet in the sense that either poems came whole or came not at all, and that she consulted nobody while the poem was in process, nor did she make any substantial revisions.[38] Like many other lyric poets Rossetti was not inspired particularly by event or scene. Mackenzie Bell astutely points out that she wrote many of her descriptive Nature poems "in the small upper back bedroom whose only outlook was to the tall dingy walls of adjacent houses."[39] All the reason more, then, to question the necessity of an actual lover as source for the love poetry.

We know also that from 1842 until about 1866 her poems were

copied, first by her sister Maria and then by Rossetti herself, into small leatherbound notebooks. From 1866 on she wrote her poems out on ruled blue paper, often quarto size. What these habits of composition reveal is that although initially her instinct was to be secretive about her writing, eventually she would share the writing process with her family. Maria transcribed Christina's verses just as in later years Christina "kept" her mother's diary—transcribed the entries at her dictation, that is. As in many Victorian families a great deal of writing went on: letters as frequent as, and serving the purpose of, telephone calls between members of the family living at different addresses in London; unpublished scholarly writing (her father's); published scholarly writing (her sister's and brother William's); and, of course, the poetry writing that engaged the brothers and sisters both privately and in their *bout-rimés* contests. With this background of the family involvement in the writing process in mind, I want to go on now to a consideration of Rossetti's life after 1860, focusing on the circumstances of publication of her work. What should emerge are the strategies that make Rossetti's poetry in an almost literal way the poetry of endurance, and the shape of a literary career informed by her "doubleness," as both a private and a public figure, as both an unassuming amateur and an assertive professional writer.

In the summer of 1847, Gaetano Polidori, who had purchased a small printing press, issued *Verses*, a collection of Rossetti's poems to that date. The volume circulated among family and friends, and, apparently, made no extraordinary impression. The poems, which are reproduced as Juvenilia in the *Collected Works*, are of interest not only as a compendium of Rossetti's literary models but also as evidence that certain themes and motifs—thwarted love, early death, desire and renunciation—are present from the beginning of Rossetti's career and do not, therefore, sustain an extended interpretation of the biographical sources. In 1850, with the founding of the Pre-Raphaelite Brotherhood and the first issue of their journal, the *Germ*, Rossetti came before the public with two poems, "Dream-Land" and "An End," both perfect models of the Pre-Raphaelite aesthetic. The second issue saw the publication of three more poems, the song beginning "Oh roses for the flush of youth," "A Pause of

Thought" (which later became the first part of "Three Stages"), and "A Testimony," one of Rossetti's early religious poems. As well represented as Dante Gabriel in these issues, Rossetti, writing under the pseudonym of Ellen Alleyne, achieved early recognition as a new and original poet. With the collapse of the magazine later in 1850, however, her work found no further avenue for publication until the 1860s, when again her brother's efforts brought her to the attention of several influential figures.

We know, then, that in the 1860s, with the writing of *Goblin Market*, Dante Gabriel took an even more active interest in getting his sister's work published. Although he was unable to interest John Ruskin in the new poem, he was able to persuade the upcoming young publisher, Alexander Macmillan, to publish "Uphill" in the February issue of *Macmillan's Magazine*. The poem was a success and Macmillan was congratulated on discovering a new poet.[40] He went on to publish "A Birthday" in April, and "An Apple-Gathering" in the August edition. In 1862 he agreed to publish a volume of poems entitled *"Goblin Market" and Other Poems*. It appeared in March 1862, less than a month after Elizabeth Siddal's death from an overdose of laudanum, and Dante Gabriel's insistence on burying the manuscript of his own poems with her. Thus while Dante Gabriel's works were at least temporarily interred, Christina's literary career was launched, with the volume a considerable critical and popular success.

During 1863 and 1864 Christina continued to write poetry but did not feel ready for another volume. Dante Gabriel, however, urged her to produce a new volume as quickly as possible, to capitalize on the success of *Goblin Market*. It is at this point that we see the nature of Dante Gabriel's influence on Christina's poetic practices and the extent to which she was able to resist his advice. With *Goblin Market* Dante Gabriel had made suggestions concerning selection and sequencing, suggestions which Christina accepted readily. In regard to the new volume, however, Dante Gabriel presumed to dictate her poetic subject. Thinking that another long narrative poem was in order, he suggested that she expand upon a short lyric, intended to stand as a poem by itself, and make it the tailpiece of a narrative which was to include certain set-pieces that Dante Gabriel thought would be arresting and, presumably, commercially viable. The result of Dante Gabriel's suggestion was that Christina undertook the title piece of the new volume, *The Prince's Progress*, a quasi epic dealing with a prince's dilatory progress through various fantastic adventures, and his arrival too late to save his repining bride from death. Although Rossetti agreed to write to Dante Gabriel's prescription, she resisted his specific suggestions, especially the idea of including a tournament scene: "How shall I express my sentiments about the terrible tournament? Not a phrase to be relied on, not a correct knowledge on the subject, not the faintest inspiration, incites me to the tilt: and looming before me in horrible bugbeardom stand two tournaments in Tennyson's *Idylls*."[41] In other words, Rossetti is resisting a masculine quest epic. In fact, her resistance was successful, somewhat at the expense of the poem, however, for *The Prince's Progress* is structurally weak and the prince himself hardly a heroic figure: the action is all a dying fall, a following out of "repining" to its inevitable conclusion.

Significantly, Dante Gabriel objected strenuously to the inclusion of two narrative poems in the volume; in both, the women characters are angry and assertive. *The Lowest Room*, in which the speaker actually learns to put aside her anger and protest and accept her lot in life, "not to be first," sustains Dante Gabriel's most persistent animus. William Rossetti cites an 1875 letter in response to the collected edition of the *Goblin Market* and *Prince's Progress*: "A real taint, to some extent, of modern vicious style, derived from that same source (Mrs. Browning)—what might be called a falsetto masculinity—always seemed to me much too prominent in the long piece called *The Lowest Room*. . . . Everything in which this tone appears is utterly foreign to your primary impulses. . . . If I were you, I would rigidly keep guard on this matter if you write in the future; and ultimately exclude from your writings everything (or almost everything) so tainted" (*Works*, pp. 460–61). As well as reacting to the poem's unwomanly tone of protest against women's lot, Dante Gabriel seems to be responding to its oblique suggestion of his sister's anger and competitiveness with him. It is important to note, however, that despite her brother's strong disapproval, Rossetti retained the poem in all subsequent editions.

The other poem Dante Gabriel objected to is *Under the Rose* (the title altered in the 1875 collected edition to *The Iniquity of the Fathers upon the Children*), which concerns the relation between a mother and her illegitimate daughter. In an 1865 letter Christina responds to Dante Gabriel's suggestions concerning the whole volume both as a sister who should "bear to learn rather than to teach," and as a poet who knows her own strengths:

> The *Prince* shall keep your modification of stanza 2, as regards the main point: though "I am I" is so strong within me that I again may modify details. . . . *Lowest Room* pray eject if you really think such a course advantageous, though I can't agree with you: still it won't dismay me that you should do so; I am not stung into obstinacy even by the Isa and Adelaide taunt in which I acknowledge an element of truth. . . . *U. the R.* . . . I meekly return to you, pruned and re-written to order. As regards the unpleasant-sided subject I freely admit it: and if you think the performance coarse or what-not, pray eject it, retaining the *Lowest Room* and *Royal Princess*; though I thought U. the R. might read its own lesson, but very likely I misjudge. But do you know, even if we throw U. the R. overboard, and whilst I endorse your opinion of the unavoidable and indeed much-to-be-desired unreality of women's work on many social matters, I yet incline to include within female range such an attempt as this: where the certainly possible circumstances are merely indicated as it were in skeleton, where the subordinate characters perform (and no more) their accessory parts, where the field is occupied by a single female figure whose internal portrait is set forth in her own words. Moreover the sketch only gives the girl's own deductions, feelings, semiresolutions; granted such premises as hers, and right or wrong it seems to me she might easily arrive at such conclusions: and whilst it may truly be urged that unless white could be black and Heaven Hell my experience (thank God) precludes me from hers, I yet don't see why "the Poet mind" should be less able to construct her from its own inner consciousness than a hundred other unknown qualities.[42]

Here we see Rossetti's "doubleness" in bold relief: she reveals and hides, asserts and retracts, accepts conventions and flouts them. Most important, she articulates—and not so tentatively—a female aesthetic which would include the heretofore unwritten and unprintable experience. The job of the poet, in her mind, is not so much to record the social injustice, as to construct an "internal portrait" of that experience and to present that deeply felt inner experience—like Rossetti's own deeply felt inner experience—as exemplary. This exemplariness is what connects her with other women, to the extent that all women's lives are exemplary, testimony not only of exclusion and alienation but of resolution and strong selfhood: "I am I" is strong within her, Rossetti says here, just as in "The Thread of Life" she would assert her self-continuity with the oracular "I am not what I have nor what I do; / But what I was I am, I am even I" (*Works*, p. 263). In *Under the Rose*, then, Rossetti presumes to cross over to the other side of the mirror, to tell what it feels like to be an illegitimate daughter, trapped in a situation of maximum alienation by the ties of patriarchy. Where Dante Gabriel flinches from the "coarseness" of the subject—and we must remember that in 1870 he was to write "Jenny," a poem having nothing to do with the female figure's inner life as a prostitute and everything to do with Dante Gabriel's finely tuned sensibilities—Christina claims that there is nothing coarse about a sexual victim's "internal portrait." In regard to the new volume, then, Rossetti was able to withstand both her own misgivings and Dante Gabriel's promptings and mark out a poetic territory all her own.

With the proofreading for *The Prince's Progress* completed, Rossetti embarked on a trip to Italy, her first visit abroad, with her mother and William. William has amply documented that trip, which at least from his perspective seems to have been a typical English tour, full of picturesque and sublime vistas and carefully logged architectural and pictorial wonders.[43] There is no mention of any contact with family members or friends, the connection having been lost, apparently, in the course of two generations in the case of her mother, one in the case of her father who, we must remember, had been a political exile. For Rossetti, as for Elizabeth Barrett Browning,[44] Italy was a "mother country," in her case a natural inheritance which had been lost, but more than that, a "mother tongue" that she still had some claim to. With the death of their father and their own taking up of adult roles in the English community, the Rossetti children had lost touch with the community of Italian exiles; for Christina, however, exile is an important trope: it expresses her particular existential situation as a woman in her culture. This personal sense of loss might well have been fertilized by her awareness of a more particular cultural exile. She must have seen, even if she did not mention, the pain of her father's exile and the pain of those lost, weary men who came to him for encouragement. For a poet who felt doubly "precursed," first by the patriarchal tradition in English poetry and secondly by her brother's "first" place in the family canon, the Italian tongue, though it was more her father's than her mother's, represented a more primary language, inaccessible in that it could not be used for her English poetry but a symbol of imaginative freedom, the freedom of invention of the improvisatore—or even the improvisatrice.

Rossetti wrote four poems in English dealing with her experience in and of Italy. In June 1865, before leaving Italy, she wrote "En Route," in which she expresses her kinship with her "motherland" as well her alienation: "Wherefore art thou strange, and not my mother?" (*Works*, p. 377). Echoing the language of sensory experience that she had used in the 1854 "Paradise" (*Works*, p. 180), Rossetti commends this "sister-land of Paradise," with its "tongue sweeter in my ears." In 1866 Rossetti was to write a poem which echoes these two and was in fact juxtaposed with "Paradise" in *The Prince's Progress*. This is "Mother Country" (*Works*, p. 245) in which Rossetti's longed-for motherland becomes paradise, a country at once hers and not hers, but a country that with its spices and cedars and gold and ivory is accessible to the senses in an imminent future.

In the second Italian poem, "Italia, Io Ti Saluto" (toward July 1865), Rossetti expresses her acceptance not only of the inevitable leave-taking but also of the inevitable partition of self: "To see no more the country half my own, / Nor hear the half familiar speech, / Amen, I say: I turn to that bleak North / Whence I came forth— / The South lies out of reach" (*Works*, p. 378). But that country is still available in memory and imagination, and especially in language, as Rossetti will still be able to name it: "The tears may come again into my eyes / . . . / And the sweet name to my mouth." In the country of language and the imagination, then, Rossetti was fully able to "taste" her motherland and in a sense to repatriate herself.

The third of the Italy poems, "Enrica, 1865," was composed July 1, 1865, when the Rossettis had returned to England. It contrasts the warmth and expressiveness of an Italian visitor—"our tongue grew sweeter in her mouth"—with the prim correctness of English women, whom Rossetti regards as masking a certain inner depth and freedom that the visitor is capable of recognizing. Despite her longing and admiration, then, Rossetti cannot abdicate her own intractable nature—the "I am even I" of "The Thread of Life"— and accepts the "doubleness" that constitutes it.

Finally, in the sonnet sequence *Later Life*, Rossetti was able to write of her experience of Italy as a doubleness that, rather than dividing, augments her experience. Writing of hearing the nightingales one June evening at Como, she asserts that "All things were in tune, myself not out of tune," and that June "that night glowed like a doubled June" (*Works*, p. 80).

We do not know to what extent the Rossetti family conversed in Italian, although Mackenzie Bell tells us that the musicality and careful enunciation of Rossetti's speech suggested the speech of someone not born to English. At any rate, while Dante Gabriel was to make a substantial contribution to English poetry by translating the Italian Pre-Petrarchan poets, Rossetti was to write a number of Italian poems which remained unpublished in her lifetime. She had been writing a few poems in Italian since 1849, the year that her grandfather had *Verses* printed up, and she continued to write a few until 1876. The most substantial of these, a sequence of love lyrics entitled *Il Rossegiar dell'Oriente*, she kept locked up in a drawer. It is unlikely, however, that this secret manuscript points to a secret love. More likely, Rossetti wanted to be known unequivocally as an English poet and did not want to be urged by anyone within or outside the family to publish in Italian. Certainly she would not have wanted to contend with the inevitable labels the critics would have attached to all her verse: its Italian "musicality," for instance, would have been both admired and subtly denigrated. The Italian poems do, in fact, point up the musicality of Rossetti's verse: the echoing repetitions and feminine rhymes, the preponderance of soft consonants, the almost overwhelming assonance.

The Italian poems also demonstrate in capsule Rossetti's method of linking and contrasting secular with religious themes, especially human and divine love. In a sense, they show how profoundly she is a *translator*: of the language of patriarchal tradition, of the language of scripture and into the language of scripture, of English into Italian into English again. The Italian poem "Finestra Mia Orientale" ("My Eastern Window," 1867), for instance, contains an image originally derived from scripture, and retranslated into an English poem, "A Bride's Song" (B. 1876, which means any time between 1866 and 1876, and therefore either at roughly the same time as the Italian poem or later). Where in the Italian poem the speaker, parted from her lover, imagines that were they together a desert might flower, the speaker in the English poem, happily anticipating union with her beloved, imagines that even were the land to turn into desert, that desert "would be / As gushing of waters to me, / The wilderness be as a rose, / If it led me to thee, / O my love" (*Works*, p. 390). Translation is also transformation—one situation inverted as its opposite, the same metaphor inserted into another context— the whole process suggesting an endless dialectic. In a way, it does not matter which comes first, the Italian or the English poem; obviously the image and the language were in Rossetti's head, ready for working and reworking.

Even more significant, however, is the extent to which *Il Rossegiar* is a preliminary sketch or a rehearsal for Rossetti's major sonnet sequence, *Monna Innominata*. Although again we have no precise dating for this sequence of fourteen sonnets which unfold the course of an unhappy love affair, it is generally believed that they were written during the sixties, after *The Prince's Progress*. The theme of both *Monna Innominata* and the twenty-one short lyrics, six of them sonnets, that comprise *Il Rossegiar* is expressed in these two lines from the last lyric of *Il Rossegiar*: "Io pù ti ama che non mi amasti tu:— / Amen, se così volle Iddio Signor" (*Works*, p. 453). (I loved you more than you loved me:— / Amen, if the Lord God wished it so," trans. Andrew McGarrell) For *Il Rossegiar* we do, however, have precise dates: three in each of 1862, 1863, and 1864, ten in 1867, and seven in 1868. This strong interconnection demonstrates that Rossetti was writing almost as productively in the sixties as in the fifties, and that she was working in a particularly interesting way, doubling her poetic material in two languages.

Although the *Monna Innominata* series was to remain unpublished until *"A Pageant" and Other Poems* in 1881 and *Il Rossegiar* was not published until after her death, between 1866 and 1875 Rossetti made several new ventures in publication. In 1870, on the advice of Dante Gabriel, she switched her publisher from Macmillan to F. S.

Ellis, Dante Gabriel's own publisher. Ellis brought out Rossetti's collection of short stories, *Commonplace* (1870), a series of cautionary tales which demonstrate that Rossetti's need to moralize produced a congealed art, except when checked by the constraints of poetic form; her strength did not, apparently, lie in narrative prose fiction. By 1872, having found the arrangement with Ellis unsatisfactory, Rossetti had switched back to Macmillan.

Writing and publishing these works must have been a great act of courage for Rossetti as well as a consolation. While she had been chronically ailing since adolescence, with diagnoses ranging from bronchitis to incipient tuberculosis, in 1871 she fell acutely ill. She was stricken by a complex of symptoms that included vomiting and total exhaustion. These were ultimately diagnosed as caused by a rare form of goiter, exophthalmic bronchocele, or Graves' disease. The disease altered her appearance terribly, causing a protrusion of the eyes and a thickening and darkening of the skin. In November of 1871 William wrote in his diary: "Poor Christina continues in a very deplorable state. . . . As regards appearance, she is a total wreck for the present, and I greatly fear this change may prove permanent."[45]

The illness persisted through 1872, and the convalescence was slow and halting. Rossetti bore the debilitation and the disfigurement courageously; the disfigurement must have been especially painful for a woman in that family—sister to her brother—where so much had been made of the mysterious appeal of the face.

In 1872 one of the peaks in Rossetti's illness coincided with a physical and mental crisis in Dante Gabriel's life. With the reissue, in March of that year, of Robert Buchanan's damaging attack on his poetry in "The Fleshly School of Poetry," Dante Gabriel's health began to deteriorate rapidly. He had become addicted to chloral taken with whiskey for his chronic insomnia, and by June was suffering from severe paranoid delusions. At the Roehampton house of Gordon Hake, the Rossettis' family doctor, who had taken him in as a patient, he apparently took an overdose of laudanum and collapsed in a coma. Christina and her mother were not informed of the suicide attempt; they believed that he had had some kind of seizure. Both Christina and Dante Gabriel, then, were critically ill at the same time, and Frances Rossetti and William and Maria had to divide their time between them. Dante Gabriel recovered from the immediate crisis, but he was to remain debilitated both physically and mentally until his death in 1882. While Christina herself seems to have been recovering by the fall of 1872, it took another year for her to achieve anything like a return to relative health.

Two further important changes in the family life took place in 1873. William announced his engagement to Lucy Madox Brown, daughter of Ford Madox Brown, and Maria entered the Anglican sisterhood, of which she and Christina had become associates while young women. This dispersal and realignment of the family, in addition to her own and Dante Gabriel's illnesses, must have made Rossetti even more conscious than in her youth of life as a succession of shocks and changes to be borne, and requiring a progressive narrowing and concentration of her energies. Although Rossetti's options at this point in her life were extremely limited, she made honorable choices: to bear suffering stoically, even cheerfully, and to maintain her commitment to her family in the best ways she could.

Like Christina, ever responsible, William insisted that he and Lucy merge households after their marriage with Christina and her mother in the family home in Euston Square. For obvious reasons, including temperamental and religious differences between Lucy and Christina, the arrangement did not work, and in 1876, with her mother and her two aunts Eliza and Charlotte, Christina moved to 30 Torrington Square, where she was to spend the remaining years of her life.

The same year of the move, Maria, who had shown some symptoms in 1873 when she made her decision to enter the sisterhood, was clearly ill with cancer. Christina and her mother visited her daily until her death in November of 1876. It was an occasion for sorrow and mourning, of course, but given the deep religious convictions of the women in the family, Christina's grief was not inconsolable. She wrote some time later of Maria's funeral: "And at a moment which was sad only for us who lost her, all turned out in harmony with her holy hope and joy. Flowers covered her, hymns were sung at her grave, the November day brightened, and the sun (I vividly remember) made a miniature rainbow in my eyelashes."[46] In this excerpt from *Time Flies* we see Rossetti as usual treating her experience as exemplary and confirming certain convictions: if life into death, then death into life; if the horror of decaying mice in gardens, then rainbows at funerals.

During these last eighteen years of her life, Rossetti was to be vigil keeper over four more family deaths. The first was the painful and drawn-out death of Dante Gabriel, who died on Easter Sunday evening, April 9, 1882, with Christina, her mother, and William all in attendance. On April 8, 1886, her mother died at the age of eighty-six, when Christina herself was fifty-six. With her mother gone, Christina was left in charge of a household which consisted of herself, her two elderly and invalid aunts, and a number of nurses and domestics. Aunt Charlotte died in 1890, Eliza in 1893, just a year before Christina's own death. Christina was deeply concerned, moreover, in Lucy Rossetti's protracted illness from tuberculosis and her tragic death in Italy in April of 1894, leaving William a widower with four children in his care.

Through these years, even before the first appearance of the cancer that was to kill her, Rossetti herself continued to be ill, although the nature of her complaints remains vague. In 1877 she wrote to Alexander Macmillan, "I am not very robust, nor do I expect to become so; but I am well content with the privileges & immunities which to attach to semi-invalidism."[47] Packer construes Rossetti's illness as psychosomatic, claiming that she "early found semi-invalidism, with its freedom from economic and social responsibilities, congenial to a life in which the production of poetry was paramount."[48] I am not so sure that Rossetti's illness was psychosomatic, and while agreeing with Packer that her poetry was of primary importance, I would stress the lack of egocentricity as well as the adaptiveness in her response to illness. Rossetti was not so much a neurotic cultivating her symptoms as a strong-minded woman responding to difficult circumstances and, as the comment to Macmillan demonstrates, wryly aware of the secondary gains.

During the times of crisis she was fully aware of the existential burden of self; writing to Dante Gabriel during his illness in 1881, she assures him that she has "heretofore gone through the same ordeal. I have borne myself till I became unbearable by myself, and then I have found help in confession and absolution and spiritual counsel, and relief inexpressible."[49] Knowing the depth of Dante Gabriel's torment, Rossetti was probably well advised to avail herself of religious consolation. A few months later she wrote to William concerning Dante Gabriel: "It is trying to have to do with him at times, but what must it be to BE himself? And he in so many ways the head of our family—it doubles the pity."[50] By 1888 Rossetti no doubt considered herself well out of swirl and tumult of putting oneself forward, of coming "first." Writing to William at this time, she explains her position: "Beautiful, delightful, noble, memorable, as is the world you and yours frequent,—*I* yet am well content in my shady crevice: which crevice enjoys the unique advantage of being to my certain knowledge the place assigned me."[51] Here again we see the Rossetti of "The Thread of Life," satisfied that she can say "I am even I," satisfied, perhaps, that she has escaped the shadow of dissipation, in all the senses of that term.

Throughout the crises of the seventies Rossetti had continued to write and publish. *Sing-Song* and *Commonplace* have already been mentioned. In 1874, *Annus Domini: A Prayer for Each Day of the Year, Founded on a Text of Holy Scripture*, the first of Rossetti's explicitly religious works, was published by James Parker and Company. The same year Macmillan published *Speaking Likenessness*, three heavily didactic tales for children. Although the dream sequence in the first tale recalls *Alice in Wonderland*, Rossetti's work is neither as inventive nor as subtle as Dodgson's. Rossetti's concern is to provide models for behavior and to suggest that a female child's development depends on painful self-awareness and self-denial. These tales are the reductio of Rossetti's own ascetic practices, and, perhaps, a mirror of her child-self, the pleasure-seeking and punishment-administering speaker of "Symbols," in effect.

In 1875 Macmillan brought out *"Goblin Market," "The Prince's Progress," and Other Poems*, an edition which collected the two previous volumes and added thirty-eight new poems. The original poems were rearranged and the new poems, ranging in date from 1858 to B. 1876, were interspersed among them. Of the new poems, only fifteen date from the seventies, the remainder mostly being poems Rossetti had not chosen to include in either of the two earlier volumes. Five poems were omitted: "A Triad" (1856), "Cousin Kate"

(1859), "Sister Maude" (1860), "Light Love" (1856), and "A Ring Posy" (1863), all dealing with rivalry and betrayal in love. The dates of the additions suggest that Rossetti, unsurprisingly, was less prolific during the difficult seventies; the omissions suggest that she felt a need to censor those poems which dealt more or less overtly with sexual passion or with the jealousy and rivalry that attend sexual passion.

In the period from 1879 to 1892 the Society for Promoting Christian Knowledge brought our five works of religious prose, interspersed with religious poems: in 1879, *Seek and Find: A Double Series of Short Stories of the Benedicte*; in 1881, *Called to be Saints: The Minor Festivals Devotionally Studied*; in 1883, *Letter and Spirit: Notes on the Commandments*; in 1885, *Time Flies: A Reading Diary*; in 1892, *The Face of the Deep: A Devotional Commentary on the Apocalypse*. Thus while Rossetti begins as a coterie writer, her first verses published by her grandfather, and her earliest public audience the readers of the *Germ* and other literary magazines and annuals, she ends by being a writer for a larger and more democratic audience whose interests are not primarily literary. This shift in her publication history marks not only her change of focus from "secular" to "religious" writing, which is not simply a narrowing, but also her discovery of a strategem that would allow her to outlast literary exhaustion, literary "decadence," if one likes. As a woman writer heavily precursed by a male literary tradition which disempowers her by declaring that she cannot write about experiences or in modes that she, as a woman, has no access to, she finds a way of going on by effacing herself within a larger tradition in which poverty of experience, poverty of a certain kind of literary originality, that is, is not an issue.

Although Rossetti turned increasingly to religious poetry and prose, 1881 saw the publication, by Macmillan, of a new volume of poetry, *"A Pageant" and Other Poems*. This collection is notable for the inclusion of the two sonnet sequences, *Monna Innominata* (as previously noted, written during the sixties) and *Later Life*, which can be dated only as B. 1882. Out of fifty-nine poems, about twenty-two, including *Later Life* as one entry, are specifically "devotional," demonstrating that Rossetti was concerned to keep the same proportion as the previous volumes. Out of the total, only one,

"Italia, Io Ti Saluto," is dated from before the seventies, and the rest are dated B. 1882, for the most part, which tells us only that they were written after 1866. Then in 1890, Macmillan published a collected edition which included the three major volumes: *"Goblin Market," "The Prince's Progress," and "A Pageant," and Other Poems.* Since the series comprising the first two volumes had been already stereotyped, Rossetti was able to make changes and additions only to the *Pageant* series. To these poems she added only fifteen poems, all clearly devotional and all dated either B. 1882 or B. 1892. Finally, in 1893, a year before Rossetti's death, the Society for Promoting Christian Knowledge brought out *Verses*, a collection of religious poems previously published in *Called to Be Saints, Time Flies*, and *The Face of the Deep*. Since Rossetti saw fit to group these poems very carefully, in an arrangement that has nothing to do with date of composition, obviously the original sequence is of significance to a correct reading.

After Rossetti's death, William Michael Rossetti issued *New Poems, Hitherto Unpublished or Uncollected* in 1896. In 1897, William oversaw the publication of an early novella, *Maude*, which appears to have been begun in 1850. Like Mary Wollstonecraft's *Mary*, it is remarkable mainly for its autobiographical references and for several lovely poems incorporated in the text. A reading of *Maude* provides convincing evidence for Gilbert's theory that Rossetti felt compelled to renounce the male "feast" of poetry, since the heroine is clearly punished for her aspirations. With the publication in 1904 of *The Political Works* under the editorship of William, the Rossetti canon would seem to have been complete. Until the recent work by Rebecca Crump this has been the only complete edition available for the Rossetti scholar. The chief problems with William's edition are that while his arrangement gives us a sense of the chronology of the poems, it gives no indication of the sequencing of the original volumes. The sequence of the 1890 volume is accessible in the *Works*, but the reader of the religious poems must refer to the 1893 *Verses* to get any idea of the sequence Rossetti intended. As regards the unpublished poems, until the Crump edition is completed, the reader must rely on Gwyneth Hatton's excellent unpublished study (Master's thesis, Oxford University 1955).

With this review of Rossetti's publishing history, I want to turn now to a consideration of Rossetti's methods of composition, her involvement in publishing and copyright matters, and her sequencing in the original volumes—all those dealings that comprise her professional life as a poet.

Although Rossetti did not revise extensively in manuscript, she was professionally concerned with the conditions of publication. Her correspondence with Macmillan over the years reveals her concern with the placement of illustrations[52] and even with the color of the binding.[53] Other letters show her politely but firmly making stipulations as to copyright matters,[54] the number of poems per page, the treatment of sonnet sequences,[55] her right to make corrections in subsequent editions,[56] and her work not being abridged or extracted in any way.[57]

To a certain extent this professionalism belies her claim to work only by inspiration, never "to order." On the other hand, the professionalism and the insistence on certain preconditions for her work are complementary: the resort to "inspiration" is, in her case, I think, by no means a lazy poet's excuse for not working but, rather, an effective stratagem for resisting external pressures that might violate her artistic integrity. As we have seen, to embark on this second volume, without waiting for "inspiration" or for her talent to mature, was to place herself in the position of submitting to Dante Gabriel's tutelage. She could resist this pressure only by refusing, in effect, to write. She did not, of course, stop writing, but she was careful to delimit the subject and scope of her poetry not so much by a leaving out as by a keeping in—a preservation of her own poetic sphere. Thus in 1877, after sending Dante Gabriel a new poem, she wrote: "You shall see one or two pieces more; but the one I sent you is a favorite of my own, and I doubt if you will unearth one to eclipse it: moreover, if I remember the mood in which I wrote it, it is something of a genuine 'lyric cry,' and such I will back against all skilled labour."[58]

Rossetti appears to have had considerable investment in claiming this broadly Romantic aesthetic. By doing so she places herself within a tradition which, for women poets, locates the source of poetry in the "heart," in emotion felt, rather than experience observed. But she was also conscious of the limitations of this aesthetic, for a poet of discernment, on output. Letitia Landon might well turn out volumes, but not so Rossetti. In 1870 she had written Dante Gabriel, presumably in response to suggestions that she write more about political and social topics: "It is impossible to go on singing out-loud to one's one-stringed lyre. It is not in me, and therefore it will never come out of me, to turn to politics or philanthropy with Mrs. Browning: such many-sidedness I leave to a greater than I, and, having said my say, may well sit silent. 'Give me withered leaves I chose' may include the dog-eared leaves of one's first, last, and only book. . . . Here is a great discovery, 'Women are not Men,' and you must not expect me to possess a tithe of your capacities, though I humbly—or proudly—lay claim to family-likeness."[59] Indeed, women are not men, and though this proposition leads immediately to a deferential shrug toward Dante Gabriel's greater "capacities," the letter is a strong articulation of Rossetti's sense of herself as a woman poet. To write other than she does would be to submit to patriarchal coercion, and thus to find herself in a double bind. If she rejects Dante Gabriel's prescriptions, then she lays herself open to his attacks—witness the previously cited letter accusing her of Jean Ingelow's and Elizabeth Barrett Browning's "falsetto muscularity." But the letter above reveals Rossetti's sense of the inappropriateness of continuing to write the poetry of renunciation. It is both impossible to go on singing to one's one-stringed lyre and impossible not to. Although she does not say so here, it would seem that Rossetti is pondering the question of how to sustain both her aesthetic and her art: if the aesthetic of renunciation is to go on generating poetry, then she must find a broader base, a wider context.

That broader base is the religious poetry which is also a logical extension of the "lyric cry": not a horizontal or historical axis but, rather, an intensification of the vertical axis, the timeless articulations of the soul's colloquy with God. No poetry is timeless, of course, and Rossetti seeks out the ground of religious poetry for important historical reasons. Having appropriated and refined upon the secular literary tradition, having exhausted, in a sense, an exhausted tradition in which women are powerful symbols but not powerful agents, she decamps to another world. At the very least, Christian ideology offers the promise of radical transformations that empower the weak. This shift in emphasis in Rossetti's work, gradual rather than abrupt, is paralleled by an almost ritualistic narrowing and refining of her role as the poet who, in order to go on writing—in order to write the poetry of endurance—makes her life and work exemplary.

It is important to remember, however, that, as a mere recounting of the events in the last two decades of Rossetti's life demonstrates. Rossetti's withdrawal from active social life seems to have as much to do with a sense of family responsibility, an assumption of real and demanding burdens, as with the spinster poet's withdrawal from life for the sake of her art. Other Victorian women, other Victorian women poets, survived by rigorous and truly eccentric withdrawals within their own households: Anna Louise Pierce, her grand-mother, directing her household from her bedroom; her female precursor, Elizabeth Barrett Browning; her American contempo-rary, Emily Dickinson. Elizabeth Barrett Browning's twelve-year retirement to her sickroom allowed her to follow a self-designed wide-ranging course of study that included the Greek Patristic writers, and to develop her poetic craft methodically and single-mindedly. Emily Dickinson, more than any other woman writer, knew how to practice the "necessary economies," as Adrienne Rich puts it,[60] and retreated to the eremetical "freedom" of her corner room. Although neither of these women abdicated completely—even Dickinson, despite her extreme withdrawal, kept up a circle of epistolary acquaintances and a select set of domestic duties—they were still centers about whom their households revolved. Choosing carefully the impingements they would allow, pearls within oysters, organizing the larger world around their private worlds, they asserted the primacy of their art. But Rossetti, who was not *of* the world, remained, except for the periods of acute illness, pretty much *in* it. She was neither a matriarchal nor an infantile center. She remained a handmaiden, a Martha who took as her role "not to be first."

In 1892 the signs of Rossetti's cancer first appeared in her left breast and shoulder. Although an operation brought some immediate relief, it did not arrest the disease, which took a critical turn in July of 1894. Rossetti remained bedridden for the next half-year, alone, except for the company of her maid and frequent visits from William. She bore her end stoically, though not without religious forebodings, as if some last fear of retributive vengeance persisted. In her last days she lay still for hours, only her lips moving as if in silent prayer. Toward daybreak on December 29, 1894, with only her maid present, she died.

On her terms and on ours, as readers of her poems, it was an exemplary life. Her sense of teaching a lesson, rather, of *being* a lesson, generates poems in which primary emotions—longing, disappointment, hope—are, as in all good poetry, both distanced and intensified. Like her contemporaries, she believed in the self, and also like her contemporaries she experienced the poetically fruitful anguish of the self divided. The biographical myth reproduced above indicates in what ways she might have been alienated as a woman and poet in her culture, as a woman and poet in her family, The polarization, the necessary refusals—but the bitter medicine swallowed at last—the ritualization of suffering, all suggest patterns common to other Victorian lives. What seems her poetic strength and uniqueness is her particular intransigence in refusing mediation: both the self who suffers and fears and the self who offers silent prayers are present to us at all times. In the poetry the mythmaking transcends the moralizing as Rossetti sets her private rituals within the larger context of the rituals—and the texts—of the Christian church, and appropriates the scriptural conventions for her myth of the deprived self who would be fulfilled, the dispossessed self who would be restored, the fragmented self who would be whole.

2 Goblin Market
Dearth and Sufficiency

Goblin Market is Rossetti's most famous poem, set off from the rest of her work by its singular narrative power and richness of texture and by the changes in literary taste that value its relative opacity over the transparency of most of the rest of her work. It was written in 1859, the manuscript inscribed to her sister Maria, and, with revisions suggested by Dante Gabriel, published in 1862 in the volume *"Goblin Market" and Other Poems* brought out by Alexander Macmillan. With the exception of Ruskin's strictures on the poem's metrical "irregularities,"[1] the poem was both a critical and a popular success, establishing Christina Rossetti as one of the "new" poets. In the early part of this century this poem was routinely anthologized, and routinely set before children. In our time, however, it has become impossible to read the poem with an innocent eye, for it has been reinvented as an unconscious erotic masterpiece, a puzzle that decodes to subversive meanings. Whatever she decides about meaning, the contemporary reader of the poem must confront crucial issues of interpretation. To the extent that the narrative hinges on contradictions and mysteries of identity that are resolved but not explained, the poem presents the same problems as a Kafka fable: the reader cannot but interpret, and no interpretation can account for all the details.[2] It is at once accessible and closed, as seductive as its goblin cries, and as resistant as its moral assertions.

Striking and innovative as the poem was for Rossetti's contemporaries, it also represented a familiar narrative mode, a blend of the fantastic and the allegorical that has come to seem peculiarly Victorian. It was at once an acceptable indulgence, something on the order of the very best cartoon animation, or the illustrations of Gustave Doré, and a fortifying lesson. Its middle-class readers would have understood it as a product of an imagination that had fed on gothic thrillers, the *Arabian Nights Entertainment*, and Keightley's *Fairy Mythology*, as well as the Bible and cautionary tales. *Goblin Market* belongs, that is, to the strain of fantastic literature that, as defined by Stephen Prickett, runs from eighteenth-century Gothic and Coleridge, through such works as Kingsley's *Water-Babies* and George Macdonald's *Lilith*. According to Prickett, the Victorian interest in the fantastic is yet another version of the Victorian divided mind; the fantastic narrative allows for the expression of unacceptable impulses and, while allegorizing, may subvert its ostensible moral.[3] Prickett's thesis is compelling, but his reading of *Goblin Market* is disasterously reductive: the poem emerges as a stunning example of the Victorians' refusal of the true fruit, knowledge of their "deepest needs and desires."[4] As we shall see, this is a mode of criticism that is often brought to bear on Rossetti's poetry. It depends heavily on either biographical speculation or formulaic analysis of the social context, with the result that either Rossetti's private erotic life or a whole culture's sexual malaise becomes the key to the poem.[5]

If *Goblin Market* is a subversive fantasy disguised as a didactic parable—and Prickett's is a useful category—then the two levels of meaning are remarkably parallel, and the poem emerges as a fully developed allegory. In both the Freudian and the Christian conceptual frameworks, that is, opposites imply each other, and symbols are the language of desire: both libido and soul thirst for fruits that are alternately paradisal and demonic, that sicken and cure. And both Christian and Freudian allegory require a similar process of decoding; like the dream analyst or the exegete of a sacred text, the reader of *Goblin Market* can claim that everything in the poem means, and things are not what they seem. What I have been implying, however, is that although the poem calls for an allegorical reading, full allegorical readings seem to miss the mark. Does it come down, finally, to rejecting any consistent interpretation, and insisting, like the resisting dreamer or the biblical fundamentalist, that the poem does not mean beyond its manifest content? Rossetti herself, as reported by William, claimed that she did not intend anything profound, that the poem would not support a detailed moralizing interpretation.[6] But William rightly points out that the incidents are "suggestive," that different minds find different meanings. This characterization of the way *Goblin Market* means sounds much like the Tennyson's own comments on the *Idylls:* "They have taken my hobby, and ridden it too hard, and have explained some things too allegorically, although there is an allegorical or perhaps rather a parabolic drift in the poem."[7] *Goblin Market,* which is a unique but not isolated poem, shares with Tennyson's *Idylls,* and with *The Ancient Mariner,* for that matter, this "parabolic drift," which suggests multiple interpretations, all tending in the same direction.

Rossetti also provides a clue to the poem's way of meaning in the strategies that characterize her other poems. In "Symbols" we saw how she presented a highly charged series of incidents within a moralizing framework: the symbols are interpreted by the speaker, literally given a speaking voice, and the reader, because of the resonance of the symbols and the baldness of the homiletic rhetoric, is pressed into an interpretation that at once parallels and goes beyond the speaker's. *Goblin Market* has a similar structure, for although it begins as an unframed fiction, it ends with a moralizing closure. No matter how thin the moral interpretation—"For there is no friend like a sister"—its presence in the poem, articulated by one of the poem's actors, signals that the poem must mean something, which the reader must interpret, just as Laura interprets. In other words, if Laura treats the events in the poem as needing a moralizing resolution, the reader is justified in treating the whole poem as a kind of exemplum requiring an interpretative resolution. Although the poem's overt moral need not be considered an adequate response to the narrative, neither can it be dismissed as a cover story for the darker implications of the poem; rather, it is a way someone might tell the story, or at least frame it. As much as the details—the goblin men, the luscious fruits, the kernel-stone, the polarized sisters—as well as the narrative structure itself, press for a systematic allegorical reading, they also repel it, and the poem is best served by framing interpretations, no one of which exhausts the poem's parabolic richness.

Goblin Market has, in fact, fared well at the hands of several modern critics: the interpretations developed by Lona Mosk Packer, Ellen Moers, Germaine Greer, and Sandra Gilbert illuminate precisely to the extent that they remain partial and falter to the extent that they aim at systematization and completeness. Packer, Rossetti's first modern biographer, has skillfully drawn together the significant sources for the poem in order to emphasize the traditionally Christian structure of the Fall in *Goblin Market*. In this view the sinner's corrupted will is more crucial than the objects and means of temptation, for where one sister is destroyed by the fruit, the other is immune.[8] Sound as her assembling of sources is, Packer's judgement fails when she moves on to the poem's "real" or hidden subject. Given the implausibility of Rossetti's official suitors as lovers or muses, as has been mentioned in chapter 1, Packer invents a secret, unrequited love for the family friend, William Bell Scott, to account for the vagaries of Rossetti's emotional life, as, supposedly, recorded in the poems. This unacknowledged, and largely undocumented, love for a married man, which is the mainspring of Packer's book, illustrates a mode of criticism of poetry by women that Ellen Moers describes as devaluing women's actual imaginative powers. In this tradition, the female poet, especially the spinster, is inevitably inspired by an undiscovered lover, and her poems are implicitly, if not explicitly referential.[9] Moers' criticism thus disencumbers a poem like *Goblin Market* of a lot of obstructive baggage; we no longer need to postulate a particular temptation or a particular renunciation to understand the poem.

While Moers sees the source for *Goblin Market* as lying deep in Rossetti's childhood, she emphasizes that those experiences are specifically female. Moers' thesis is that *Goblin Market* belongs to the genre of "female gothic," reflecting the sexuality and sadism of a Victorian childhood, in which the "rough and tumble" of the Victorian nursery was the locus of not only erotic stimulation but also a physical freedom that the female child was soon bound to relinquish.[10] Moers rescues the poem from the fallacies of biographical criticism and, in the course of developing a range of theses about "literary women," provides a brilliant but not comprehensive interpretation. Interestingly enough, in developing her thesis about *Goblin Market*, Moers starts by saying that there is something "more" about the poem than is accounted for by its sources, that "suggests" to her the connection between goblins and brothers.[11] This is evidence that the poem works as William Michael says it does; it is deeply *suggestive*.

Like Moers, Germaine Greer also recognizes that the poem's power comes from its disguised but immediate expression of impulses and experiences belonging to childhood. For Greer, the poem is both an inversion of the Eucharistic feast and a celebration of infantile libido, illustrating the pleasure and pain of oral satiety.[12] In order to make her claims, Greer, like most other Rossetti critics, reconstructs Rossetti's biography, dismissing the suitors and hypothetical lover in order to establish the pathological progress of the Victorian spinster's unconscious through hysteria and masochism to this singular instance of sublimation. By Greer's lights, as well as Prickett's, *Goblin Market* is not only a deeply perverse poem but a largely unconscious one. Greer's insights into the literary contexts of the poem, and its source in infantile sexuality, are as useful as they are provocative. Her reading as a whole, however, much as she claims to leave the poem intact, is basically assaultive; the poem is battered, its juices are rendered.

In the most brilliant and polemical of recent interpretations, Sandra Gilbert uncovers a level of meaning that lies below or beyond the "sexual/religious" allegorical meaning of the poem. Gilbert speculates whether the goblins "incarnate anything besides beastly and exploitative male sexuality," and whether the fruits might not represent something more than carnal pleasure.[13] She claims Milton as the most important source for the poem: the fruits are intellectual, and Laura in eating them is asserting her poetic, as well as sexual, power. As evidence Gilbert uses Rossetti's early prose work, *Maude*, in which the poet-heroine's abrupt death suggests that Rossetti knew already she would have to renounce the "goblin fruit of art," learning to become the poet who sings "selflessly, despite pain, rather than selfishly, in celebration of pleasure."[14] Gilbert's reading is impressively coherent; not only are the fruits and the goblin men accounted for, but also the ritual eating of Lizzie, which Gilbert interprets as an "ingestion of bitter repressive wisdom."[15] But ingenious and resonant as Gilbert's reading is, it fails to convince to the extent that it substitutes one allegorical-didactic reading for another presumptive one. Although *Goblin Market* is an important poem in the forging of Rossetti's aesthetic, it is not a poem about poetry, or even about the powers of imagination, in any of the ways we usually understand such poems. If Rossetti is drawing on Milton and the Bible, then the fruits are significant primarily as objects of a certain kind of act. They are neither intellectual nor carnal, but both, and what signifies is the pattern of transgression, renunciation, and redemption or, in secular terms, acting, suffering, and recovering. The poem no doubt reflects Rossetti's frustrations as a woman and a poet, as well as her infantile experiences, just as it also exemplifies her absorption of certain literary and sacred texts. But in *Goblin Market* Rossetti is attempting to project an imaginative vision whose meaning is neither as "polymorphous" as Greer implies nor as selectively encoded as Gilbert claims. Whatever fruits Rossetti may have thirsted and hungered for, she found that in literature and the Bible everybody feels this way or, at least, writes this way; that is, the language of thirst and satisfaction, of fruits that cloy and fasts that cure, is widely distributed in Western literature. Still we might ask, what motivates Rossetti to use these metaphors with such persistence and consistency? As suggested in chapter 1, Rossetti may have had a lifelong need to define herself against her talented brother, to set her abstemiousness against his self-indulgence. One of the enactments of this self-defining opposition is the poetry itself, which is pervasively concerned with what is enough and what is not enough, with the inexhaustible feast and the irremediable famine. But a biographical interpretation cannot go further. While Rossetti's exclusion from the male banquet of poetry, as well as her abstention from the fruits of life, are real enough, Rossetti uses these experiences to write *Goblin Market*, which goes beyond these experiences.

The first part of this chapter offers an exegetical commentary on *Goblin Market*, unfolding its structure and elaborating its key motifs. This commentary is roughly psychological-phenomenological. It asks, that is, what is the "world" of this poem? What is the system of its language? In the second part this commentary is extended to include more systematically the poems which echo *Goblin Market*'s concerns in whole or in part. Much of this poetry postdates *Goblin Market* and can thus be read legitimately as commentary on this crucial poem. This section groups poems according to neither chronology nor Rossetti's own system of sequencing. Rather it returns to the "pool" from which Rossetti took her sequences, selecting poems according to motifs keyed into a total structure.

Ostensibly nothing like *Goblin Market,* the devotional poems, in particular, suggest ways in which we might follow out the "drift" of a poem that appears highly idiosyncratic but hints at communal meaning. If the experiences that give rise to Rossetti's poems derive from a specific historical situation (but not isolated biographical events), the language she often chooses, the language of scripture and religious orthodoxy, is superficially, at least, transhistorical. As in "Symbols," where the moralizing frame both distances the experience of frustration and anger and preserves it unmitigated, so the religious poems provide a frame that both distances and intensifies the central experience of *Goblin Market*. Much as Rossetti might shrink from such a metaphor, *Goblin Market* can be seen as a narrative text—gospel or epistle—in a long poetic service, the constant parts of which are the devotional poems—prayers and hymns. Just as the text is "expanded" by these unvarying comments, so the comments vary in their symbolic force according to the text. *Goblin Market,* with its vivid representation of demonic/divine oppositions—between feast and famine, garden and wilderness—makes many of the highly conventional invocations of paradisal bliss seem richly allusive, while conversely, against the background of the emblematic vision of Paradise in the religious poems, *Goblin Market* takes on an ironic flavor. Without the context of the religious poems, that is, Laura's wrong inferences tend toward comedy: the villainy is so undisguised, how can she be so greedy, so monomaniacal, so obstinately blind? Set against the soul's yearning for bliss, however, Laura's longings look like—indeed are—immortal longings. We learn that the impulse to merge with the object of desire by incorporating it and becoming part of it is independent of the valuation of the object, that hunger is hunger: "Eye hath not seen, nor ear hath heard, nor heart conceived that full 'enough'" is a biblical tag that appears explicitly in three poems[16] and resonates in many others, including *Goblin Market*. Laura may want the wrong fruits, but her attitude is correct. She wants with the right degree of single-mindedness and intensity. The opposition between "enough" and "not enough" is a crucial one for the poem, and around it cluster several other conceptual and linguistic oppositions: between gardens and antigardens; between the self's growth and the self's resistance to growth, pruned but hardened by the exile from the garden; between feasts that leave one hungry and antifeasts—either fasts or the bitter cup—that satisfy.

The oppositions which are the mainspring of the poem generate a process of re-vision, or redefinition. Laura emerges from one kind of community with its conventional wisdom—she must not listen, must not look—experiences the risks of her individuation and returns to another kind of community. In the course of her individuation her familiar universe of meaning is made strange and her lexicon expanded. By the end of the poem the reader knows something more about what is "natural," what is "change," what is "action," and what is "will." Although this process is an archetypal one, common to allegorical and epic quest, in *Goblin Market* the pattern is given, implicitly but surely, a gendered dimension; the poem explores what "nature," "change," and "self" are to a woman, and what constitutes a female community. By appropriating and reinforcing the paradoxes and inversions of scriptural language, Rossetti opposes to the inevitable decline into natural womanhood the stark decline that precedes a startling paradisal transformation. Ultimately the poem redefines female action as endurance: on the one hand, blind tenacity, as exemplified by Laura's obsession with the fruits; on the other, heroic perseverance, as exemplified by Lizzie's standing firm against the goblins' assault.

I

Who knows upon what soil they fed / Their hungry thirsty roots?

(Ll. 44–45)

Early in the poem Laura delivers this admonition which is also a speculation about origins. In this, "curious" Laura is Eve's daughter, making a critical mistake but asking a crucial question. If we cannot know origins, then we are doomed to our ends. If we live in nature, a part of nature, then we are subject to strange, inhuman, that is, metamorphoses. The purely natural is, in effect, magical, for things in nature change shape—blossom, wither, and decay into unrecognizability—as if gods or goblins did in fact fashion and inhabit them. The gods promise renewal, but all they give is endless change, and Laura may want to escape nature, but all she gets is a speeded-up natural decline. Like other myths and fairy tales, *Goblin Market* is also about the fall from innocence into experience, a "natural" process which leads to the "unnatural" and purely human growth into self-consciousness and freely chosen participation in communal life. At the beginning of the poem we have two clonelike sisters, the same but different, opposed aspects of the self, both of whom act purely according to their natures. Laura is curious and greedy; Lizzie has neither curiosity nor appetites: at the beginning, at least, she is a repository of received opinion, village gossip, superstitious lore, the collective voice of the parents and the community. Laura, of course, is intent on finding out and getting things for herself, like a folk or epic hero. But her quest and her calamity demystify the heroic thrust towards self-definition. There is another way, Rossetti seems to be saying: there are situations in which standing firm and being for another are more integrative and potent than going forth and being for oneself. What the sisters acquire and demonstrate by the end of the poem is particularly female—but not necessarily renunciatory—wisdom. Self-consciousness begins with questions about origins: What is this new experience like? What does this challenge remind me of? It is always possible to come up with the wrong answers, to see Duessa as Fidessa, and this is exactly what happens to Laura who, through her "mistake," lapses into the kind of sterile self-consciousness that terrified so many of the Victorian poets, Tennyson and Arnold being the chief. For the nineteenth-century woman poet this static as well as sterile self-consciousness is doubly terrifying, because often she is already alone with herself and already immobilized. For her the answers to the questions about origins— and ends—are foreknown, and the meanings of nature quite different than for the male poet. Her task may be not to cultivate (her) nature but to will herself beyond it.

The poem begins, like all fairy tales, with time rather than space and with voice rather than vision. The time is not "once upon a time," a point in a narrative past, but a recurring present, morning following evening, and a cycle that is moving swiftly: "Morns that pass by, / Fair eves that fly." The goblin voices speak in an imperative, as voices usually do, and they inventory their wares. These fruits are not as yet visible to the eye; they are a word feast of the imagination. "Listening" to the goblins' pitch, we cannot deny the accuracy of Sandra Gilbert's insight: it is the fruits of the literary imagination that are renounced in the poem. But as well as the imagination, Rossetti's parable—always the something "more"— has to do with nature, human and inhuman, and with deep structure of motivation and action.

By the second verse paragraph time is moving more quickly and darkness and endings are moving closer: the sisters hear the cries come "evening by evening," and the summer weather is "cooling." Maids in general have become identified as "Laura and Lizzie," now actors for the first time in the poem, both hiding from danger, and both voyeurs putting themselves in the way of temptation. Soon Laura and Lizzie act, entirely according to their natures, and Laura reveals her divided nature—by lifting up her head in curiosity at the same time that she admonishes Lizzie not to look, in a tone that suggests rote learning. But it is at this moment, when Laura is mouthing parental admonitions—"We must not look at goblin men, / We must not buy their fruits"—that the poem takes its metaphysical direction. We cannot choose but hear, and voices must be obeyed or ignored; the feast is purely imaginary, and though it can make our mouths water, we remain sceptical of the mind's productions. "Who knows upon what soil they fed / Their hungry thirsty roots?" is a legitimate question: What is the provenance of these fruits? Are they natural or unnatural, and if the latter, demonic or divine? When Laura raises her head and looks she instantly knows, for to see is to know, and is instantly deceived, for visions are both more convincing and more unstable than voices. Now Laura is sure of the fruits' source as in language that recalls the *hortus conclusus* of the Song of Songs she invokes the rich garden of her own imaginative vision: "How fair the vine must grow / Whose grapes are so luscious; / How warm the wind must blow / Thro' those fruit bushes" (Ll. 60–63). The origin of these fruits is an Eden-garden, she thinks.

Out of her own nature Lizzie resists the siren call of the goblins and, repeating communal wisdom—"Their offers should not charm us, / Their evil gifts would harm us"—as well as sealing off her senses, flees from the scene. Out of *her* nature, "curious" Laura chooses to "linger," the prototype of Rossetti's liminal persona, the woman hovering on the threshold between two opposed states, here the unfallen and the fallen, elsewhere this world and the next. If the fruits are both strange and familiar, plausible contents of a greengrocer's or a streetseller's wares, so are the goblins, exotic but benign metamorphoses of domestic menageries. Like Disney cartoons, they are winningly animated; also like Disney cartoons, they offer a harmonious chorus—"They sounded kind and full of loves / In the pleasant weather"—a phony and childish conception of the peaceable kingdom. Finding the goblins as well as the fruits irresistible, Laura makes herself known to them in an almost phallic thrust of curiosity and desire: "Laura stretched her gleaming neck." Because she spies them, they spy her—in this poem to look is enough. When the goblins return to her, now "brother with queer brother," they are less demonic forces than opportunistic tricksters, and both strange and familiar analogues of brothers. What happens then is that Laura must be initiated, must pay with a totemic part of herself, the golden curl that enables the goblins to have magical power over her. Once tasting, she truly *knows* the fruits, like Eve, however, thoroughly deceived, and aflame with manic triumph and hysterical denial. The peculiar quality of the fruits is that they are both enough and not enough. One can never have enough of them, but neither can one have too much: "She never tasted such before, / How should it cloy with length of use?" Later we shall see how Laura's feast is a parodic version of the divine feast of Love that is offered the Christian soul, that full "enough" that is available only in paradise. Here, the immediate irony is that although Laura cannot have enough, the fruits are quickly exhausted, and from now on especially unavailable to her.

But gathered up one kernel-stone, / And knew not was it night or day /
As she turned home alone   (Ll. 138–40)

When Laura has devoured the feast, she turns homeward, no
longer sustained by the diurnal round but trapped in the no-time of
demonic possession, or, more in key with Rossetti's poetic world,
obsession. Her singleness of mind is encapsulated in a symbolic
object: the "one kernel-stone" which she seizes as a token of the
goblin feast. The kernel-stone represents another important opposi-
tion in Rossetti's lexicon: the opposition not only between feast and
fast, enough and not enough, but also between growth and steril-
ity—death before death. This opposition will be modified in later
poems to contrast the unchecked growth of nature's abundance with
the stunted but hearty growth of the ascetic Christian—and the
ascetic female self—which precedes full flowering in the afterlife.
Although Laura is wrong about the nature of the kernel-stone, she is
not wrong in wanting something all her own, something to plant
and cultivate: a well-rooted and inviolable self.

This particular kernel, however, is more like a stone than a seed,
and a symbol of the obstinacy of obsession. When Laura returns
home, Lizzie tells her the monitory story of Jeanie, whose addiction
to goblin fruits led to natural sterility: where she lies buried neither
grass nor daisies will grow. But Laura is still full of the feast and still
insatiable. The Laura who declares "I ate and ate my fill, / Yet my
mouth waters still," is a parody of the Christian soul that cannot have
enough of Jesus, that still hungers and thirsts with an appetite that
can be satisfied only by that full "enough" itself. And in a parody of
Eve, Laura offers her sister—tomorrow—the fruit of the tree, once
again bringing to bear her imaginative and intellectual powers.
Reveling in a sensuous description of the fruits, she again speculates
about origins: "Odorous indeed must be the mead / Whereupon
they grow, and pure the wave they drink." Although her inferences
are all wrong, they are not implausible, for such divine fruits might
well have divine origins. When Laura muses on the odorous mead
she indulges in the same imaginative act as this speaker of this early
poem:

There cometh not the wind nor rain
   Nor sun nor snow:

> The Trees of Knowledge and of Life
> Bud there and blow,
> Their leaves and fruit
> Fed from an undecaying root.
>
>   ("Eye Hath Not Seen," *Works*, p. 149)

This is the garden in which such fruits as Laura describes might well grow. This is the paradisal garden, the garden all Christian souls hunger and thirst for, and Laura is at this point a tragic actor, making inevitable—but misleading—imaginative connections.

But Laura's imaginative speculations have diminished into narrow obsessions. By night the sisters are twins—two pigeons, two blossoms, two snowflakes, two ivory wands—a wonder in nature that enchants the moon and stars and night creatures. Their sameness is freakish, but still a part of nature, a harmony like that of the cooing goblins: delusive appearance. By day they go about their domestic duties as usual, the endless, repetitive tasks that follow the diurnal round and also distinguish the human community from nature. Laura, however, has stepped outside the community to become the self-seeker and has gotten stuck at a particular moment in time that she needs to repeat incessantly. She thus becomes Rossetti's prototypical *repining* woman, alone with her ruminative obsessions. She is outside of time, but also, paradoxically, the victim of time as well as of nature—and her own nature. What befalls Laura next is poetic justice, a *contrapasso*-like punishment. While Lizzie "watches *out*" for the goblins, Laura "watches *for*" them, but bidden fantasies will not come, and she experiences literal disenchantment, fallen into a world that no longer speaks, that is no longer alive. Once she *knows*, this time without creative imaginings or daring speculations, the essential nature of her situation, that she is famine-struck, a hungry exile, possessed by appetites she cannot possibly quench, Laura turns completely inward, falling into the depression of mourning: "Laura turned cold as stone / To find her sister heard that cry alone." From now on Laura's feast will not only cloy, but also devour her, while she becomes consumed by her appetite.

> *Her tree of life drooped from the root*   (L. 260)

Just as Laura suddenly freezes in despair, she has the potential to melt, to break down in anguish, but not before she has discovered the full meaning of impotence. After she turns cold as stone to learn that she is blind and deaf to the goblin world, Laura undergoes a rapid and vivid decline. The image of the drooping tree, over-obviously a phallus that detumesces, invites a psychosexual reading. Certainly at the first onset of curiosity and desire Laura had raised up her head in a sequence of images that signify both female defloration and male excitement:

> Laura stretched her gleaming neck
> Like a rush-imbedded swan,
> Like a lily from the beck,
> Like a moonlit poplar branch,
> Like a vessel at the launch
> When its last restraint is gone.   (Ll. 81–86)

But in a culture that polarizes male and female functions so that the female is rooted, immobilized, languidly statuesque yet a "vine," a weak vessel, a broken bowl, what way to imagine knowing and striving except as phallic thrust? The tree is not exclusively phallic, of course; as Freud suggests, "wood" is a natural female symbol,[17] and the fruit tree, if anything, is more properly an androgyne, towering on its root like a man, exfoliating and bearing fruit like a woman. Both Christian and Freudian orthodoxy, in fact, would find Laura guilty of spiritual or psychic onanism, persisting in her doomed endeavor to do it all by herself, appropriating patriarchal/phallic power for her own sufficiency. Certainly this is what seems to be going on when Laura attempts to germinate the kernel-stone in sterile solitude. But the possible Freudian substructure of these images remains skeletal and vague: these ambiguities are self-canceling rather than enriching. Laura's tree of life is more usefully seen as an offshoot of the tree of Genesis that includes as its offshoots all the other biblical trees—the fig-bearing and the barren, the tree marked for the axe, the "tree" on which Christ died—as well as the synecdochic parts of the tree—the root, the branch, the leaf. Against this allusive background, Laura's tree has the capacity to survive devastation.

For the moment, however, this promise is only a potential in the texture of the poem's language, and Laura has experienced a radical disintegration. She and Lizzie are no longer undifferentiated parts of a whole but a separate self and other. This is not to say that the undifferentiated double selves represent a superior state; the twinness belongs more to the realm of nature than of human activity, and moreover, the similarity was delusive, as the sisters clearly have different "natures" right from the beginning. Still, to diverge in this way is almost literally to tear oneself in two and to suffer horribly as a consequence. On one level *Goblin Market* is identical to scriptural and literary myth, for having attempted self-transcendence by becoming one with the fruit, Laura will discover instead the hellish pain of self-consciousness as experienced by Tennyson's personae in "The Two Voices" and "The Palace of Art." But in Rossetti's obsessive dialectic, individuation is not simply a difficult human process; rather, there seem to be only two possibilities, both of them equally undesirable: either total fusion or total, possessed, anxiety-driven separation. It is possible to see this either-or situation as a particularly female dilemma. For women in Victorian culture, at least, to act out individuation, to be different from their mothers and sisters, to separate from the familial matrix, was dangerous, if not impossible. It is not that you cannot go back home again, but that you can never leave, except for another "nest," this time the matrimonial, childbearing one. Further, if gender is extremely polarized, to desire and act is masculine-marked behavior, "unnatural" for a woman who, if she acts on her curiosity, on speculation, as Laura does, becomes a parody man—here a mock phallus ripe for castration.

After she "wilts" in this way, Laura acts out all the torments of the rejected and repining woman, except that she is more active, more childishly—and comically—driven. While Lizzie sleeps, the no longer blossom- or dovelike Laura "sat up in a passionate yearning, / And gnashed her teeth for baulked desire, and wept / As if her heart would break." This is the furious child of "Symbols" again, but after this passion she becomes secretive and mute, more sullen than exaltedly stricken. The only thing she can do while unnatural nature has its way with her, causing her to "dwindle" like the moon, is to keep watch, to become a vigil keeper, that is, a parodic version of one of Rossetti's central figures, the indomitable, unmoved soul who watches for the end, when all desire shall be fulfilled. Laura's attitude once again is correct, although her end is delusive and her watch in vain, both futile and part of the passing vanities of the temporal world.

One day remembering her kernel-stone   (L. 281)

Again like a child, Laura fastens on the magical transitional object that may bring back or duplicate the feast. The kernel-stone is a version of all the seeds, stones, buds and shoots that grow or *do not grow* in Rossetti's poems. In planting it, Laura is at once submitting to natural processes and trying to subvert them. Cut off from the fruit that would give her life, she is as good as dead; out of this death she tries to breed new life. What she hopes to achieve is what happens in "Spring," where frost-locked "Seeds, and roots, and stones of fruits" put forth shoots that reveal "the hidden life / . . . / Life nursed in its grave by Death" (*Works,* p. 345, August 17, 1859). And yet to involve oneself in the life process in this way is to let "it" happen: in "May," for instance, the speaker cannot tell us "how it was"; it simply "came to pass" on a day when the poppies had not yet germinated, nor the last eggs hatched, nor any bird left its mate. With the month, "it" passed away, leaving her "old, and cold, and grey" (*Works,* p. 318, November 20, 1855). It is "natural," then, for loss to follow possession, decay fruition, and Laura's last phase is like this speaker's. But Laura does not want "it" to happen to her; she does not want to pine away and die as is natural in the cycle that carries along roses, poppies and birds from seed or egg to maturity and death. As a consequence she commits an "unnatural" act, planting the kernel-stone that she hopes will return the cycle to the beginning.

The seed's failure to germinate represents not only Laura's hardness in sin and the hostility of mortal soil to immortal fruits but also Laura's hard and unnatural refusal to submit to the natural cycle. Like the stone-coldness she feels, it represents a core of resistance: Laura plants, but she does not really want to "grow" because growth at this point means only decline. In her efforts, Laura mimics God, who plants us in our garden-graves so we may live anew, who sends dew, rain and sunshine "To nourish one small seed" ("Consider the Lilies of the Field," *Works,* p. 156, October 21, 1853). Like the exile from the promised land Laura hopes for restitution: "Our seed shall yet strike root / And shall shoot up from the dust" ("By the Waters of Babylon," *Works*, p. 234, December 1, 1861). As this parallel text suggests, restitution is not implausible, but Laura cannot usurp patriarchal creativity; she must wait for a sister's Christ-like mediation.

And for the first time in her life / Began to listen and look (L. 328)

While Laura keeps vigil over her seed, Lizzie keeps vigil over Laura. Torn between her wish to help her sister—by supplying her with the magical fruit—and her fear that she will suffer the same fate as Laura and Jeanie, "who for joys brides hope to have in earliest winter time / Fell sick and died / In her gay prime," Lizzie also chooses to act. Whether or not in Jeanie's case the joys represent sexual delights, they are clearly the kind of joys that turn to ashes, that isolate Jeanie from her community role: she who should have been a bride becomes the bride of death and returns to (un)nature. But Lizzie's care for her sister enables her to overcome the powerful prohibitions and to take risks. The Lizzie who goes in search of the goblins "for the first time in her life / Began to listen and look." Began to act, that is, without the benefit of unreflective communal wisdom. No longer a Greek chorus, Lizzie becomes more like a tragic protagonist or a heroic quester who must risk her life to prevail over evil forces, and who must draw upon her own resources, including guile as well as strength of will. It is mainly endurance that Lizzie demonstrates in the goblins' assault upon her. But what other way, other than fleeing, to deal with this humiliating—"barking, mewing, hissing, mocking"—assault and still win the restorative antidote? This *is* typical female strength, the strength of a mother, for instance, who will not only fight like a tiger but also, when the circumstances demand it, use guile and endure *humiliation* to save her child. Lizzie's heroic fortitude transforms the eroticized similes that have been used to illustrate Laura's downfall into images of resplendent female power, images that will find echoes in Rossetti's later work in the figure of the "wonder" woman who endures to the end, the vigil keeper transformed into the apocalyptic woman clothed in the sun:

> White and golden Lizzie stood,
> Like a lily in a flood,—
> Like a rock of blue-veined stone
> Lashed by tides obstreperously,—
> Like a beacon left alone
> In a hoary soaring sea,
> Sending up a golden fire,—
> Like a fruit-crowned orange-tree
> White with blossoms honey-sweet
> Sore beset by wasp and bee
> Like a royal virgin town
> Topped with gilded dome and spire
> Close beleaguered by a fleet
> Mad to tug her standard down.   (Ll. 408–21)

Although Lizzie is speechless—"Lizzie uttered not a word"—she is no patient Griselda. She keeps her mouth shut pragmatically rather than symbolically—so that she will not be forced to eat the fruit—and she "laughs in her heart" at the triumph of her endurance which is also the triumph of the strategic guile that forces the goblins into their childish passion. Like Rumpelstilskin, the goblins stamp their feet and disappear, while Lizzie, sensorily alive—"in a smart, ache, tingle"—runs home to Laura, urged not by fear, but by a "kind heart" and "inward laughter."

Her ensuing passionate speech is the liberating revel of comedy, with permission replacing prohibition. "Laura," she cries,

> Come and kiss me.
> Never mind my bruises,
> Hug me, kiss me, suck my juices
> Squeezed from goblin fruits for you,
> Goblin pulp and goblin dew.
> Eat me, drink me, love me;
> Laura, make much of me:
> For your sake I have braved the glen
> And had to do with goblin merchant men.   (Ll. 466–74)

This speech is not only exuberant and comic but erotically innocent or, rather, beyond eroticism. At the heart of the feast is the Eucharistic feast, in which the man-god's flesh and blood are eaten. Lizzie has endured a physical passion on the order of Christ's passion, and as a female Christ for her sister, for another, she makes an entirely appropriate offer. This is not to say that the transactions in *Goblin Market* are spiritual rather than physical; they are, in fact, profoundly physical, as physical as the nourishment, delight, and corruption of the body can be. Laura's dis-ease is profound and it can be cured only by another leap of the imagination. The earlier travesty feast is undone by comedy, as Laura, falling on Lizzie in an access of sisterly anxiety—"Lizzie, Lizzie, have you tasted / For my sake the fruit forbidden?"—feasts both unintentionally and of necessity.

Her lips began to scorch, / That juice was wormwood to her tongue, / She loathed the feast   (Ll. 493–95)

Immediately, however, Laura experiences the ravages of the new feast. Just as the Eucharist repeats and corrects the feast that marks the fall, this feast replaces the addictive poison with restorative antidote. Although the original food was sweet to taste—Laura thought it would never cloy—its consequences were terribly bitter: Laura dried up and turned to stone as a result of eating. This cathartic repetition reveals the true taste of goblin fruits, but where those had bitter residue, this poison will bring refreshment. As we shall see in the second section of this chapter, Rossetti develops a complex dialectic between the feast and the fast, the full and the poisoned cup, that has to do with the ambiguities of what is "enough," and with how one can avoid hellish self-absorption by the paradisal feast of Love, in which the self is absorbed into the divine All.

Laura has experienced a version of self-absorption that Rossetti calls "self-consuming care," the obsessive anxiety that befalls the soul whenever it becomes possessed, not by demons, but by demonic aspirations toward total self-sufficiency. Although there is in Rossetti's dialectic a heroic form of self-possession, the quality that Lizzie displays, self-consumed Laura must be broken down. Here Rossetti uses a series of similes that pose the single thing against the multitudinous, the individuated structure—really the individuated self—against chaotic energies. Laura's senses, which appeared to constitute her integral self but which led her astray, here literally fail. Overwhelmed by the cataclysm within her, she loses consciousness and dies to her old self:

> Like the watchtower of a town
> Which an earthquake shatters down,
> Like a lightning-stricken mast,
> Like a wind-uprooted tree
> Spun about,
> Like a foam-topped waterspout
> Cast down headlong in the sea,
> She fell at last.   (Ll. 514–21)

Again the similes go beyond their initial eroticism; in one sense Laura is here "castrated," but all along she has been spiritually as well as physically impotent: she cannot get enough of what she wants and needs, and she wants the wrong thing. This metaphorical—and internal—fall doubles and corrects the initial fall just as the wormwood feast doubles and corrects the initial goblin feast.

Hovering in a liminal state, between life and death, Laura is finally restored to herself through the vigilance of her sister. Here Lizzie performs the act that is almost the exclusive function of the female community, keeping vigil by the side of the sick or dying person. In the course of the poem both sisters have lost track of night and day, but Laura, after her dark night of the soul, wakes to the diurnal round that includes both nature and humans, both "golden sheaves" and "reapers." Laura awakes "as if from a dream" to a "new day," her physical decline magically reversed. The "dream" has been not simply a demonic visitation but a true lapse of attention, a falling away from self by nightmarish absorption into the self that is the opposite of self-possession, and that is also a fall into unnatural—inhuman—nature. While Laura, by a "masculine" act falls into the "female" world of decay, Lizzie stands fast in her self-possession, discovering the uses of goblin adversity, and achieves her highest self-realization in being for another. Laura's attempts to escape the cycle of "natural" womanhood only plant her further in it, but Lizzie succeeds in transcending nature—and Laura's death in nature—by a sisterly and womanly act of self-transcendence. Laura cannot do it all by herself, but Lizzie can do it for another, and thus for "herself," the female self. The wormwood feast cancels female self-division, and division from one another, as two sisters fuse in one purpose, and no singular *one* flourishes while another pines.

For there is no friend like a sister   (L. 562)

At the end of her restorative sleep Laura is reborn as an integrated self: not a sister-twin, but a sister-friend. The sisters now marry—it doesn't matter whom, for simply the act of marriage signifies their participation in communal life and their transformation into "mothers"—and produce children for whom they articulate their myth. But can the domestic world and its myth compete with exotic adventure and wild, sensuous dreams? Is it possible to say that antithetical selves have been reconciled and that the sisters are now actors who share a unique female history? Or, as Sandra Gilbert asserts, does the ending of the poem represent a regressive vision, a backing away from the male literary fruits and a return to the childhood garden?[18]

"For there is no friend like a sister" may seem like an oversimplification at best, a pious banality at worst, a sugarcoating for the bitter pill of domestic exile. But the poem has led inevitably and surely to this conclusion: there *is* no friend like a sister, there is no power like that of the female community—which already exists for every woman and does not have to be proven or sought. *Goblin Market* represents a rediscovery of true female origins and a rejection of the patriarchal quest myth or, rather, a reappropriation of it as a female myth. Laura and Lizzie narrate their story within a world where mothers educate children, passing on a mother's version of *res gestae*. If the old myths show women setting themselves in deadly peril and devastating the world by Eve's "mistake," then Rossetti will append a saving closure, showing women saving themselves through sisterhood and narrating their own "harmless"—demystified, that is—version of that myth. The poem that begins with streetseller's cries ends with a nursery chant that constitutes a reframing of mythic truth as gnomic, yet practical and adaptive wisdom.

II

The elaboration and reframing of Rossetti's female myth goes on in images and structures scattered throughout the rest of her career.

In order to follow out the parabolic drift of Rossetti's major poem, I have selected some central paradoxes and binary oppositions around which groups of poems can be clustered. The first opposition concerns gardens and antigardens, including exile from the garden and destruction of the garden. The second derives from the question "What is enough?" and revolves around two metaphors: the denial or satisfaction of appetite and the transaction or barter of "all" for "All." The third focuses on two metaphors for the self, the ungerminating kernel-stone and the fruit-bearing tree. The final takes up the peculiar logic of the relation between poison and antidote. This reading rests on the two central premises which underlie my whole critical reading of Rossetti's poems: that the religious poems "correct" without canceling the experiences of the fallen world rendered in the so-called secular poems, and that Rossetti's rewriting or doubling of her own poems, as well as the texts of biblical and Romantic literary tradition, contributes to a female myth and, ultimately, a female aesthetic.

Gardens and Antigardens

At work in *Goblin Market* as in other Rossetti poems is a language of gardens and antigardens in which the same sign may stand for opposed referents, and in which signs are strongly linked to their opposites. Like the language of scripture and scriptural commentary it is rooted in ambiguity and paradox: "graves" turn out to be "gardens," and "without change" reads differently depending on whether it signifies hellish nullity or celestial plenitude. Within this framework, any reference to an earthly garden brings into play the Edenic or paradisal garden, as well as the enclosed garden of the Song of Songs, and also their opposite, the exile or the desert—the "wilderness." The invariance of the connection makes it possible to automatically transform "wilderness" into "garden" and "garden" into "wilderness," to the extent that the symbolic meanings of these terms are present to the reader at all times. As seen in "A Bride Song," the fulfillment of married love is imaged as a land "like a garden to smell and to sight," but even if this land "were turned to a desert of sand," it would retain its paradisal attributes, with the desert transformed into waters, the wilderness into a rose. Conversely, in the somber "I Have a Message Unto Thee (Written in Sickness)," Rossetti inventories the spring profusion among which, like Laura, the speaker pines, "ruinously pale," only in order to assert that this paradise is ephemeral, and Earth's gardens are valuable only as symbols to remind us of "heaven's own harvest field / With undecaying saps" (*Works,* p. 316). Earth's gardens may in fact be wildernesses, for in our garden walks we find ruins everywhere: "a hundred subtle stings / To prick us in our daily walk: / A young fruit cankered on its stalk" ("Yet a Little While," *Works,* p. 343, August 6, 1858). It is easy to speculate that Rossetti felt herself blighted and thwarted, and so made a virtue out of necessity. More likely, however, her mistrust of "easy" gardens stems from her awareness of the deep connection, in language and so in thought, between women and gardens—women as ripe buds, or full-blown roses, or fruits to be plucked—and the particular mortality that this sign system imparts to women: "all things that pass are woman's looking-glass" ("Passing and Glassing"). As these examples demonstrate, both before and after *Goblin Market* Rossetti was employing the symbolic transformations that give that poem its poetic logic: Laura's imagined "odorous mead" is a travesty of the Edenic garden, and her own little garden plainly a desert. These transformations also underlie the asceticism of Rossetti's aesthetic: the garden is valueless because it is actually a wilderness; the wilderness is valuable because it is potentially a garden.[19]

The earthly paradise is not always a travesty or a mere emblem of the heavenly garden, however, nor is Rossetti always so eager to renounce it. The garden of "Symbols," for instance, is a ruined paradise to be set off against the celestial garden; it is also obviously the garden of self, and belongs with the self-gardens of "Shut-Out," *The Prince's Progress,* and *From House to Home.* Characteristically, Rossetti deploys the garden as image of self in a double way: in "Symbols" the ruination of the garden, its transformation into wilderness, stands for thwarted potential and the fallen self; elsewhere the garden remains whole and stands for the ideal self, while exile stands for thwarted potential. That mythic selfhood is the obvious subject of a garden poem that predates *Goblin Market*, "Shut-Out" (*Works,* p. 320, January 21, 1856). Here the exile is radical and causeless, the garden unambiguously Edenic:

> The door was shut. I looked between
> Its iron bars: and saw it lie,
> My garden, mine, beneath the sky,
> Pied with all flowers bedewed and green.
> . . . .
> With all its nests and stately trees
> It had been mine, and it was lost.

"My garden" cannot be anything other than "my self." Either the garden is despoiled, as in "Symbols,"or the self is dispossessed as in this poem. Like both speakers Laura is exiled from her innocence and from further "knowledge," and in her mistaken attempt to attain an ideal self becomes the fallen self.

While in her garden speculations Laura is completely wrong, in the same way that Eve is wrong in Genesis, in these other garden poems the garden of the ideal self is represented as an undeserved loss. This kind of garden is valuable not only because it is delightful but because it is "mine." Retrospectively, the garden of *From House to Home* (1858) is a solipsistic delusion, like Tennyson's "Palace of Art:" it is a "pleasure place" within the soul, "an earthly paradise supremely fair / That lured me from my goal." In the language of the poem, however, this paradise is represented as anything but delusive; the structure that most resembles the delusive palace of art is a "glittering and frail" castle, but this is dismissed in a stanza, while seven stanzas are given over to a description of what the speaker calls her "pleasaunce," a rich and extensive landscape:

> My pleasaunce was an undulating green,
> Stately with trees whose shadows
> slept below,
> With glimpses of smooth garden-beds
> between
> Like flame or sky or snow.   (*Works,* p. 21)

This pleasaunce supports varied life, including a number of small

phallic creatures—lizards, frogs, toads, caterpillars, snails, slugs—
that can be seen as an earlier evolutionary stage of the goblins. In
contrast to the terrified and enraged speaker of "Symbols," who
rampages through the aborted garden, the keeper of the pleasaunce
is marked by godlike forbearance. She tolerates all forms of "queer"
life: "I never marred the curious sudden stool / That perfects in a
night." Rossetti is perfectly at home in this mental-physical land-
scape: she possesses it and lets it be, promoting ideal conditions for
the ideal self. But there is also trouble in the garden. Although the
mole and the hedgehog are not in danger from the speaker, the
speaker is in danger from her angelic companion, the animus who
has the power to fulfill ("With spirit discerning eyes like flames of fire
/ But deep as the unfathomed endless sea, / Fulfilling my desire") and
to deprive, and who ultimately devastates the garden, simply by
withdrawing his presence—and his power. If we regard the angelic
companion as a projection of self, then Rossetti has completed the
garden of female—and polymorphous—selfhood by the addition of
a masculine "active" power. He is angelic because he represents
"mind" or "spirit," as opposed to the physicality of the garden
which, although it appears remarkably complete and self-sustaining,
must be conceived of as a lack—female nature and female Nature.
When the "active" power is withdrawn, the female garden is de-
stroyed. What follows is an allegorical vision of the suffering renun-
ciatory woman, a female Christ who weeps and bleeds, and whose
torment—she walks on flowers whose stalks are thorns—is prepara-
tion for a paradisal apotheosis. By the end of the poem, then, the
speaker has entered the exile of the wilderness-garden, where cul-
tivation for a heavenly flowering must go on. This cultivating in-
volves pain—the speaker-self is a tree whose branches must be
pruned—and clearly a contraction, or even dessication, of the speak-
er's prior expansiveness. What remains, however, is radically strong,
a tree fed at the root by Christ's blood. This, then, is the true female
garden, not waste, but waiting.

There is an obvious complementary relation between *Goblin Mar-
ket* and *From House to Home,* written a year earlier. Beyond the
similarities in pattern and tone—the luxurance of the garden, the
intensity of the "famine," the "bitterness" of the redemption—there

is the question of the protagonist's relation to the garden of self. Though distanced, Laura, too, has her pleasaunce: the unknown "odorous mead" and the goblins and fruit which are its "life." Despite the canonical answers, the question remains: why must that garden be renounced or destroyed? Obviously because something very dangerous enters or is present in the garden: to *have* and to *do* are both very dangerous. Again there seem to be obvious and traditional answers, both religious and psychosexual. What seems more dangerous than spiritual or sexual transgression, however, is simply the violent power sweeping through both poems, coursing through veins and devastating gardens. Again one is reminded of the wrathful child in "Symbols," who violates the natural symbols that have disappointed her. In line with Sandra Gilbert and Susan Gubar's general argument about nineteenth-century women's literature, I think that there is powerful, subversive rage at work in the poem, and it is the rage, perhaps, that is the real danger. Since the rage can go nowhere, since it gets directed inward and smashes or poisons what has been despoiled already, or marked for despoilation, Rossetti then attempts to define what *remains*: however barren or thorny the ground, it is inalienably hers. While the speaker of *From House to Home* comes to her estrangement, Laura is from the beginning estranged from her pleasaunce, and her attempt to regain it through eating the fruits is no less futile and parodic than her attempt to regain the fruits after eating them. Both poems offer similar definitions of the female garden: it can be possessed only temporarily; it is defined by loss and lack; and it is ravaged both by the exertion of power and the withdrawal of power, both the eating of the fruits and their denial. What remains in both cases is the wilderness-garden which must be strenuously, even cruelly, pruned.

The pleasaunce of *From House to Home* turns up as a more obviously eroticized garden in the later allegory of loss and frustration, *The Prince's Progress* (*Works*, p. 26). Here the garden is the wasting princess's "own country," which the prince achieves after a prolonged series of vicissitudes and diversions. Having negotiated a Childe Roland wasteland, countries of "famine," the prince passes through a "fissure barren and black" to come upon a remarkably fecund country:

Before his face a valley spread
Where fatness laughed, wine, oil, and bread,
Where all fruit-trees their sweetness shed,
    Where all birds made love to their kind,
Where jewels twinkled, and gold lay red
    And not hard to find.   (*Works*, p. 33)

This valley is as obvious and as liberal as the "pleasaunce," on one
level simply the vulva lying open to the fatal worm:

Rose, will she open the crimson core
Of her heart to him?
Above his head a tangle glows
Of wine-red roses, blushes, snows,
Closed buds and buds that unclose,
    Leaves, and moss, and prickles too;
His hand shook as he plucked a rose,
    And the rose dropped dew.   (*Works*, p. 33)

Like Laura, then, the prince makes the gesture that breaks off the
dormancy period, and marks the fall. The princess dies shortly after
this symbolic violation, and although no cause and effect relation is
made, the death may on one level be construed as sexual. Ostensibly,
however, she simply fades away because the prince has come "too
late." Symbolically, perhaps, the princess dies because the arrival of
the prince means the end of her as virgin princess, because she exists
only insofar as she "lacks." She pines because her garden is incom-
plete without him; she dies because his coming means the end of her
garden: the phallic power that she lacks is also the phallic power that
destroys. Similarly Laura perishes, or comes close to perishing, both
for lack of the fruits and because of the fruits. Either way, the garden
of self-sufficiency and self-possession is impossible to maintain.

Although exile from the garden, dispossession from one's rightful
inheritance, is a universal human experience, this myth is particularly
suited to Rossetti's situation as a woman and poet in Victorian
England. As she makes the shift from childhood to adulthood she
must give up the diffusely erotic garden of self for a constrained and
dependent, even subservient, role. As a woman she must learn how
to be a "vine"; as a poet and sister to her brother she must learn how
not to be "first." On all levels, she has to deal with her sense of

dispossession by making do with a much smaller and sparser territory than had once been hers in fantasy or reality. Instead of letting her garden with all its rosebushes, lizards, and snails simply *be*, she must, in the absence or failure of phallic power which *appears* to sustain but always destroys, cultivate what has been left to her: "My vineyard that is mine I have to keep, / Pruning for fruit the pleasant twigs and leaves," says the speaker of "Yea I Have a Goodly Heritage" (*Works*, p. 280, ca. 1890). All Rossetti's "late" gardens are wilderness gardens of this type, images of the self-sufficiency that depends on self-restraint. Christian symbolism rationalizes the choice to remain "athirst and hungering on a barren spot," hedged with a "thorny hedge" ("From Sunset to Rise Star," *Works*, p. 375, February 22, 1865). Yet Christian symbolism also allows for the opposite, for the exile's longing after the garden of which she has been dispossessed: "To them my trees, to them my gardens yield / Their sweets and spices and their tender green" (*Works*, p. 239, June 29, 1864). In developing her myth of self Rossetti repeatedly recounts how the dispossession inevitably takes place, how the painful cultivation goes on, and how the appetites persist undiminished.

Sufficiency and the Nature of Appetite

Eye hath not seen, nor ear heard, nor heart conceived that full "enough."

On her return from the goblin feast Laura tells Lizzie: "I ate and ate my fill, / Yet my mouth waters still" (l. 165). Later she will feel deprived, painfully insatiable, but at this moment she is at one with the object of her desire, the infant at the breast who is perfectly self-sufficient, or so she thinks. As in the case of the garden, the language of feast and famine, of oral appetite, that is, runs through all of Rossetti's poetry: it is both a synecdoche for a full range of sensual appetites and a metaphor for spiritual aspirations, the soul hungering and thirsting for the feast that is God. Yet Rossetti's insistence on the metaphor, like all her repetitions, suggests that something special is at stake, an early fantasy, perhaps, if not an actual experience. One of the few poems that has any reference to contemporary events concerns the plights of starving lambs whose mothers could not feed them, and were fed by shepherds with teapots ("The Lambs of Grasmere, 1860," *Works*, p. 350). Rossetti's sympathy for animals does not alone account for this poem; its rather grotesque subject seems fraught with special anxieties, despite the happy ending. Nothing, it seems to be saying, is more terrible than death by starvation and a mother's inability to feed the child. Another poem that precedes *Goblin Market* tells of a mother who has obscurely neglected her baby and is about to die. The baby answers the mother, who has expressed a wish to kiss her baby: "You shall kiss and kiss your fill, mother, / In the nest of Paradise" (*Works*, p. 311, January 7, 1854) Although this kissing, which recalls Laura's sucking, is ascribed to the mother, it seems more likely that the baby—and Rossetti's baby-self—wishes to suck its fill, a gratification possible only in "the nest of Paradise." We must not, however, imagine the grown Rossetti as a monstrously greedy child hankering after forbidden sweets or converting them into self-consuming poison. More important is the way instinctual desires are filtered through traditional biblical figures. In the translation of Eros into Agape, appetitive desires are transformed into spiritual desires, and the inexhaustible feast that satisfies without cloying is fully achieved.

In "St. Peter," for instance, Rossetti reworks traditional figures for the soul's longing for Christ to create an intense expression of personal longing:

> Like as the hart the water-brooks I Thee
>   Desire, my hands
> I stretch to Thee, O kind Lord, pity me:
> Lord, I have wept, wept bitterly,
>   I driest of dry lands.   (*Works*, p. 177, ca. 1877)

What is remarkable is the collocation of figures; the way the traditional associations act upon one another, and the way the self is imaged as both weeper and dry lands recalls other such images for the self in Rossetti's poetry. But it is also the aspects of form—the enjambment in lines 1–3, the assonance, the caesuras, the repetition of "wept," the rhyme—that give St. Peter's cry its controlled passion. Just as the conception of the spiritual appetite overpowers the conception of the physical appetite, converting it into a strong metaphor, so the formal design overcomes the allusions, converting the conventional "hart/brook" metaphor into a fresh and powerful metaphor of the dry land weeping.

The intertextual allusions—between poems, between the poem and other texts—are part of the poem's original meaning, however. There is a network of connection, for instance, between St. Peter and the Prodigal Son of the New Testament and the Babylonian exiles of the Old Testament. The Prodigal Son hungers for the perpetual feast of home, a land not unlike the princess' own land in *The Prince's Progress*:

> Hungry here with the crunching swine,
> Hungry harvest have I to reap;
> ....
> There is plenty of bread at home,
>   His servants have bread enough and to spare,
> The purple wine-fat froths with foam,
>   Oil and spices make sweet the air,
>   While I perish hungry and bare.   (*Works*, p. 251, B. 1882)

Here even proportion tells us something: this description of the prodigal's hunger takes up exactly half the poem; the second half deals with his resolve to return. This exiled, but chiefly *hungry*, prodigal is keenly aware of what he is missing: the feast is as sensuously detailed as Laura's fruits, and he is as destitute as the ravaged speaker of *From House to Home*. Similarly, the Babylonian exiles recall with masochistic voluptuousness the ripe pleasures of the land toward which they kneel with "famished" faces. There "milk and honey flow," "waters spring," and there dwell the fig tree and the fruitful vine; there also strangers reap the harvest and "make their fat hearts wanton with my wishes" (*Works*, pp. 239, 240).[20] Both prodigal and Babylonian exile hunger, parabolically, for what St. Peter hungers for, and Laura's appetite is a parodic version of these appetites. The objects of these appetites compose a spectrum with Laura's fruits at one end, St. Peter's crucified Christ at the other, and Laura becomes a kind of typological figure from a "fallen" fictional world, prefiguring the desirous Christian soul.

The progress of Rossetti's appetite for Christ can be anatomized in a group of devotional poems extending across her career. In these she addresses herself specifically to what will satisfy without cloying. The lyric speaker typically expresses her need as unalloyed oral appetite: "I thirst for Thee, full fount and flood" (*Works*, p. 243).[21] This insatiable appetite is projected onto the symbolic landscape; "All earth's full rivers cannot fill / The sea, that drinking thirsteth still" (*Works*, p. 343); and the ocean announces itself as thirsting "from long ago, / Because earth's rivers cannot fill the main" (*Works*, p. 413). In other poems the soul is compared explicitly with the river, longing to merge with God as the river longs to merge with the ocean.[22] These are oceanic appetites, then, and the "feast" itself is voracious; ultimately the hungry, thirsty self can be satisfied only by being itself swallowed up. In the Eucharist this paradox is fully realized: He who hungers for the human soul gives Himself to eat, while the feaster both consumes the source of nourishment and is absorbed by the feast.

With this end to appetite as a model, it becomes clear why the soul is "Beset by hunger earth can never feed" (*Later Life*, no. 25, *Works*, p. 81). Earth is death-ridden; here "Men heap up pleasures and enlarge desire, / Outlive desire, and famished evermore / Consume themselves within the undying fire" (*Works*, p. 227). This hellish fire is opposed to the fire that refines the soul, leading it upward to heaven, the purgative fire that burns away Laura's torment. It is also possible, however, to achieve a kind of satiety on earth. The speaker of *Later Life* is "sick of fasting" and "sick of food," indeed sick of "self" (p. 78), while another speaker asserts: "Long have I longed, till I am tired / Of longing and desire" (*Works*, p. 402). For this speaker the only alternative is to accept Christ's invitation to "joy the joys *unsatiate*" (*Works*, p. 164, my emphasis).

To enjoy the "joys unsatiate" fulfills a deep infantile wish, for to partake in the endless feast is to become one with the nurturer. But this is not possible, nor even desirable, in this fallen world, where individuation and separation from the world are necessary conditions for "salvation," for the movement toward the fusion of death and transcendence. The lack of mediacy in Rossetti's poetry raises certain questions: Why in her image system, is separation equivalent to starvation? Is appetite so threatening because it can be satisfied only by a fusion that is annihilating?

For the female self, it would seem, starvation and eating can be equally dangerous. If starvation means self-denial, a self defined by "want," then eating can mean a horrifying fusion, a self absorbed by the feast and by the self. In "A Triad" (*Works,* p. 329, December 18, 1856, written three years before *Goblin Market*), Rossetti categorizes three women "on the threshold" in terms of feeding and starving. One of the three is a fallen woman, one a wife, and one an unrequited virgin. The first two ostensibly flourish; the third is "blue with famine after love," the repining woman who turns up in so many of Rossetti's poems. None of the alternatives is ultimately satisfactory, however, for even the wife grows "gross in soulless love, a sluggish wife," while the virgin dies, and the shamed woman is as good as dead. Significantly, Rossetti is most scornful not of the fallen woman but of the "sluggish" wife, whose spiritual torpor is imaged as mindless gluttony: "One droned in sweetness like a fattened bee." Rossetti's fastidious nature finds it repugnant that the wife gets fat, whether from overeating, or pregnancy or from abandonment to the sweets of married—sexual—love. Sexual appetite, then, can be satisfied only at the expense of becoming wife or whore, either grossly self-absorbed or spiritually and socially dead. Here the images which ultimately derive from a personal psychological situation serve to embody the historical situation: Rossetti succinctly anatomizes female roles as defined by Victorian patriarchy—wife, virgin-spinster, whore—and demonstrates how all are deadly falsifications of female selfhood.

Beyond the threat of loss of self, desire satisfied in this fallen world poses specific moral problems: How do you get what you want without depriving others? If the starving exile pines while others flourish, then how can the exile flourish except at another's expense? In "Cannot Sweeten" (*Works,* p. 381, March 8, 1866), Rossetti explores the psychology of a ballad heroine who has in effect devoured her lover:

> I ate his life as a banquet,
>   I drank his life as new wine,
>   I fattened upon his leanness,
> Mine to flourish and his to pine.

This vivid inversion of the Eucharistic feast possibly reflects Rossetti's sense of the consequences of "monstrous" appetite: if she devours, if she suits *herself* like the woman in the poem, she may wind up devoured, like the man in the poem. Once again this generalized psychological reality intersects with a particular social reality, for the poem may also be read as a projection of others' devouring needs as much as her own terrifying appetites. "Mine to flourish and his to pine" is a simple reversal, after all, of "His to flourish and mine to pine." If Dante Gabriel flourishes, that is, he in some way eats up her power, her allotment. While he feasts and grows aesthetically "fat," she fasts and grows aesthetically "thin," not only because she fears the consequences of her own appetites, but because she fears the consequences of his; for if his physical appetites are poisonous to himself and damaging to others, his aesthetic appetites are specifically cannibalistic. In "In an Artist's Studio" (*Works*, p. 330, December 24, 1856), the artist, here Dante Gabriel, "feeds" on his model's beauty, draining the actual woman, Elizabeth Siddal, of her vitality, and even more, obliterating her individual selfhood. This indictment of the artist sounds like the usual Victorian expostulation against solipsism in art, but the imagery that links "In an Artist's Studio" with "Cannot Sweeten" suggests that more is at stake, that as a woman who stood be "fed upon" and as an artist who must "feed" Rossetti had a special horror of the kind of self-indulgence that consumes both the feaster and the feast. Although Laura's feast harms no one but herself, it does involve the abrogation of relationships and responsibilities; it will have to be annulled by another feast that mimes but does not travesty the Eucharistic feast.

If the satisfaction of hungers in the fallen world is so problematic as to lead either to hellish self-absorption or to cannibalization of others, then rigorous self-denial becomes not merely reactive but morally imperative. In the early poem "The World" (*Works*, p. 182, June 27, 1854), a woman offers a treacherous feast: "Ripe fruits, sweet flowers, and *full satiety*" (my emphasis). But just as the female garden is delusive, so this fair woman is a "lie"; by night she is monstrous in her need, "With pushing horns and clawed and clutching hands." If the "true" female garden is wilderness ground, then the "true" female feast is the fast that turns leavings into divine food. As an aesthetic, this is accounted for not simply by the Tractarian doctrine of Reserve,[23] for although Rossetti might well find that rubric useful as sanction for her poetic austerity, her paradoxical leaps, such as that from feast to famine, are often bold rather than "reserved."

Again, the audacity of this aesthetic derives from Christian symbolism itself: just as expulsion from the garden makes possible the reversal by which wilderness or desert becomes garden, so exclusion from, or rejection of, the feast makes possible the spiritual nourishment of the fast. In Christ's abstemiousness Rossetti finds the ultimate model for the self-restraint that annuls self-absorption: "He hungered Who the hungry thousands fed, / And thirsted Who the world's refreshment bore" (*Works,* p. 227). Rossetti chooses to identify not with the human artist, the narcissistic lover gazing in the woman-mirror that gives him back himself, but with the human sufferer who looks into the mirror of "grief" and sees two suffering faces, "Christ's Face and man's in some sort made alike." Contemplating this resemblance, the sufferer can take pleasure at last: "Then grief is pleasure with a subtle taste" (*Works,* p. 227). This sufferer has chosen a refined epicureanism: she would not "drug with sweets the bitterness I drank, / Or break by feasting my perpetual fast" (*Works,* p. 383, B. 1870).

Starting from the position of the hungry exile who has been forced to abandon the garden of self, Rossetti pursues, over the course of the poetry, a logic of desire, the final terms being the righteous faster who feasts on her hunger and the complementary figure of the sinning feaster who is consumed by her appetite. Although this pattern is strongly synchronic, with the same relation between appetite and its fulfillment operative throughout her poetic career, Rossetti does, in a sense, develop, in that the hungry man and the saint can be seen as the final incarnations of the desiring self: stylized, Byzantine refinements of the earlier exiles and prodigals.

Even as late as "before 1882," however, Rossetti persists in questioning the reality of the distinction between feaster and faster in the fallen world. In the person of "Maiden May" she asks: "Wherefore greatest? Wherefore least? / Hearts that starve and hearts that feast? /

You and I?" (*Works,* p. 401, B. 1882, my emphasis). The "you" and "I" could be anyone, of course, a self relative to an other. It is significant, however, that Rossetti thinks of difference, possibly even of individuation, as inequality, and it is impossible not to speculate that the "you" is her brother, Dante Gabriel Rossetti, even if by now his life was ended. He feasts and is consumed by his own appetite, but he feasts at her expense, simply by virtue of being the oldest male child and the designated family genius. She, as a consequence, takes up an equally extreme position as the faster who finds nourishment in bitterness, in frugal fare, and in hunger itself.

The Metaphor of Barter

Behind Laura, pondering the insatiate nature of goblin food, stands the self-abnegating but desirous lyric speaker, evaluating what has been allotted, what suffices, what is more than enough, what is offered and what she has to offer, what can be measured and what cannot. At worst, this sufferer has nothing but her suffering, like the female figure at the end of *From House to Home* who is set the Augean task of measuring "measureless sorrow toward its length, / And breadth, and depth, and height." No sorrow is too much: she cannot have enough, just as Laura cannot have enough of the goblin feast. At best, the sufferer wagers an earthly "nothing" against a heavenly "all," for the correlative of insatiable need is inexhaustible supply. Like the metaphor of feast and fast, the metaphor of barter or transaction raises issues of differentiation, inequality, and fusion. The metaphor in this case moves from the unequal distribution between a self and another—the "I" is too poor or has too much to give, the other gives too much or has too little to give—to the cancellation of distinctions, the absorption of individual differences into an "all."

In a sense the movement is chronological; the metaphor of barter has a meaning in the late religious poems different from that of the early love laments. The speaker of the love lyrics may, on the one hand, long for the full transaction of earthly love, finding herself "Ready to spend and be spent for your sake" (*Monna Innominata* 9, *Works,* p. 62); on the other hand, she may find the transaction empty: "Still spending for that thing which is not bought" ("After All," *Works,* p. 304, October 24, 1852). By the time of the devotional poem "Lent," however, the speaker discovers that the same wager leads to more certain recompense: it is good to "spend and be spent" so long as this depletion of resources leads to "Easter Day" (*Works,* p. 163, 1886). Rossetti has revived the metaphor for a new purpose, doubling it in effect, and has achieved something like irony: the assertion of faith gains depth by similarity to, and contrast with, the romantic avowal of the *Monna Innominata* sonnet, and, if we read synchronically, the romantic avowal is strongly qualified by a religious context.

But the movement—from unequal and partial exchange to equal and total exchange—is present also in individual poems and individual sequences. In a sequence of four sonnets entitled "By Way of Remembrance" (*Works,* p. 384, toward October 1870) the speaker goes through a series of ruminations on the nature of love's transactions. In the first, the speaker, though fully aware of what is due to her and from her, considers herself "poor" in that she has too little to give: the accounts must be settled in the next life. In the second and third she meditates on the nature of the reunion after death, in particular the awfulness of the *individuation* of the final resurrection. In the fourth, however, she takes comfort in the fact that loving is its own end, that love's mere self is a continual feast, sufficient until the time when "love reborn annuls / Loss and decay and death—and all is love."

Returning to the context of the body of Rossetti's work, we find that as in the single sequence, the ultimately satisfying transaction involves exchanging "all" for the "all in all" ("At Last," *Works,* p. 405, B. 1882). But this Love which is the full "enough" is present from the beginning in Rossetti's work as a telos that shapes her images. In "Who Have a Form of Godliness?" (*Works,* p. 156, December 18, 1853) the divine love feast will be available in the times of restitution, "the sweet times refreshing" when "my God shall fill my longings to the brim." And in the slightly later "What Good Shall My Life Do Me?" (*Works,* p. 346, August 27, 1859) the speaker advises the hopeless soul that Love, which offers full restitution in death—"Shall not this infinite Love suffice / To feed thy dearth?"—is the potent generative force that fertilizes and feeds the natural universe, satisfying the most basic hungers. Ultimately Love is not only "all in all" but the "better part," the part that can be everything, and that can be obtained only "at the cost of all things here." For that sufficiency the suppliant is willing to offer her "all": she gives up everything, including her burdensome selfhood, but in return she gets, "at last," enough.

The demonic version of Love's absorbing feast is the cannibalizing that transpires when the human lover "feeds" on the beloved as object, as in "In an Artist's Studio" and "Cannot Sweeten." If such absorption of one ego by another is an inevitable consequence of individuation—"Wherefore . . . / Hearts that starve and hearts that feast / You and I?"—then Rossetti must imagine another kind of feast for desire. The inequity that seems to follow upon individuation is canceled by the absorption of the self into an all that is never depleted; the more Christ gives, for instance, the more he has to give: "Who givest more the more Thyself hast given" ("Ascension Eve," *Works*, p. 169). Typically, we see Rossetti translating a set of terms—starve, feast, give, enough, all, I, you—*as if* into another language by restating them in a different context. Rossetti recapitulates the Romantic attempt to transcend and realize, or realize by transcending, the self. But in her insistence on retaining the same terms while inventing a new meaning, we see her grappling with some of the problems posed by phallocentric discourse: writing as a female subject she is both the traditional—and phallocentric—lyric "I," the subject who desires and lacks, and the female who experiences herself as object of desire, as the lack itself. It is that second identity that gets expressed not by the cancellation of the "I" but by the images of absorption or dissolution, which exert a strong pull on the "I," and by the translation of terms into another sphere where everything remains the same but is reconstituted as incalculably different. The "I" remains part of her integral female identity, for of course the linguistic and cultural barriers cannot be transcended, and that identity consists of the *play* between an instransigent "I," the seed-stone of self, and various forms of fusion or "translation."

The Kernel-Stone and the Tree of Exile

The self who survives exile and famine, and who only hopes for the fusion of "all in all," is something like the Laura who turns "cold as stone" when she realizes that only Lizzie hears the goblins, and who plants her kernel-stone, stubbornly watching it not grow. What is suggested by Laura's arrestation and rigidity is the obstinacy and rigidity of the stoic sufferer, the woman frozen in a pose, as in "A Soul": "She stands as pale as Parian statues stand / . . . a wonder, deathly-white" (*Works*, p. 311, February 7, 1854). This is the frozen statue-woman who will appear as vigil keeper and watcher in a group of poems discussed in chapter 3. Courageous as it seems, the resistance of this stoic sufferer neighbors on death and despair. This kind of cold and stony resistance shows up as pure negation in "Once for All" (*Works*, p. 380, January 8, 1866), where it is a patch of garden snow encountered on a spring walk: "So walking in a garden of delight / I came upon one sheltered shadowed nook / . . . / And there lay snow unmelted by the sun." This patch of snow is an image of dread comparable to Emily Dickinson's snake who inspires "the zero at the bone." Internalized, this patch of coldness belongs to the hardened sinner: the vampirish woman of "Cannot Sweeten" must bear a heart as "cold as stone, as hard, as heavy." But it may also be the appropriate response to the shocks of living: "My heart within me like a stone / Is numbed too much for hopes or fears" ("A Better Resurrection," *Works*, p. 191, June 30, 1857). Whatever the situation, the cold hardness not only defines a bedrock of self but also exists only to be broken down. In the devotional lyrics Rossetti fills in the other term of the dialectic—resist/give up—by begging Christ to melt her stone heart, to rescue her from the despair in which she bears what the speaker of *An Old World Thicket* calls the "actual self of lead" (*Works*, p. 66). Laura is all of these figures in a continuum: the woman suddenly chilled and panicked in her garden, the stoic sufferer, the hardened sinner. And all of these figures, as encountered in the rest of the poems, resonate with Laura's predicament.

In the devotional lyrics Rossetti also lays down the conditions under which germination from the kernel is possible. Laura's kernel-stone represents a wish to turn time back to the beginning, to make the "same" thing return. She cannot know that this kind of growth, the return of the same, occurs only under one condition, the seed-time of death. Earth in the poem "Advent," for instance, is a Great Mother bearing "millions more" between "inner swathings of her fold" (*Works*, p. 157, B. 1886), and in the general resurrection each saint will ascend to his proper goal, "As seeds their proper bodies all upthrust" (*Works,* p. 215, B. 1893). In the meantime, the dead lie dormant in God's Acre, "the garden of confident hope," "where sweet seeds are quickening in darkness and cold" (Hail, garden of confident hope!" *Works*, p. 135, B. 1893). We plant young girls, like Laura or Jeanie, in "garden plots of death," and Rossetti will go so far as to say that graveyards bear a resemblance to Lost Eden ("Young girls wear flowers," *Works*, p. 135, March 26, 1855). Dead women may in fact look to a miraculous second growth, a self-creating pregnancy: "Another Sun / Than this of ours / Has withered up indeed her flowers / But ripened her grapes every one" ("A Dirge," *Works*, p. 302, January 18, 1852). This startling and radical metamorphosis, modeled on Christ's death and resurrection, is the obverse of the progress of natural womanhood. If Rossetti found the drive toward autonomy and self-realization in the fallen world was a presumption that toppled over into decay, then in relocating "growth" at the end of life, she was able to postulate a truly bold metamorphosis that would supersede the natural cycle.

The Tree of Life and the Tree of Exile

Laura needs the kernel stone to grow so that she can regenerate her own fruit-bearing tree of life. As a natural symbol for the integrated self, the tree is especially appropriate because it is the most extensive exfoliation of the seed; because it is both earthbound and sky-directed; because it is both vulnerable and strong: in strug-gling upward it risks being buffeted or felled.[24] As I have suggested earlier, however, Laura's tree is a branch of the tree of the New Testament as well as the Old, and therefore a variant of Christ's "tree" of sacrifice. Just as the kernel-stone germinates a range of selves or, rather, strategies for establishing and maintaining a self, so Laura's wilted and would-be tree exfoliates into another range of possibilities for the self explored throughout Rossetti's work.

In Rossetti's poems the tree image for the most part serves to illuminate problematic aspects of the female self. In a poem with the curious and sardonic title "A Dumb Friend" (*Works*, p. 358, March 24, 1863), Rossetti overtly identifies the tree as an image for self. This tree, however, is her parodic double, for as it flourishes, she declines; ultimately, of course, the tree will outlast her, still going on with the seasonal cycle when she lies under the cypress. The tree is, in fact, a sister-self very like the second sister in *The Lowest Room*, who flourishes by cultivating her "natural" womanhood, while the articulate, discontented speaker declines. Thus although the tree is this speaker's "friend," representing the realization of maturity rather than old age, this natural fulfillment is not a likelihood for the speaker. By a severe dialectic in which female maturity is projected onto silent nature while actual female growth is represented as a decline that bypasses maturity, Rossetti indicates the limitations on female potential.

If the tree in "A Dumb Friend" is an image for unattainable—and undesirable—"maturity," then the tree in the earlier "An Apple-Gathering" (*Works*, p. 335, November 23, 1857) is an image for aborted potential, a more usual condition for the female figures in Rossetti's poems. This speaker gathers apple blossoms from a tree designated as "mine"; when she goes for apples there are none, of course. This loss of apples parallels her rejection by her beloved in favor of a woman with a "full" basket. At the end, while the speaker lets her neighbors pass her by, returning to their homes, she lingers: "but I loitered; while the dews / Fell fast I loitered still." In her disappointment and in her tenacious, brooding, loitering, this figure is a prototype for Laura returning disconsolate from her evening walk. Like Laura, this speaker acts hastily and imprudently, unable to operate according to basic rules, unable to make correct inferences. Within Rossetti's myth of self, to act at all is to act prematurely, to abort potential; what remains is to endure consequences. Thus whether the symbolic tree flourishes or declines, whether it represents what might have been or what can never be, the self that emerges from the relation between speaker and symbol is a depleted or miscarried one. If she cannot act, the female self must be acted upon and swept along by the cycle of decay, like the Princess of *The Prince's Progress*, who declines in an almost exact inversion of Laura's first motion toward knowledge and action:

> As a lily drooping to death,
> As a drought-worn bird with a failing breath,
> As a lovely vine without a stay,
> As a tree whereof the owner saith,
> "Hew it down to-day."   (*Works*, p. 32)

Alternatively, she may try to remain a seed, all dormancy—"poppies unborn"—and by that obdurate refusal to grow and branch out, preserve the kernel of self. Since she cannot forever remain as seed in the garden, however, she is forever exiled, making do with the minimal, enduring stoically.

It is the tree of exile that serves as a more viable emblem for female identity, as in "Introspective," where the self withstands both "the shattering ruining blow" and "the probing steady and slow" to

> . . . stand like a blasted tree
> By the shore of the shivering sea.
>
> On my boughs neither leaf nor fruit,
> No sap in my uttermost root,
> Brooding in an anguish dumb
> On the short past and the long to-come.
>   (*Works*, p. 331, June 20, 1857)

This self both declines and stands firm; or, rather, the declining is already over: this tree is the fundamental self, and, however impossibly, the site of a new germination. The woman at the end of *From House to Home*, for instance, having won through to stoic self-possession, is able to see herself as the "cultivated" tree, a child in nature being trained up toward another kind of maturity ("ripe eternity" [*Works*, p. 317], Rossetti calls it elsewhere):

> Although to-day He prunes my twigs with pain,
> Yet doth His blood nourish and warm my root:
> To-morrow I shall put forth buds again
> And clothe myself with fruit.   (*Works*, p. 25)

Like Laura, this speaker craves nourishment, but having paid the price—she treads on sharp thorns, drinks the loathsome cup—she becomes the fruit-bearing tree herself, containing her own kernel-stone. In "Ash-Wednesday" (*Works*, p. 217, March 21, 1859) the barren tree as an image for self reappears, this time as a "fig-tree fruit-unbearing" that God's justice condemns while his love saves. Significantly the speaker asks as a gift from God the ability to love. The self that needs so much can get only by giving, by branching out, in effect. In "Long Barren" (*Works*, p. 244, February 21, 1865), in an extended conceit rare in her poems, Rossetti invokes a metamorphic tree:

> Thou who didst hang upon a barren tree
> My God, for me;
> > Though I till now be barren, now at length,
> > Lord, give me strength
> To bring forth fruit to Thee.

In an apostrophe to Christ the barren tree is transformed into the "Rose of Sharon, Cedar of broad roots, / Vine of sweet fruits," from which the speaker asks basic nourishment: "Feed thou my feeble shoots." This is a different opportunity for growth, then. This tree of self neither droops nor is felled but, like the "planted" dead woman, grows toward a radical transformation. The tree that stands to undergo this change is not the full tree of natural womanhood, but rather the blasted or withered tree of female negation: by refusing to grow and by standing fast, this female self grows to completion by Christ's redemptive act.

Poison and Antidote: The Restorative Feast

Laura's purgative feast on goblin juices is, as I have pointed out earlier, a Eucharistic feast that corrects the feast that occasioned her fall. It is also Christ's metaphorical cup ("The cup I drink He drank of long before," *Works*, p. 227), both the cup of Gethsemane and the gall of the Cross. If Laura's "cup" is taken inadvertently, elsewhere in Rossetti's poetry taking the bitter cup is represented as a strong

that one and one make two: / Later, Love rules that one and one make one." Rossetti goes on to uphold the paradox by asserting that both statements are true: while most people subscribe to the first equation, the second "total" is perceived by the few. Rossetti's "one" is surely not the "one" in which the wife disappears as a legal identity but, rather, the Platonic "One," the androgynous fusion in which the inequity of female identity is canceled. Love's illogic is really esoteric knowledge which restores the Edenic relation between woman and man. Both Eve's mistake and Laura's speculative curiosity belong to the category of commonsense logic, the category of "one plus one makes two." To be Eve, betrayed and betraying by intellectual curiosity, is intolerable, and so there must be another kind of "logic" that cancels this terrible mistake. This logic is the verbal sleight-of-hand which repeats and undoes the original trickery and rescues the female actor from an untenable position. The sestet of this sonnet in fact posits the power of words as a refuge:

> Befogged and witless, in a wordy maze
>   A groping stroll perhaps may do us good;
>   If cloyed we are with much we have understood,
> If tired of half our dusty world and ways,
>   If sick of fasting, and if sick of food;—
> And how about these long still-lengthening days?

Laura before her "cure" and the speaker of the *Later Life* sequence are in exactly the same situation in that they are "sick" of everything, both the feast and the fast, of "all I have and all I see—" (*Later Life*, no. 17, *Works*, p. 78). Wanting *more*, wanting to incorporate or add on, gets you nowhere in the finite, exhaustible world of reason where one plus one equals two. But there is an esoteric knowledge reached by a "wordy maze" or by a symbolic act that works like a riddle or a trick—Lizzie's obtaining of the fruits, Laura's inadvertent feasting—and that reverses meanings, turning bitter into sweet, sweet into bitter. These conversions are tautological and hence finite, closed yet infinitely repeatable and hence inexhaustible—One, or All. In this scheme Laura is no more than a token shuffling from one pole to another. What the pattern of her fate represents, however, is the poet's determination to retell the old story of Eve's fall and to impose the arbitrary on what seems "natural"—not only man's firing of the world but woman's decline *in* nature, the decay that seems to follow on fruition. This is the fate of Eve's daughters as signs, as markers of the "mistake." Although this fate really is inescapable for Rossetti—both as a social role and an aesthetic—she achieves something like control by setting up her own system of determinacy: if the garden is a wilderness, than in wildernesses she will make her garden; if the feast collapses into famine, then the fast and the bitter cup become the feast; if the barter of earthly love is always unequal, she will exchange her all for the All; if the seed stone of potential cannot grow then she will cultivate her own thorny and pruned tree of life: "I am even I."

3 The Female Pose
Model and Artist, Spectacle and Witness

In chapter 2 we saw how the methods of a species of prefigural symbolism allowed Rossetti to construct a system of allusions between *Goblin Market* and the rest of her poems so that the situations of *Goblin Market* can be seen as figures for situations in the fallen and redeemed worlds of the lyric poems. The "odorous mead" and the feast on ripe fruits recall the Edenic feast and prefigure the Eucharistic feast, as well as the divine feast in which all is absorbed into the All. Not only does like call up like, but also one symbol or situation implies its opposite. The Edenic garden signifies in relation to the wilderness garden of exile, which in turn refers to the paradisal garden. By establishing this polarized system Rossetti expresses, without mediation or compromise, the division that is at the heart of female experience: the garden of self must always become a devastated wilderness which will one day turn into a garden again. At the same time that the system emphasizes division—between feast and fast, garden and wilderness—the paradoxical relation between terms tends to cancel all differences: the feast is really a fast, a fast is really a feast. This kind of play on words cancels not only the cycle of mortality but, more specifically, the cycle of natural womanhood: the cycle of Eve's "mistake" and Eve's fall. Rossetti's paradoxical strategies can thus be seen as comprising a verbal artifice to set against the "teeming generations" that threaten to absorb her female identity.

This chapter follows out the process by which Rossetti adapts or translates another traditional metaphor for the purpose of her female myth, bringing into play yet another configuration of female personae. That metaphor is the visual metaphor which, in Western culture, expresses fundamental experiences of presence and absence in terms of "seeing" and "being seen." The metaphor is profoundly involved in issues of identity, for the subjects who see are conscious of being seen, indeed base their identity on being seen. This double awareness—awareness of self as other—which is a crucial issue for women, is represented in Rossetti's poems by a range of seeing acts and visual "positions." The range is exemplified by Laura and Lizzie: Laura takes the position of the artist-voyeur who tries to appropriate the object of vision, while Lizzie, who refuses to look at the goblin men, becomes a type of model watcher who looks out for the object of her desire, in the sense of taking care and keeping vigil. Laura's kind of looking is bound to falsify female identity, not only because women are not supposed to "see," but also because it is precisely the creative I/eye that reifies women as objects of vision. Lizzie's kind of looking, on the other hand, becomes an exemplary female stance: the figure who looks out in this way strikes a pose that dramatizes her strategic passivity and protects her female selfhood. In what follows the tension between Laura as a true "seer" and Lizzie as a type of "watcher" remains a central axis.

Seeing and Being Seen

Like the metaphor of feast and fast, the visual metaphor is profoundly paradoxical: the phenomena we see are signs of the godhead, but earthly sight is blind compared to inward sight, and spiritual insight is fostered by blindness to earthly spectacles. Many nineteenth-century poets are drawn to this metaphor precisely because it plays between immanence and transcendence, because it spiritualizes the material and puts a human face on the ineffable, as is dramatized in the Pauline text that resonates throughout the century: "For now we see darkly, as in a glass, but then face to face."

"Face to face," a common locution in the period as well as a strong metaphor for presence, suggests the removal of not only the veil of the flesh, but also the social masks and veils that conceal personality. Something lies beyond the face that can only be expressed as the immanence of "face to face." This is the paradox that haunts Rossetti and her contemporaries. Like Tennyson, who longs to see Hallam and dreams back his "fair face,"[1] Rossetti longs for the embodied yet transcendent intimacy of "Thou Face to face with me and Eye to eye (*Works*, p. 267)," while Elizabeth Barrett Browning, who deliberately eroticizes this mode of knowing, celebrates Robert Browning's power to "look through and behind this mask of me /.... and behold my soul's true face."[2] In each of these instances the face-to-face encounter—between the dead and the living, between god and mortal, between lovers—suggests the possibility of mutual recognition, one subject knowing another without reifying the other, distance closed without annihilating fusion.

But for the nineteenth-century woman poet the metaphor is uniquely complicated by her social role, her "Otherness" in patriarchal culture. The division in the metaphor, between seen and hidden and between seer and seen, reflects more than the Neo-platonic split between spirit and matter, or the Victorian divided self. Even if she shares with many of her male contemporaries a sense of self as separate from its roles, as a woman she is more radically divided between a "true" self and an apparent one than her male counterpart. The visual metaphor focuses acutely, even painfully, the female split between subject and sign: as seeing subject what she sees is *herself being seen*.[3] Expressed as visual metaphor, female otherness takes the form of action frozen in a pose; the woman whose beauty or monstrousness transfixes the beholder is herself immobilized. "Face to face," then, becomes fraught with paradoxical significance for women, promising the recognition that frees them while delivering the alienation that binds them. The woman who wants to see and be seen as only God sees her is trapped behind an effigy or icon of herself. Behind the smiling face stands the frozen woman of Rossetti's "Dead before Death," "with stiffened smiling lips and cold calm eyes" (*Works*, p. 313), or the captive soul of Barrett Browning's

"The Mask." These images of women trapped within their own bodies suggest not only the existential continuum of Barrett Brownings's and Rossetti's lives as women but also the constraints of their historical moment: the voluminous and restrictive clothing that hampers movement while highlighting and eroticizing the face; the fascination with physiognomy that further structures and moralizes the encoding of the face; the anxieties about death that focus on the liminal maternal figure as bringer of death as comfort.[4] For the women themselves, however, the crucial aspect of their life as signs is that whatever they gain in power to impress, to influence through their "looks," they lose in mobility and expressivity. Their life as signs signifies their symbolic death as persons. Thus much as the visual metaphor promises intimacy, in the Romantic tradition it often renders distance and alienation.

Rossetti's, as well as Barrett Browning's, deployment of the visual metaphor is bound up with Romantic "vision" and the particular reification the female figure undergoes in the Romantic poet's quest for self. In this tradition the beautiful female face is often the means to visionary experience: a veil to be penetrated, like the monolithic sibylline faces of Keats' Moneta and Mnemosyne, or a mirror that reflects, like Dorothy in Wordsworth's "Tintern Abbey," in whom Wordsworth longs to "behold" "what I was once."[5] The imaging of the female face, either as itemized parts or as a schematic whole, is not new, of course: it belongs to a long tradition in English poetry, stretching at least from sixteenth-century sentimental or satiric portraits.[6] Within the Petrarchan tradition the female face tends always to become an emblem of transcendence, but prior to the nineteenth century, in English poetry, at least, the particularized context of the lover's tribute or plea allows for mobility of expression and assigns influence to the lady's active "looks." Even though this female face is quite literally a sign to be read, a "lecture," as Sidney would have it, the beloved in some sense directs the reading. No less other than any female figure who is an ideal object, she is at least made to mime volition. The Romantic gazer, on the other hand, contemplates a face that is simultaneously enlarged—often literally —and reduced: a monolithic, mute face, something like a natural vista. Like nature, this female sight becomes freighted with crucial doubts and expectations. In part it is a maternal face, focusing the yearning for lost wholeness; in part it is a death's head for an empty universe. It haunts the nineteenth-century male poet because it can be made to stand for anything. It haunts the female poet, too, because she sees in it an image of herself that is capable of fantastic transformations, but unchanging and inexpressive in any human sense. What Sandra Gilbert has described as the problem of "lyric assertion"[7] in poets like Rossetti and Barrett Browning comes to an acute focus in the visual metaphor: face to face with the iconic faces of literary tradition the female poet confronts female silence, the negation of her capacity to originate meaning. The internal split between "self" and "other" becomes the split between the writer who sees and speaks, and the image/woman who is seen and is mute; the woman writer's subjectivity is implicated in a self-image whose subjectivity and expressivity are denied by the writers whose tradition she has no choice but to appropriate.

Neither Rossetti nor Barrett Browning can, or want, to cast off their "faces"; both write within a tradition that requires they present a face as well as look upon one. In *Aurora Leigh* and "Lord Walter's Wife," Barrett Browning was able to reclaim the beautiful female face as woman's "true" face and to give that face an expressive voice.[8] For Rossetti, however, that degree of mobility was neither an existential nor a literary option. Rather, she explores a range of static female types in their relation to symbolic power. One kind of mobility derives from the apocalyptic transformation of the dead woman into the woman "clothed in the sun." A more viable mobility is to be found in Christ's suffering face which becomes an appropriate model for the female face; the only look that does not reify the object of vision is the *exchange* of looks between suppliant and Christ. Otherwise, Rossetti adapts and adjusts the pose of the immobilized woman to derive the figure of the watcher. In the watcher's pose the dualism between the "active" see-er and the "passive" seen is overcome: the model transcends the artist, and the spectacle for all eyes becomes the witness of her own restitution. The comparison between Barrett Browning and Rossetti stops here. Barrett Browning had her own unique life situation, of course, but Rossetti's was strongly "visually" marked. She was sister to her brother, who in poetry looked long into the mirror of the beautiful face, and in his painting enshrined images of cataleptically immobilized women.[9] She was his model, and, I shall suggest, his most intimate mirror. Finally, she was a woman in deep conflict about her own problematic appearance.

Artist and Model

Like any woman in her culture, Rossetti was subject to appraisal as a beautiful—marriageable, that is—woman, or not. Indeed, the progress of her "looks" seems to parallel her prospects: as with other women in a culture that strongly equates beauty with marriageability, her prospects fade as her looks decline. But in Rossetti's case the problems of composing a face for the eye of the beholder-lover are compounded by the actual situation of posing. From her earliest years she sat for some forty-five portraits and photographs, ranging from a watercolor when she was seven to Dante Gabriel's last chalk portrait of her, done when she was forty-six. This prolific documentation of her physical appearance is not so unusual in the case of a woman from an artistic family, moving in artistic circles: one thinks of Edith Sitwell, for instance. But where in the context of modernism Sitwell's "strangeness" was taken for granted, glorified even, Rossetti's deviations from the Victorian norm were registered as just that—deviations, inadequacies. William's comment in his preface to the *Collected Works* reveals the extent to which Rossetti's looks were problematic:

A question has sometimes been raised as to the amount of good looks with which Christina Rossetti should be credited. She was certainly not what one understands to be "a beauty"; the term handsome did not apply to her, nor yet the term pretty. Neither was she "a fine woman." She has sometimes been called "lovely" in youth; and this is true, if a refined and correct mould of face, along with elevated and deep expression, is loveliness. She was assuredly much nearer to being beautiful than ugly; and this, in my opinion, remained true of her throughout life, for in advanced years her expression naturally deepened, although the traces left upon her by disease, as well as by time, marred her comeliness.   (*Works*, p. ix)

The comedy of William's scrupulosity warring with family pride, his struggle to find the right term for what resists categorization, his commitment to an unstated yet fixed ideal, all emphasize what must have been a painful reality in Rossetti's life: her awareness that she was constantly being appraised, and for tactfully undefined reasons found wanting.

The lack that William could not quite put his finger on had more to do with her deviations from the norms of female expressivity than with her facial conformation. Even in this, it seems, Rossetti manifested her characteristic doubleness, for her biographer Mackenzie Bell, writing in 1898, describes a woman with two faces:

> When I first met her she had acquired much of the portliness of middle age, and her face *in repose* was sometimes rather heavy and even unemotional. But her smile was always delightful, and sometimes irresistibly sweet, and, when in animated conversation on some especially congenial theme, her face to the last was comely.
>
> It is this marked difference between the comparatively unattractive aspect of her features *in repose*, and the great change which came over their lineaments during animation, that make her photographs taken in later life seem so unsatisfactory.[10] (My emphasis)

When she smiles and speaks, then, her face invites; when her features are merely in repose, not composed, her face repels. Bell's description accords with Rossetti's description, in her autobiographical novel *Maude*, of a young woman whose features "were regular and pleasing. . . . as a child she had been very pretty; and might have continued so but for a fixed paleness, and an expression, not exactly of pain, but languid and preoccupied to a painful degree. Yet even now if at any time she became thoroughly aroused and interested, her sleepy eyes would light up with wonderful brilliancy, her cheeks glow with warm colour."[11] The "languid and preoccupied" face, like the face "in repose" described by Bell, clearly represents its bearer's depression, and boredom, which are transformed by thought and speech. But this inexpressivity is also a protective mask, a refusal to meet the demands of the actual and symbolic posing situation: she will not make herself into an attractive female object. To a certain extent, it appears, Rossetti attempted to control others' responses to her; not in the way the sexually available woman does, but in the way that the sexually forbidden—and forbidding—woman does. The mask of impassivity, which caricatures the erotic immobility of her brother's models, becomes a means of asserting her own sibylline power.

When we look at the portraits themselves we are struck by her melancholy and beauty. The portraits, in fact, reveal what the face in the verbal descriptions chooses not to show. It is easy to see the "pensive beauty" ascribed to the young woman by Watts-Dunton[12] and to credit the claim that it was "the fascinating mystery and soft melancholy of his sister's eyes" that influenced Dante Gabriel's choice of the "sad female face" as a pictorial subject.[13] The 1846 and 1847 profiles show a young girl expectant as any other; the 1848 full-face head shows a young woman with a sober and penetrating look, not unlike that of the seven-year-old in Pistrucci's portrait; the 1866 chalk portrait shows the poet in a contemplative pose, withdrawn into her own thought, the expression suggests, rather than absorbed in erotic reverie, as Jane Morris in *Reverie* and *The Daydream* of about the same period seems to be; the last chalk heads and the double portrait of Christina and her mother are shockingly uncompromising visions of both Dante Gabriel's suffering and her own.

Rossetti is not the creator of the portraits, of course; Dante Gabriel remains the artist and she the model. But to the extent that his representations shaped her presentation of herself, they tell us something useful about her. In all of these representations of her there is a tension, as there is in all portraiture, between exposure and concealment: the subject who has been "caught" by the painter has also somehow eluded him. This tension is especially strong in the representation of women in painting. As erotic *objects*, signs, they are symbolically dead: they have no existence as erotic—or thinking—*subjects*. In their objectified body they are exposed; in their dreamy withdrawal from this body, they are hidden. Dante Gabriel's female subjects are strongly marked by this simultaneous presence and absence. Whether the subject is Beata Beatrix, Prosperpina, or Lilith, the figures both offer and withdraw, all accessible/inaccessible female objects. The woman whom the artist has *not* captured lives somewhere in an unpicturable realm of mystery and transcendence: this, too, is implied by what is pictured in the male painter's art, especially in Romantic art. From the point of view of the female model, or even the female spectator, however, it is possible to fantasize that the female subject has abandoned this image of herself so that she can carry on her own life as a person: she is not here, but elsewhere. This is what is suggested in Dante Gabriel's portraits of his sister. Where the absence of Dante Gabriel's other female subjects belongs to the realm of female eroticization and female transcendence, Rossetti's pictured withdrawal can be imagined, at least, to belong to the realm of creative withdrawal. Her impassivity, the resistance of her face in repose, is due in part to the generic demands of portraiture, in part to Dante Gabriel's aesthetic, and in part to her own will to possess herself as an artist, to retrieve the "seer" from the blind fate of the "seen." The expressionless face in repose looks like a woman thinking, and a woman thinking is not an erotic object.

In claiming that a tension between a normative representation of women as erotic objects and Rossetti's "resistance" to this norm generates the face we see in the portraits, I do not mean to suggest that Dante Gabriel did not, in fact, subtly and powerfully eroticize her. Underlying the tension between norm and deviation (erotic woman vs. thinking woman) is a more specific tension between the expression and the repression of the erotic in the relation between brother and sister *as painter and subject*. What is striking from the beginning of Dante Gabriel's career is his conflation of mother and sister in powerful Oedipal images of sexual longing and prohibition. Christina's symbolic fate is forecast in Dante Gabriel's epochal Pre-Raphaelite paintings, *The Girlhood of Mary Virgin* and *Ecce Ancilla Domini*, in both of which she models for the virgin. She thus presides, actually and symbolically, at the "birth" of his art, which is dominated by images of women who are both extremely powerful in their allurement and extremely powerless in their pictorial confinement and langorous poses. Christina becomes, in effect, the repressed mother of these images, which function as symbolic projections of Dante Gabriel's sexual-aesthetic anxieties, as well as role-casting for his models. Christina, like the other women in his life, takes up the role of the enigmatic woman who inspires and mirrors his art. If she is the author of the role, her impassive mask resists eroticization because she thinks her own thoughts; if he is the author, the mask of virgin and sibyl represent his repression of powerful erotic drives in the service of his art. If they are "co-authors," then he, perhaps, acknowledges her presence as her own subject, while she assimilates his erotic symbols to her own mask in life and art.

The repressive mask functions somewhat differently in the late portraits, the double portrait of Christina and Mrs. Rossetti and the two chalk heads of Christina, which were executed in 1876–77, when Dante Gabriel was recovering from a serious illness in the care of the two women. The double portrait repeats the configuration of mother and sister (mother and virgin mother) in the early *The Girlhood of Mary Virgin*, but this time the heads are aligned. Christina is thus a perfect double for a mother in a composite image that suggests sibylline power. The women appear to prophesy and preside over his death; they are versions of the Medusa, their faces set toward the light. William's comment on this portrait seems particularly apt:

This profile is markedly like a certain aspect of Christina's face which was not exactly unwonted, but still was exceptional; there is a rather inscrutable sphinx-like look about it. Whenever I set eyes upon it, the lines from her poem, "From House to Home," come into my mind—

> Therefore in patiences I possess my soul;
> Yea therefore as a flint I set my face.   (*Works*, p. lxv)

The flint-faced woman is the essence of *self*-possession, the masked woman who resists any attempt by the eye to make her over into an attractive object. This is the poet that Edmund Gosse saw, "sitting alone, in the midst of a noisy drawing-room, like a pillar of cloud, a Sibyl whom no one had the audacity to approach."[14] In this portrait, as in Gosse's account, we see the convergence of the viewer's and painter's will with the model's: she is seen as she wills to be seen.

The full face of the 1877 portraits, a remarkable image of melancholy reproach as well as self-possession, shows another potential of the sibylline mask. This is the face of the witness, who both displays her suffering and, Christ-like, sees the sufferer. This face of Rossetti's shows traces—in the slightly protruding eyes and the puffiness—of the thyroid disease that raged during the years 1871–74, distorting her face in actuality into a frightening mask. If the sibyl-line mask was within her control, signifying inhuman self-posses-sion, the mask of illness was beyond her control, signifying female monstrousness, the Medusa rampant. But in these portraits the latent image of the Medusa is submerged in the face of the suffering and compassionate Christ: female monstrosity is displaced by female disfigurement, and female horror by female pathos, as both Chris-tina and Dante Gabriel take up their final positions vis-à-vis one another, attempting to rescue compassion from the ruins of sexual figuration.

As a model for her painter-poet brother, Rossetti saw herself as the repressive/repressed virgin who doubles for the mother in the begetting of art; as the terrifying Medusa-mother who possesses herself at the cost of appearing monstrous; and finally as the female Christ who witnesses the sufferings of sex: her brother's failure to love the woman as she "is"; her own reification as a female icon. In the last, Christ-like version of her face Rossetti casts her own role, with Dante Gabriel assenting in her myth. If the face of erotic love in his story is potentially the face of horror,[15] in her story the face of horror, her own "disfigurement," can become the face of love.

Whoever authors her face, the impression of unease persists, a function of both Christina Rossetti's problematic meaning in Dante Gabriel's aesthetic, and her own resistance to meaning anything in his art. Her situation as model is always implicated, however, in her role as artist, as she struggles to appropriate images of female im-mobilization for her own aesthetic. Although she often explores the disjunction between the outward pose and inward mobility, she primarily uses the immobile pose as an image of inward resolve and courage. The pose can either entomb or fortify the living self. The following sections explore ways in which Rossetti adapts various poses in her poetry, playing upon different kinds of "seeing" in order to create a fairly systematic myth of the female self. The first section, "Model and Artist," shows how the modeling situation as such gets articulated in the poetry. The following sections, "Dead Women," "The Whore of Babylon," and "Masks of Life and Art," explore a number of specific female poses, to show how crucial for Rossetti the presentation of self as spectacle was. All of these poems suggest how the "appearance" is at odds with the "reality," but all make clear that appearance is inescapable, that women are seen as signs. "Watching, Looking, Keeping Vigil," the last section, shows how in the religious poems Rossetti finds something like an answer, deriving a strategic variant of the immobilized model, the watcher-witness who testifies to and transcends her reification, and discovers a "seeing" act—the interchange of looks between suppliant and Christ—that does not reify the female subject.

Model and Artist

In 1880 Dante Gabriel Rossetti completed *The Daydream*, an oil version of an 1878 chalk sketch, which shows Jane Morris, the model, in an attitude of reverie, framed by the branches of the tree in which she sits, an open book under her left hand which rather slackly holds a flower. The languorousness, the sadness, the *absence* of the female figure, differ little from the qualities of other portraits of the period, like *La Donna Della Finestra*, for instance. At that time Dante Gabriel was in fact turning out paintings to suit the tastes which he himself had created, and so it is not surprising that *The Daydream* should be highly conventionalized, a particularly apt example of the dreamy immobilization that characterizes images of women in Victorian art. Not unlike the Mona Lisa, the work raises certain conventional questions, as well. What does that lack of a smile mean? Is the woman herself a semiallegorical figure, the daydream itself? Does she dream, like Tennyson's Mariana, of an absent lover, and again like Mariana, does she represent the artist's own paralysis? Has the book inspired her daydream or is it merely a decorative prop? Is she an enigma guarding her own secret, independent of the specta-tor/artist's reading? Or is she an enigma without a secret, a sign signifying nothing of the self?

These are also the kinds of questions raised by a poem Christina Rossetti wrote some twenty years earlier. "Day-Dreams" (*Works*, p. 332, September 8, 1857) represents both the perfect realization of the Pre-Raphaelite ideal and its deconstruction. The speaker alter-nately describes and addresses a female figure named only as "my soul's soul." This mute epipsyche sits at her "chamber window," framed like the figures in Dante Gabriel's paintings, unmoved by the speaker's pleas:

> I have strewn thy path, beloved,
>   With plumed meadowsweet,
> Iris and pale perfumed lilies,
>   Roses most complete:
> Wherefore pause on listless feet?

> But she sits and never answers,
>   Gazing, gazing still
> On swift fountain, shadowed valley,
>   Cedared sunlit hill:
> Who can guess or read her will?

What does this woman want? The speaker goes on to "guess" and "read" but without any satisfactory conclusion: "Is it love she looks and longs for / . . . . / Is it slumber self-forgetful / . . . . / Is it one or all of these?" Does she want to live or die, that is? Is she possibly a Galatea who refuses to come to life?

The only "answer" is her adamant refusal to speak or to move, like a glassily smiling doll. As the speaker irascibly turns away from this stupefyingly indifferent beloved, the poem shifts in tone, becoming a parody of the love lament:

> Now if I could guess her secret,
>   Were it worth the guess?—
> Time is lessening, hope is lessening,
>   Love grows less and less:
> What care I for no or yes?

From the perspective of the male seeker the sphinx who has no secrets is a worthless object for appropriation. But from the perspective of the idolized or devalued woman, as well as the author who is manipulating both these puppets—the stony woman, the stereotypically faithless suitor—the sphinx has her revenge on those who would read her as a conventional sign: rather than mean what the lover wants, she will mean nothing at all.

In the last two stanzas, however, Rossetti suggests what meaning can be made out of women-as-empty-idols. Already artifacts of a culture's making, they can be turned into funerary statuary, monuments to their death-in-life. The speaker vows to give this already stony woman a stately burial and a gravestone that duplicates her "life" pose:

> I will give her stately burial,
>   Stately willow-branches bent:
> Have her carved in alabaster,
>   As she dreamed and leant
> While I wondered what she meant.

The persona of the suitor thus can stand for the artist, who projects his desires and fears on the woman-as-idol, an empty screen, as it turns out. Ultimately he kills off this idol/model, who is already "dead" anyway, in order to make an art object that commemorates her fixity and his obsession, like Keats' urn: "For ever wilt thou love, and she be fair!" But this persona also stands for Christina Rossetti herself, the artist who is model as well. Out of the artifacts of the patriarchal tradition, the immobilized female figure who can be "read" as indifferent, like Swinburne's sphinx in "A Leave-Taking," or abandoned, like Tennyson's Mariana, or reified in nature, like Wordsworth's insensate Lucy, Rossetti creates first a parody of that artifact (a parody inherent in the type itself, for even male poets can express anger and frustration at the inanition of the image they have created) and then her own artifact. "My soul's soul," a toy, becomes my soul's soul's effigy, a copy of a copy, a conclusion to the process of reification already underway when the poem begins. Out of female death in art, that is, Rossetti makes her own art object, here a poem that both exemplifies and parodies the poetic relation between lover and beloved, artist and model, poet and muse.

I have already suggested, in discussing Dante Gabriel's portraits of Christina, how the model's pose and the female mask may afford the female subject a paradoxical freedom. Rossetti herself comments more explicitly—and playfully—on the usefulness of masks in a poem written only two months after "Day-Dreams." In "Winter: My Secret" (*Works*, p. 336, November 23, 1857) Rossetti suggests that she wears her "mask" for "warmth," and that "my secret's mine, and I won't tell. / Or, after all, perhaps there's none." Like the sphinx of "Day-Dreams" this enigma may be empty as enigma, but more important, the speaker, the owner of the "mask," asserts her right to think her own thoughts. If we place the 1867 portrait of Rossetti beside the 1880 painting *The Daydream* and entitle the former *Woman Thinking* or, perhaps, *Woman Composing*, we see considerable formal similarity and considerable conceptual difference. As I have already pointed out, this portrait resists eroticization, precisely because a woman thinking is not an erotic subject. The pose is close enough, however, to other, more erotic proses, to encourage certain conventional ways of seeing. Neither obtrusively erotic nor obtrusively unerotic, this disengaged but attractive pose provides a useful cover for a woman who wants to be free to think her own thoughts.

It is also apparently a pose that Rossetti sometimes assumed in life. From Arthur Hughes' account, on her visits to Penkill castle, William Bell Scott's residence in Scotland, she could often be seen framed in a turret window, "elbows on the sill, hands supporting her face," assumed by Hughes to be "meditating and composing." Packer, who passes on this anecdote, adds that Rossetti could "see as well as be seen" and goes on to sketch in the scene Rossetti must have observed.[16] Here we can see Rossetti duplicating and exploiting the female pose in art: she can say the pose hides nothing and even further secrete herself within the pose, free to observe, ruminate, even write poems. The self-display that falsifies the self becomes a means to compose a self that sees while being seen, and the model turns out to be none other than the artist. That double figure is the central figure of the "witness" who presents the self as "spectacle," converting female reification into an inward pose of female courage and endurance.

The nature of that inward pose can be seen most clearly in "A Soul" (*Works*, p. 311, February 7, 1854), a poem that antedates "Day-Dreams" by about three years. The female figure in "A Soul," a prototype for the vigilant watchers of Rossetti's religious poems, is an antitype of the erotic figure of "Day-Dreams." Significantly, however, both poems focus on statuesque immobility as a sign equally of female power and female powerlessness. The erotic sphinx who has power over her suitor but is powerless to "move" becomes a statue signifying her "death"—her emptiness, that is—as symbol. The statue-woman in "A Soul" similarly demonstrates female power and female weakness, but her—or, rather, her creator's—triumph over the symbolic system that generates her is rather different in this case. It is as though Rossetti is moving around the statuary she has inherited from the literary tradition, trying to see what can and cannot be brought to life. The symbolic woman in "A Soul" lives, but only with great strain:

> She stands as pale as Parian statues stand;
> Like Cleopatra when she turned at bay,
> ....
> She stands alone, a wonder deathly-white:
> She stands there patient nerved with inner might,
> Indomitable in her feebleness,
> Her face and will athirst against the light.

Like the figure carved in alabaster, this statue-woman is also an artifact, crafted from literary and biblical traditions. As "model" for her "soul" Rossetti has chosen an archetypal fatal woman, legendary for her licentiousness and her queenly power. Purified of her eroticism and blended with the seekers who set their faces toward Jerusalem, Cleopatra becomes the perfect exemplar of heroic abdication and stoic endurance. Rossetti fixes her at her penultimate moment, as she chooses liberty and death over servitude and life. Thus the woman "indomitable in her feebleness," who gives up her life, opts for freedom, and the woman who freezes in a pose testifies to her inner strength. Although she cannot move because she is helpless, she also *will not be moved*—in a different sense from the effigy of "Day-Dreams"—because she is tenacious, persevering. She holds a pose that invites our gaze while she herself looks out for something beyond the "shadowy land." She is thus both a cover and a display, both conventional in her heroic-meditative pose and a subversive icon of protest against symbolic systems that require spectacular women.

This, then, is the kind of inward pose that Rossetti extracts from the external situation of posing. The pose in "A Soul" is no less external than the pose in "Day-Dreams" in that both poems are concerned with the symbolic representation of women in art. "A Soul," however, suggests a possible way of adapting traditional models for inward states that is closer to authentic female experience as Rossetti conceived it. While the dreamy woman of "Day-Dreams" eludes the symbolic system by her inanition, the tenacious figure of "A Soul" represents an attempt to work through and live with the symbolic representations that fix female freedom. The Cleopatra-soul's freedom consists in the choice to enact the isolation of female iconicity, the solitary "wonder deathly-white." Like Lot's wife, she is a spectacle of female obduracy, female will to self-possession, but also like Lot's wife, like spectacles and heroines, she is absolutely alone.

Dead Women

In "Day-Dreams" and "A Soul" Rossetti explores two female poses that are generated by a patriarchal aesthetic and hints at ways on which a female subject might reclaim those images. The external pose is inescapable—women are always seen posed as objects—but Rossetti adapts it as a model for the internal pose: a woman possesses herself by constructing her own image of herself, by translating the pose of stony indifference, for instance, into the pose of stoic endurance. Rossetti's poetry is populated, then, with "spiritual" female figures, "souls," who mime, or double, the immobile poses of "physical" women imprisoned in art or trapped by life. The next stage for the woman frozen in a pose is, as the two poems above suggest, death itself. As a poetic subject, the process of death—the woman on her deathbed or laid out on the bier or buried in the earth—fascinates Rossetti, as, indeed, it fascinated many of her contemporaries. To the extent that Rossetti shares the metaphysical uncertainties of her contemporaries, that is, she dwells on the liminal moment. Like Tennyson in *In Memoriam*, for instance, she focuses on the last look and the farewell touch. Also like her contemporaries, Rossetti is influenced in her aesthetic of death by a complex of literary traditions: ballad conventions, for instance, in which the pathos of early death is generated by a narrative of betrayal, religious conventions in which the pathos of early death illustrates an Ecclesiastes-based moral, and the female sentimental tradition in which the pathos of early death meets the demand for pathos in and of itself. Rossetti writes "death" poems illustrating all three of these rhetorical strands, but it is the last which exerts the strongest influence on her aesthetic. As Sandra Gilbert has pointed out, women write about death as a metaphor for their cultural powerlessness: unlike the Byronic outcast who might long for death as an end to a self-canceling string of events, the female outcast longs for death as an end to an eventless life, as in Rossetti's "From the Antique" (*Works*, p. 312, June 28, 1854):

> It's a weary life, it is, she said:—
>   Doubly blank in a woman's lot:
> I wish and I wish I were a man:
>   Or, better than any being, were not:

Death, here, cancels what has been already canceled, "doubly blank." Rossetti, then, is one of the company of poets who, like L. E. L. in Rossetti's sonnet (*Works*, p. 345, February 15, 1859), whether dying for lack of "love" or starved for lack of life, symbolically turn their faces to the wall. For women, then, the symbol of the dead woman is doubly paradoxical: the power of the symbol symbolizes actual powerlessness. In Victorian culture, the doubleness of the symbol is heightened. As Alexander Welsh points out, the woman who presides over death in actuality can become symbolically either the bearer of death or the savior from death. Either way, she rules over the realm of the powerless, a powerful symbol of negation and lack. The subject of female death, then, serves Rossetti's own strongly dialectical mode in predictable ways. Typically, that is, she will reverse the paradox: the dead woman really lives; the powerless woman, like the immobile soul, has power. The symbol thus means the way it always has, signifying power-in-powerlessness, but rather than reflecting male projections, it represents the female poet's power to reclaim this image of herself from the male tradition and to restate her own position as a female consciousness contemplating its most absolute reification.

More than this, however, the subject of early death suits Rossetti's aesthetic because it is projected strongly as the pose of death. It is yet another manifestation, that is, of the visual metaphor that focuses female alienation so acutely. The time of vigil and mourning becomes the time of the "last look," the last confrontation between the dead woman who ostensibly sees nothing and the spectator for whom, like the model, she is a spectacle. The title of one of Rossetti's earliest death poems, the poem that William Michael Rossetti places first in the "General" section of the *Poetical Works* is "A Portrait," which suggests how Rossetti was drawn to the idea of "portraiture," the staged but revelatory gesture, as a way of accomplishing her poetic goals. The subject is a woman's brief renunciatory life and her deathbed apotheosis. As the mourners look on, she, unseeing, undergoes a double transformation; while she stiffens in the pose of death, she simultaneously breaks free, apostrophized as the Heavenly Bride in a litany the speaker borrows from the Song of Songs. The poem emphasizes the discrepancy between the woman as she seems, or *as she is seen*, and the woman as she "is," for the mourners can see only the edifying spectacle of the deathbed. The "real" woman escapes to a realm that is inaccessible except by hyperbolic metaphor. This "progress" typifies the development of all Rossetti's death poems, poems with titles like "Dream-Land," "Rest," "Life Hidden," "Sound Sleep," "A Dirge," "Buried," "The Last Look." All of these represent a split between the visual spectacle and the invisible reality, or between a present immobility and a future transfiguration. In Rossetti's canon, then, "death" is a vehicle for expressing not only profound alienation but self-possession—and something like erotic power.

These early poems stress not so much the corruption of death as an inviolable stasis. It is as though these brides of death really are Snow White, seen through a glass coffin even when buried under the earth:

> Roses and lilies grow above the place
>   Where she sleeps the long sleep that doth not dream.
> If we could look upon her hidden face,
>   Nor shadow would be there, nor garish gleam
> Of light; . . .   (*Works*, "Life Hidden," p. 294)

Is this pose of death an erotic display? To what end is Rossetti exploiting the conventions that eroticize deathlike passivity? Certainly the dead woman in these early poems is an attractive object, seeing herself being seen, and deriving gratification from the exhibitionistic—as well as voyeuristic—act. More to the point, however, is the fact that Rossetti is writing from the perspective of a Pre-Raphaelite aesthetic. "Dream-Land," for instance, was published in the first issue of the *Germ*, along with Dante Gabriel's "The Blessed Damozel" and "My Sister's Sleep." As a canonical Pre-Raphaelite poem it reflects an aesthetic that depends on images of entranced, "fatally" passive women. At first glance, Rossetti appears to have succeeded in writing a poem that looks something like Dante Gabriel's two. Sleeping her charmed sleep till the end of time, the dead woman is peculiarly undead. Like the Blessed Damozel, that is, she inhabits a transitional state awaiting a further transformation, and like the subject of "My Sister's Sleep" her passage from one state to another is the focus of intense aesthetic concentration. Rossetti would thus seem to be in thrall to the same powerful image of lady death, gateway to life and death, as her male contemporaries are. But there are a few indications that she may have something different in mind from the erotic reverie of "The Blessed Damozel," say, or the aesthetic trance of "My Sister's Sleep."

From the beginning of the poem the landscape is peculiarly familiar:

> Where sunless rivers weep
> Their waves unto the deep
> She sleeps a charmèd sleep:
>   Awake her not.
> Led by a single star,
> She came from very far
> To seek where shadows are
>   Her pleasant lot.   (*Works*, p. 292)

The literary echoes are intricate: the single star faintly echoes Wordsworth's "She dwelt among the untrodden ways," while the emphasis later in the poem on the woman's lack of sensation—"She cannot see the grain / . . . / She cannot feel the rain"—recalls "A slumber did my spirit steal." On the other hand, the diction and the syntactic structure of lines like "She left the rosy morn, / She left the fields of corn" recall the Lady of Shalott, who "left the web" and "left the loom." But there are other literary echoes that undercut these images of the passive woman, submerged in Nature like Lucy or doom-ridden like the Lady of Shalott. The sunless rivers of the opening lines, in association with the "deep," recall the "sunless sea" of Coleridge's "Kubla Khan," while the general syntactic structure and the rhymes (although certainly not the meter) suggest Tennyson's "The Kraken": "Below the thunders of the upper deep: / Far, far beneath in the absymal sea, / His ancient dreamless, uninvaded sleep / The Kraken sleepeth." The poem may, of course, be read as a pastiche of Romantic vocabulary and coloration or an attempt to move in Swinburne's direction toward the aestheticism of the sunken garden and Proserpine's sleep. Yet these particular allusions to "Kubla Khan" and resemblances to "The Kraken," which mesh with Rossetti's scriptural preoccupations, seem to invoke the power of origins and endings purposefully. The allusion to Coleridge's poem suggests the Edenic garden of self, while resemblance to Tennyson's suggests the apocalypse, the violent eruption of both demonic and divine power. Taken together, the allusions provide the "plot" for a transfiguration, a "rising" that will produce not only the beast and the whore of Babylon but also the woman clothed in the sun. What is more, while she awaits this awakening, the dead woman is less Lucy, insensate in Nature, than the biblical watcher: "Her face is toward the west, / The purple land." This female figure is the product, then, of the play of biblical models against Romantic ones, and of one set of Romantic motifs against another. Thus although the dreaming woman, whether the corpse of "Dream-Land" or the effigy of "Day-Dreams," is generated by an aesthetic that feeds on images of female dormancy and unconsciousness, Rossetti to an extent empties out this aesthetic for her own purposes. By a network of allusions she at least hints that the dreamer is a kind of visionary who will awake to "joy."

The double nature of the death pose, as image of alienation, as image of transfiguration, is dramatically evident in two poems, "A Pause" (June 10, 1853) and "After Death" (April 28, 1849). Both poems exploit Pre-Raphaelite and sentimental conventions: the woman is a liminal figure, lingering between life and death; she is laid out attractively on a floral deathbed; she is a pathetic, misunderstood figure who is set up to stir regret in the neglectful mourner. But she is also acutely conscious in a way that the other dead women we have been discussing are not. She feels and sees and hears everything; she narrates in the past tense from some omniscient perspective, seeing, as always, herself being seen. Like the wraith who haunts the scene of her exclusion in "At Home," she is the quintessential outsider, both eavesdropper and voyeur. What the intensity of her perception affirms, in the one poem, is the pathos of her *invisibility*; in the other, it is its power.

In the earlier poem the confrontation between the lover-mourner and the dead woman leads to pathos, but nothing like recognition: "He did not touch the shroud, or raise the fold / That hid my face, or take my hand in his, / Or ruffle the smooth pillows for my head" (*Works*, p. 293). The Pre-Raphaelite clarity of detail recalls other clear moments of desolation, like Tennyson's "Mariana," like Emily Dickinson's "I heard a fly buzz when I died," and a striking sense of the woman's fragmentation: the body that arrests and repels the viewer; the consciousness that lies in wait, tenacious, possibly vindictive, but certainly entrapped. The later poem inverts these propositions. In "A Pause" the dead woman similarly awaits her beloved, whose arrival is also described with naturalistic particularity: "At length there came the step upon the stair, / Upon the lock the old familiar hand." These are the kinds of details that Dante Gabriel Rossetti uses in "My Sister's Sleep" to indicate the pathos—and the aesthetic tension—of the moment of the woman's death. In Christina Rossetti's poem it is just at this point of highest tension that the imagery veers from the "naturalistic" Pre-Raphaelite world of "My Sister's Sleep." In language that recalls the woman clothed in the sun of Revelation, the invisible woman makes her appearance, seen only by herself:

> Then first my spirit to scent the air
>   Of Paradise; then first the tardy sand
> Of time ran golden; and I felt my hair
>   Put on a glory, and my soul expand.   (*Works*, p. 308)

The moment of passage is the occasion not for pathos but for apotheosis, as the dead woman makes an extraordinary escape from the body. Rather than await her human lover, she leaves for a timeless realm that might include the woman Rossetti calls "a great wonder," the woman who represents "weakness made strong and shame swallowed up in celestial glory."

In Rossetti's repertory of female images this basic opposition between the visible death and the invisible transfiguration represents her attempt to deal with an aesthetic which surrounds her with images of women displayed in congealed poses, while locating consciousness—"vision"—in the artist-lover-spectator. Like all transfigurations, Rossetti's signify an end to dialectic: the transfigured woman escapes forever the cycle of desire and renunciation, the disjunction between visible and invisible, "appearance" and "reality." While awaiting this imagined end, the woman trapped in the body, trapped behind the cultural mask, can maintain an inward pose. This is the watcher's pose, which differs from the pose struck by the repining woman, the object of vision who, in a masculine aesthetic, waits and dreams her life away. The watcher's face is set toward Jerusalem, the site of her transfiguration; she is less a dreamer than a visionary.

The Whore of Babylon

The dialectic does not entirely end with the translation of female spectacle to a visionary realm. The female spectacle at the end of time includes also the Whore of Babylon, the figure who represents both the female "lie," and the female "truth," one as horrifying as the other. On the one hand, she belies female innocence and stands ready to seduce the beholder; on the other, she tells the truth about female depravity. Rising from the ages-long sleep entails facing this image as well; the antitype of the woman clothed in the sun, she may, in fact, represent one direction female "awakening" might take. In her prose commentary on Revelation, *The Face of the Deep*, Rossetti was forced to confront not simply the biblical figure itself, "Mystery, Babylon the Great, the Mother of Harlots and Abominations of the Earth," but a range of Old and New Testament diatribes against women. In line with the patriarchs, Rossetti asserts that the Whore can be studied as illustrating "the particular foulness, degradation, loathsomeness, to which a perverse rebellious woman because feminine not masculine is liable." "Solomon," Rossetti goes on, "by warning man against woman has virtually warned woman against herself." These authoritative texts sanction, in other words, woman's separation from herself, her perception of herself as a spectacle of corruption. Rossetti wrote only two poems that hold this mirror up to female nature, but they are strikingly revelatory of the ways in which her sense of the illustrative female image reflects a deep cultural bias. Everywhere she looks, she must, like the Royal Princess in the poem of the same name, see only "mirrors," and the terrifying images must be assimilated along with the rest.

In the earlier poem, "The World" (June 27, 1854), the images in fact suggest less the specific figure in Revelation than the kind of denunciations against female sinfulness Rossetti must have read in writers like St. Paul. This figure is characterized by her duplicity. By day she is beautiful, "soft, exceeding fair"; she woos the speaker with "ripe fruits, sweet flowers, and full satiety" (*Works*, p. 182). By night she is a phantasm of loathsomeness, a Medusa figure with "subtle serpents" in her hair. Rossetti sums up her doubleness as the opposition between lies and truth: "By day she stands a lie: by night she stands / In all the naked horror of the truth" (*Works*, p. 182). It is not difficult to read the return of the repressed into this recognition: the sexuality Rossetti has ostensibly denied returns as a monstrous Medusa, symbol of female castration, and of the power to castrate, and therefore of both female powerlessness and female destructiveness. But that "truth" is not really "hidden" for Rossetti, not a nightmare vision. Rather it is a cultural truth in plain sight, codified by scripture and the patristic diatribes. Rossetti is responding less, I think, to psychic pressures than to conventional ideas and images that warn women against themselves.

The Whore turns up once more as a transfixing image in "Babylon the Great" (*Works*, p. 284, B. 1893). The double lie-truth woman in this portrait is "Foul . . . and ill-favored, set askew," revealed in her "truth," that is. But the viewer can be mesmerized by her, as by a Medusa, and dream another image, the "lie" into existence; the speaker warns: "Gaze not upon her till thou dream her fair, / Lest she should mesh thee in her wanton hair." This terrifying spectacle is the opposite of the statue-woman; she is, in fact, one of the few female figures in Rossetti's poetry who moves. At the end of the poem Rossetti represents her as dancing wildly and again warns the reader not to *look*, lest one be caught up in the final destruction, "When, at the far end of her long desire / Her scarlet vest and gold and gem and pearl / And she amid her pomp are set on fire." This extraordinary image suggests that Rossetti might have been unconsciously exploiting the subversive "truth" of the apocalyptic-demonic woman: she is the witch, the wicked Queen who dances to her death, a symbol of female rage and power, unleashed in the ways that Sandra Gilbert and Susan Gubar suggest. But if she identified with the monstrous woman as an avatar of female power on an unconscious level, on a conscious level she certainly repudiated the identification, except to the extent that every woman is inhabited by the patriarchal images: in the Whore every woman is warned against herself. Inevitably, given her culture, and in particular her relation to scriptural authority, Rossetti had to contend with this image, working it into her exploration of female "doubleness." Ultimately, what is of most interest is that the female spectacle, whatever its origin, falsifies and betrays: she who gazes is betrayed by a dream-nightmare no less then she who embodies the vision.

Masks of Life and Art

Everywhere she looks, it seems, Rossetti sees mirrors that reflect her female deformity—"All things that pass are woman's looking-glass"—or masks that signify female inanition. A woman behind the mask or pose may be a horror, as in the two Whore of Babylon poems, or a woman arrested in another pose, that of the watcher awaiting her transfiguration, as in "A Soul" and "A Pause." The mask may, however, be totally empty, either because the "real" woman has somehow made her escape, as is a possibility in "Day-Dreams," or because of the horrifying possibility that the woman has grown one with her mask. The persisting consciousness that afflicts the subjects in poems like "After Death" and "A Pause" suggests that Rossetti means to convey what it is like to be buried alive, stifled by a life which demands and gives too little. Along with their intense consciousness, these buried women retain the expectation that an apocalyptic realization of their powers awaits them. The worst horror that Rossetti can imagine, however, is the spiritual death of a woman who freezes in a lifelong pose of social decorum, as in Rossetti's most desolate poem, "Dead before Death" (*Works*, p. 313). Here the cold mask of convention is almost as frightening as the apocalyptic Whore's face, for it is not only a death mask but also a Medusa's head, belonging to a woman who is herself petrified: "Ah changed and cold, how changed and very cold, / With stiffened smiling lips and cold calm eyes!" The woman who, in the first line, parodies the indifferent beloved, has turned into a corpse by the second line, suggesting erotic and deathly affinities between the two kinds of "indifference," that go beyond the traditional associations. "Grown rigid in the sham of life-long lies," this woman has been robbed of life by the cultural mask; she must endure, "cold and lost," until death overtakes her "death."

The mask of decorum must have been familiar to Rossetti as her own mask; William Michael speculates that the poem is addressed to herself as she "might become if 'Amor Mundi' were to supersede the aspiration after divine grace" (*Works*, p. 479). With just a shift in emphasis we can see the aptness of his judgment: all of Rossetti's poems say this, in effect, for to live as a woman in the world, as a cultural sign, is to risk becoming a corpse; the only escape is to another realm altogether. Occasionally however, it is just possible to get a glimpse of the invisible woman, the woman as she "is" behind the mask. Only another woman, perhaps, can witness the truth, as in "Enrica, 1865", where the warm-blooded Italian woman sees through the Englishwomen's icy rigidity to their hidden mobility and depth:

> But, if she found us like our sea,
>   Of aspect colourless and chill,
>   Rock-girt,—like it she found us still
> Deep at our deepest, strong and free.
>
> (*Works*, p. 378, July 1, 1865)

This female spectator has a double focus that sees the other woman's double nature. In this case the surface appearance does not belie the "real" woman but, rather, comes to be read differently, as inscribing another kind of metaphor.

But if the surface appearance does belie the woman as she "is," the female witness has the ability to see that, too, as in Rossetti's tribute to the pathos of Elizabeth Siddal's life, "In an Artist's Studio." Here one woman is the model or, rather, the pictured woman, while another is the watching consciousness. The relation between them, however, can be taken to stand for the relation between the self who sees and the self who is seen. Looking at the portraits, the speaker is struck by their reductive sameness:

> One face looks out from all his canvases,
> One selfsame figure sits or walks or leans:
> . . . .
> . . . every canvas means
> The same one meaning, neither more nor less.

Unlike the artist, whose vision is single, indeed monomaniacal, the speaker witnesses the discrepancy between the artist's frail illusion and the woman's unpicturable reality and testifies to the pathos of both:

> He feeds upon her face by day and night
> And she with true kind eyes looks back on him,
> Fair as the moon and joyful as the light:
> Not wan with waiting, not with sorrow dim;
> Not as she is, but was when hope shone bright;
> Not as she is, but as she fills his dream.
>
> (*Works*, p. 330, December 24, 1856)

This beautiful woman vampirized by art is a version of the woman dead before death. The difference is that she lives, however weakly, detached from her image, and that the speaker has the capacity to see the woman unmasked.

Whether the female subject of these secular lyrics is the woman dead before death or trapped by the mask of art, the poet claims the power to hold both the mask and the inner reality in focus. Given just the right focus, she finds it possible to see a woman who is normally invisible. The subject of "In Progress" (*Works*, p. 352, March 31, 1862), unlike the petrified woman "changed, yet the same," and unlike the model who changes for the worse behind the scenes while her portraits stay the same, is at one with her changes. Her calmness and silence signify not spiritual death but, rather, self-possession: "centered in self and yet not unpleased to please." After a realistic catalogue of this woman's evident virtues, "wearied perhaps but strenuous certainly," Rossetti suddenly makes a visionary leap to the last stage of this "progress": "Sometimes I fancy we may one day see / Her head shoot forth seven stars from where they lurk / And her eyes lightnings and her shoulders wings." If she persists in her stoic heroism, Rossetti implies, this is what we can expect to see: a woman clothed in the sun, a woman *grown* to this power. This transfiguration bypasses the death pose, illustrating how, still within traditional parameters, enlightened vision can bypass deadening images to reconstruct a vocabulary of female power.

Watching, Looking, Keeping Vigil

The transfigured woman, the walker in white ("Of My Life," *Works*, p. 312, May 15, 1866) is still a spectacle, object of the verb "to see," still an image of a woman seeing herself being seen. In a sense, she is a product of a failure of vision, a splendid icon invoked to offset other, damaging female icons. In some of Rossetti's devotional poems that reification is intensified, in the figure of the watcher-witness who, like the Cleopatra soul, offers herself as a spectacle for God's view. In this poetry of "watching," the emphasis is on the frozen pose and the unseeing look. Typically, the watcher's face is rigid and impassive, the "set" face derived from Jeremiah and Isaiah, as in "Yea, therefore as a flint I set my face" (*From House to Home, Works*, p. 25, November 19, 1858), "Our face is set to reach Jerusalem" (*Works*, p. 122, ca. 1877), and "Set faces full against the light" (*Works*, p. 145, B. 1886). The watcher's face may in fact be both obscured and unseeing: "Therefore to Thee I lift my darkened face; / Upward I look with eyes that fail to see, / Athirst for future light and present grace" (*Works*, p. 227, B. 1886). What matters here is the fixed, straining position, the watcher's pose rather than spectacular woman's display.

What the watcher does long for is the apocalyptic dissolution of roles and the transcendent vision "face to face." Throughout her career Rossetti focuses on the divine Face as the watcher's fulfillment, for "Who looks on Thee looks full on his desire" (*Works*, p. 269, B. 1893). At the apocalyptic end, when all spectacles have passed away, those who are now "cast down, in want," will see "in the eternal noon / Thy Face" (*Works*, p. 128, ca. 1877). It is to this vision that the devotional speaker offers herself as spectacle and witness, a figure carved in stone, "Thy Mercy's all-amazing monument" (*Works*, p. 266, B. 1893). Again, what signifies is not so much the quality of vision as the act of self-display, the watcher watching herself observed. As generated by the watcher's pose, then, the religious poetry would seem to be poetry of alienation, the self conscious only of its division and its separation from a distant God. In the pattern of Christ's life and death, Rossetti finds the perfect analogue for the self isolated as object of vision. "None with Him" (*Works*, p. 238, June 14, 1864) represents Christ's extreme loneliness in life as a consequence of a human failure of vision:

> My God, to live: how didst Thou bear to live,
> . . . .
> Few men prepared to know
> Thy Face, to see the truth Thou cam'st to show.

The loneliness of His death is similarly intensified by a visual failure, as Christ becomes a grotesque spectacle: "A curse and an astonishment, past by, / Pointed at, mocked again." Rossetti concludes that by comparison her own suffering is inconsequential, her response cowardly. But the analogy works the other way as well. Because she experiences the isolation of self as spectacle, whether derided, or misunderstood, or merely appraised, she can comprehend Christ's isolation. Christ's isolation thus becomes the adequate symbol for the female predicament. Similarly, she can write of the martyr's ordeal as primarily the ordeal of a woman seeing herself stared at unfeelingly: "a gazing-stock" for "pitiless eyes" (*Works*, "A Martyr: the Vigil of the Feast," p. 259, B. 1882). The self as "gazing-stock" is the opposite, but complementary, pole of self as "amazing monument." Both situations are equally desperate, and equally isolated.

Yet although Rossetti's primary impulse may be to "freeze" in a submissive yet self-displaying pose while awaiting an apocalyptic dissolution of roles, many of her religious poems render a more integrative experience of self. In a group of poems dealing with the soul's relation to Christ, Rossetti explores the more integrative variant of the visual metaphor, compassionate "looking." In over twenty of the devotional poems the speaker asks Christ to look on or upon, look down, look back: that is, to respond actively to the sinner in her need. On the one hand, then, the persona of the religious poems "sets" her face both to withstand hostile or falsifying stares and to keep watch for the transcendent union "face to Face"; on the other, she achieves now, in her imperfect mortal state, an intimate and reciprocal relation:

> Yea, Lord, be mindful how out of the dust
> I look to Thee while Thou dost look on me,
> Thou Face to face with me and Eye to eye.
>
> (*Works*, p. 267, B. 1893)

The divine face that participates in this type of encounter is not the beatified countenance but the disfigured face of the crucified Christ. In "The Descent from the Cross" Rossetti discovers the face that requires her to look with compassion:

> Is this the Face that thrills with awe
>   Seraphs who veil their face above?
> Is this the Face without a flaw,
>   The Face that is the Face of Love?
> Yea, this defaced, a lifeless clod,
>   Hath all creation's love sufficed,
> Hath satisfied the love of God,
>   This Face the Face of Jesus Christ.   (*Works*, p. 254, B. 1882)

Although the face that awes seraphs is in no way a false abstraction, like the idealized portraits of Elizabeth Siddal, there are structural parallels between this poem and "In an Artist's Studio." "The Descent from the Cross" can, in fact, be read as an inversion of the secular poem. While in "In an Artist's Studio" it is the idealized face that replaces the living, suffering face, in "The Descent from the Cross" it is the idealized face that is absent, displaced by the reality of the dead Christ's disfigured face. Although the change in Christ's face is perceived as shocking "defacement," it is also a change through which transcendent value persists—this face is still "the face of Love." The speaker recognizes this face, just as she recognizes Elizabeth Siddal's marred face, because it is the face that is most like her own: the face of suffering, and mortal change.

Looking upon this face of suffering can become a means of rescuing a relation, and thus a self. For although the woman fixed in art appears to look back at the artist-spectator, she is not present in a relation. Her image reflects *his* need, but *she*, as Christina Rossetti makes clear, is elsewhere. In the religious poems, however, if the watcher looks steadfastly upon Christ's suffering, there is a chance that looks will really go both ways, that Christ will respond to the spectacle of the watcher's suffering. Christ's suffering face is thus a proper revision of the fair face of the ideal beloved: it mirrors human suffering, it looks back with "true kind eyes."

Although Rossetti can imagine Christ actively looking for her "Elsewhere and nearer Me" (*Works*, p. 221, B. 1893), His look may be averted, and the speaker's utterance aimed at turning that look: "Lord, wilt thou turn and look upon me then" (*Works*, p. 228, September 30, 1863); "Turn, look upon me, let me hear Thee speak" (*Works*, p. 230, B. 1886); "Turn, as once turning / Thou didst behold Thy Saint" (*Works*, p. 231, B. 1893). The speaker seems to beseech Christ as if He were a fixed and silent icon, projecting upon Him that fatal stillness which she experiences as part of her persona. But Christ's answering look, when the speaker does succeed in evoking it, breaks down her own iconicity. By His look Christ calls forth the speaker's integrated self. When, for instance, she asks the Lord to "look" and "see" what she has to offer, Christ answers that he looks not so much for flawed attributes—a "marred" will, a heart "crushed and hard"—as for a whole self: "I crave not thine but thee" (*Works*, p. 220, b. 1886). Because her whole self, even marred and suffering, finds acceptance in Christ's expectant look, the speaker can imagine a relation of intense mutuality, represented as an exchange of looks:

> Lord, dost Thou *look on* me, and will not I
>   Launch out my heart to Heaven to *look on* Thee?
>   Here if one loved me I should *turn to see*,
> And often think on him and often sigh.
>
>   (*Works*, p. 229, B. 1893, my emphasis)

The analogy with lovers' looks is compelling, not because it demonstrates Rossetti's thwarted erotic impulses, but because it so clearly demonstrates in what ways a relation is adequate. Rossetti expects from God no more than she would expect from a human relation. In her secular poetry, however, the human relation appears most often as failed:

> He looked at her with a smile,
>   She looked at him with a sigh,
> Both paused to look awhile:
>   Then he passed by,—
>   (*Works*, "Under Willows," p. 368, July 11, 1864)

But while earthly lovers pass by, put off by what they "see," and the would-be beloved remains "silent and still," transfixed again in the watcher's pose, Christ looks persistently and stirs the speaker out of her immobility. Christ's look calls forth not only a whole self but an active one. Thus in a brief poem for the Vigil of St. Peter, Rossetti, while retaining the visual metaphor, links it with movement:

> O Jesus, gone so far apart
>   Only my heart can follow Thee,
> That look which pierced St. Peter's heart
>   Turn now on me.
>
> Thou who dost search me thro' and thro'
>   And mark the crooked ways I went,
> Look on me, Lord, and make me too
>   Thy penitent.   (*Works*, p. 175, B. 1893)

As a prayer, the poem assumes that words can have effect, that both the one who speaks and the one who is spoken to can be moved from fixed positions. If words bridge the distance between the speaker and Jesus, the speaker will attempt to establish a relation by working through a series of verbal definitions. Jesus' defining characteristic is His removal to a distance—"gone so far apart." Although both as lyric speaker and as watcher the suppliant maintains a fixed position, she moves synecdochically: her "heart" follows the spatial route as far as it extends. But at this limit, like the heart, the poem itself has to turn back through the historical moment of Peter's denial and Christ's reproach to the present of "Turn now on me." As readers, we are expected to know the exact nature of St. Peter's sin, but not in what particular way his "heart" was "pierced"—whether with shame, remorse, sorrow, love, or all of these. All we know is that the speaker means to bring that piercing look into the present, purely as an act of attention.

The second stanza establishes a present context for the relation by extending the visual figure. Jesu has already looked piercingly at the speaker and judged her past goings, the "crooked ways" as opposed to the heart following. Now the speaker asks Him to supersede those seeing acts with the look that not only judges but also binds the one looked at in a relation to the one who looks. Jesu's attentive look will transform the speaker from a distant spectacle of sin and guilt into a self who is intimately related to God as "Thy penitent." God's penitent "moves" inwardly: she changes position within a relation; she knows and is known, loves and is loved.

In the "look" that registers compassion and compels a relation, Rossetti finds a way out of both her usual predicament and her usual defense against the pain of her predicament, as expressed in the figure who is both spectacle and watcher. Earlier I suggested that "witness" was a useful term for the compounded watched-watcher. The witness testifies to her predicament by displaying a self in isolated immobility; she also testifies to the resolution of that predicament by describing what she sees: both God's glories and His sufferings, both woman's iconic mask and her changing, marred face. *One day*, then, not now, all distinctions will be subsumed in light, and we shall see and be seen "face to Face." Although the witness takes a stand, she or he still has the status of onlooker, distanced from the spectacle—whether of self or another—even in the act of representing it. But Rossetti discovers that the spectacle of suffering requires her to abandon the solipsism of the watcher-witness and to commemorate other sufferers by "looking" compassionately. "Looking" can thus transform the act of witnessing into "keeping vigil." The vigil keeper, as in "The Vigil of St. Peter," looks back as well as forward. By commemorating the dead, the vigil keeper establishes a community of suffering that links the living with the dead and constitutes a meaningful present.

Thus in the poem that begins "Our Mothers, lovely women

pitiful; / Our Sisters, gracious in their life and death" (*Works*, p. 214,
B. 1893), Rossetti keeps vigil for the dead while they, perhaps, watch
over her. Like Tennyson, who speculates about Hallam's continuing
participation in the concerns of the living, Rossetti cannot be sure
that the dead women remain aware of their living sisters and daugh-
ters. But "if they see us in our painful day, / How looking back to
earth from Paradise / Do tears not gather in those loving eyes?" In
the community of sufferers, even paradisal women cannot look at
the spectacle of other women's pain without feeling identity. The
poem ends with the consolation: "Ah happy eyes! whose tears are
wiped away / Whether or not you bear to look on me." Rossetti can
endure the possibility that looks do not go both ways, that she keeps
vigil in isolation, by postulating heavenly consolation: eventually,
too, her tears will be wiped away.

In poems like "Our Mothers," vigil takes the form of valediction,
the mode that both acknowledges and overcomes loss. In 1858, when
she was twenty-eight, Rossetti wrote "A Burden," a valediction for
"her" dead. Lying "at rest asleep and dead," the dead in "A Burden"
exert a strong pull on the living. While the dead are fulfilled, the
living still "hope and love with throbbing breast," and long for the
"nest of love beneath / The sod." A coherent pattern breaks through
these effusions: the dead are both present and absent, they forget
and remember, and, as the speaker extols them, "They watch across
the parting wall" (*Works*, p. 205).

Some time "before 1886" Rossetti refined "A Burden" to a twelve-
line lyric, much less speculative and melodramatic than the earlier
poem. In the later poem Rossetti wisely refrains from ruminations
about the vanity of human wishes, and simply celebrates the dead as
irrevocably absent and firmly unforgotten:

> They lie at rest, our blessed dead;
> The dews drop cool above their head,
> They knew not when fleet summer fled.
>
> Together all, yet each alone;
> Each laid at rest beneath his own
> Smooth turf or white allotted stone.

When shall our slumber sink so deep,
And eyes that wept and eyes that weep
Weep not in the sufficient sleep?

God be with you, our great and small,
Our loves, our best beloved of all,
Our own beyond the salt sea-wall.   (*Works*, p. 127)

Although these dead do not look back, the speaker does not suffer in isolation; she takes her place as vigil keeper within the community in which all are "together" and yet "alone." No longer images of female powerlessness, these dead represent her communal life as sister, daughter, friend, and member of the Christian church.

In taking on the responsibility of keeping the dead "unforgotten," Rossetti both commemorated the pain of her own history and transcended that pain by imagining it absorbed within a communal history. Thus she could write movingly of the separation between Paul and Barnabas: "For saints in life-long exile yearn to touch / Warm human hands, and commune face to face; / But these we know not ever met again" (*Works*, p. 174, ca. 1877). What Rossetti always wanted was the kind of mutuality in which no one is object or other; thus the final resurrection is imaged as the most complete reintegration: each soul will return "bone to his bone," "Each with his own not with another's face." "O faces unforgotten!" she says, "if to part / Wrung sore, what will it be to re-embrace?" (*Works*, p. 215, B. 1893). Only the final reintegration makes the present separation, self from self, self from other, endurable.

Thus Rossetti always comes full circle. By keeping vigil she testifies to the final outcome, but only the final restitution gives meaning to the vigil. Within this circle, however, she discovers a range of poetic stances. As model, as dead woman, as the Whore of Babylon, and as the woman clothed in the sun, she explores the varieties of female spectacle that issue from a body of conventions that depend on a reification of the female subject: these spectacular women can only see themselves being seen. As watcher-witness she extends the role of the spectacular woman to the speaker of the devotional poems, exploring the ways in which the desiring soul experiences isolation and longs for transcendence "face to Face." As the sufferer who looks upon Christ's suffering face and is looked at in return she discovers the possibility of intersubjective recognition, a mode of looking by which the self is not reified. Finally by looking for her fellow sufferers she transforms isolated gazing into a collective act. Over this range of seeing acts, then, Rossetti is able to express not only fragmentation and isolation but something like integration and community.

4 Self-Sisters
The Rhetorical Crisis

Through the motif of the watcher watched, the exemplary woman who displays herself as spectacle and testifies to her reification, Rossetti gives form both to her self-division and her self-possession. The statue-woman who witnesses and is witnessed is both a beginning and an end, both a seed-stone of potential selves and a monument-stone to unrealized selves. After all the possibilities have been closed, she remains and endures, providing the poet with a stance for regarding and demonstrating the shape of her life. This monolithic figure is surrounded by—and realized in—a range of female projections, both "strong" and "weak" sisters. All are actors in the psychic theater, a company that includes lyric and dramatic speakers, as well as narrative subjects. All are descended from the prototypical Laura and Lizzie, each alternately the sister who ventures forth and the sister who sits and waits, and all exhibit the obduracy of the stone-woman in varying degrees. The lyric speaker yearns, suffers, and endures; the dramatic monologuist posits and rejects alternatives, protests and renounces, strikes an inward pose; the narrator creates a company of women—mothers, daughters, sisters, brides, nuns, corpses, ghosts—who spurn or are spurned, who linger on the threshold or stand rooted to the spot. By exhorting, lamenting, and commemorating these women, by giving them voices, Rossetti creates what Winston Weathers has called "the sisterhood of self."[1]

In outlining Rossetti's myth of "the fragmented self moving or struggling toward harmony and balance," Weathers distinguishes three groups of poems of sisterhood: "those that simply analyze the self into its parts, those that present the conflict within the self, and those that deal with some sort of integration of self."[2] Weathers' extremely useful schema is somewhat misleading to the extent that he implies that the groups are equally weighted. I would argue that integration plays a small part in Rossetti's total myth, and that Weathers' first two categories predominate: the sister-selves either coexist as antithetical types or compete as sexual rivals and as ideological antagonists. Indeed, integration expressed as consummation, whether sexual or spiritual, may signify the death of self, for to achieve the object of desire is to incorporate it or to be incorporated in it, and to lose the keen edge of desire. There is a sense in which Rossetti must, as a poet, stay "hungry" and incomplete, her persona of the unsatisfied watcher a female version of the yearning quester.

As we have seen in chapter 3, Rossetti expresses her deep sense of self-division in the system of visual imagery that generates the motif of the watcher watched. In the sisterhood poems we see how this doubleness extends to structures and themes as well. By dividing "sisters" in narrative poems and by opposing the self who desires to the self who renounces in the lyric poems, Rossetti articulates her version of Romantic-Victorian divided consciousness:[3] not the split between hero and villain, or between reason and emotion, but between the sister who is chosen and the sister who is spurned, and between the self who romantically asserts and the self who stoically denies. Sexual rivalry can be resolved only by subordination. For if two or more compete, then one must win and one must lose; as the speaker of *The Lowest Room* would have it, "Some must be second and not first; / All cannot be the first of all" (*Works*, p. 16). The spurned sister, though outwardly invalidated, endures as the authentic consciousness, while the rival becomes the "other," reduced to her function as usurper. Through the structure of rivalry Rossetti expresses her deep sense of displacement. She asks for "the lowest place" because no other has been reserved for her, and because, perhaps, only the first or last will do.

As in all instances of literary doubling, a psychobiographical interpretation is unavoidable, and Christina Rossetti can be seen as working out in her poetry her poetic and Oedipal rivalry with her brother and her Oedipal rivalry with her mother. Although Frances

Rossetti was, from all accounts, a model Victorian wife and mother, there is some indication that she lacked warmth.[4] Christina was greatly dependent upon this strong and demanding woman all their long life together and certainly unambiguous in her expressions of devotion.[5] Precisely to the extent that she was unable to achieve autonomy from this controlling matriarch, however, Rossetti must have had ambivalent feelings toward her, and likely the negative feelings found their way, obliquely, into the poetry. Thus the sexual rival, the fair woman who always wins, can be construed as the mother who wins by overcontrolling her child and by taking away the father in the Oedipal triangle.

But the "other" is also Dante Gabriel Rossetti, for the rivalry between Christina and her brother, again unexpressed, is fairly evident. As children they are alike in temperament and gifts. As they grow up, however, they must conform to sharply divergent expectations. Dante Gabriel becomes the romantically excessive artist, Christina the ascetic spinster, the sister who tends the hearth and ministers at deathbeds.[6] Their sexual roles extend to their poetry, as Dante Gabriel enacts risk and excess, Christina conformity and restraint. At worst, he is decadent, she rigid. Mostly, however, he is always "first," the quintessential precursor, whether as gifted and beloved son, or as poet. Moreover, brother and sister, "twins" in their position in the family, can be seen as preoccupied with one another in an almost incestuous way: as we have seen, Christina is Dante Gabriel's first model, even a prototype of subsequent models.[7] Further, Christina's antipathy toward Elizabeth Siddal looks very much like jealousy of a rival in love and in art, for Siddal replaces her simultaneously as model, as ideal "beloved," and as protégé. Thus the other "sister" is either the mother or the erotic rival for the brother or the brother himself in a narcissistic doubling. The ambiguity of erotic rivalry is fully realized in the 1863 "The Queen of Hearts" (*Works*, p. 353) in which the speaker is constantly outplayed by the rival in a card game. The antagonist picks up the queen of hearts unfailingly, even when the speaker cheats. Stanley Weintraub relates that the Rossetti children identified themselves with specific suits: William with spades, Maria with clubs, Dante Gabriel with hearts, and Christina with diamonds.[8] Here although the speaker identifies with clubs (the weakest suit) rather than with diamonds, the identification of hearts with Dante Gabriel is still plausible, and the erotic rival, the demonic Queen, is either Dante Gabriel or a woman loved by Dante Gabriel (and thus the mother).

Lastly, Rossetti's sisterhood poems must be considered in the light of their narcissistic component. Although she does not write poems that could be categorized as literature of the double, strictly considered, she does write about clearly opposing selves, whether they are the antithetical but symbiotic Laura and Lizzie, or the antagonistic cardplayers in "The Queen of Hearts." Rossetti projects her self-love upon the other, the "twin" brother masked as sister (but really a sister-self), as a defense against the threat of death and loss of self, whereupon, by the logic of the "return of the repressed," the second self originally asserted as a defense comes to embody the threat. As Otto Rank explains this transformation: "So it happens that the double who personifies narcissistic self-love, becomes an unequivocal rival in sexual love."[9] Despite the plausibility of these speculations, it would be misleading to represent the Rossetti family as actors in a family romance written by Eugene O'Neill. Whatever the underlying ambiguities of their relations, from all evidence they acted generously and responsibly toward one another. And whatever the unconscious source of the conflict in Christina's case, in the poems it has been recast as a recognizable drama of self engaged with self, struggling toward self-knowledge and self-mastery.

For there is a sense in which that second self, the winning rival, *is* external to the "true" self, and the split reflects the subject's experience of herself as "other" in de Beauvoir's sense. The subject, or first self, has been usurped, not by an actual rival, not even by a domineering older brother, but by both a narcissistic double and a collective projection that defines woman as everything that is other, everything that the subject desires and fears. Thus the woman poet is both she who stands apart, desiring, and she who is desired. She—the subject, the first self—experiences herself not only as her own narcissistic love object but as another's, as a generic object. She cannot, of course, really integrate with this other self, although she cannot disclaim responsibility for it, any more than a mother can disclaim responsibility for a freakish birth.

Rivalry and Language

Rossetti's lifelong identity crisis is bound up with a language crisis. Just as in the poems the subject has been displaced by a sexual rival, a "sister," so in life the poet has been usurped by a brother poet, indeed a whole brotherhood of poets, specifically the Pre-Raphaelite Brotherhood,[10] or more broadly, the whole Romantic tradition. Christina Rossetti has to make do with and also make over a language which is in a sense not her "mother tongue." Therefore just as there is a split in the poet-subject's identity, so there is a split between her "own" language of ascetic self-denial and the "other" language of romantic passion and romantic self-assertion: the language of old ballads, of Gothic Romance, of English and Italian Petrarchism, and, most important, the language of Keats, Shelley, and Byron. Nearly overwhelmed by this babble of voices—romance mixed with eighteenth-century hymns and Italian opera libretti—Rossetti struggles to recover a language. She cannot begin to invent one (a feat no Victorian poet could accomplish) because she is too ill educated, despite poring over Hone's *Everyday Book*, to grasp how others build their own models of the world out of borrowed materials, because she sees that for her, originality is at best futile, at worst dangerous. She can, however, mount a criticism of dead or falsifying conventions from inside the conventions, from within the form of the ballad, for instance, or the Petrarchan love sonnet.

In her religious poetry, however, Rossetti finds a way to express sincere feeling, as her voice merges with a more public and impersonal voice. Sensing that the language of romantic feeling and romantic individualism is inappropriate to her vision, Rossetti takes up the officially sacred language partly in order to drown out that other language. As a religious poet her solution to self-division does not lie with reconciling selves but, rather, with the discovery that the self must be *for* another; the religious lyrics are all rhetorical situations in which an "I" lays claim to a "Thou." As Freud tells us, "in the last resort we must begin to love in order that we may not fall ill."[11] Thus Rossetti's substitution of the divine love object or otherworldly ego ideal for a human love is a healthy response, even a noble narcissism.

In the secular poems, specifically the poems that render sister-selves either simply divided or explicitly at odds, Rossetti speaks both in the "other's" voice and her own, as different voices and different "songs" compete. The subjects of ballad narratives are drawn into a critique of the language of love and sexual alliance, specifically the metaphors of the fruit, the flower, and the gift. The speakers of the secular lyrics develop a language of suffering that pares away and parodies romantic expressiveness; like Romantic lyrics, these poems raise the possibility of stony silence. In both the secular and the religious lyrics the speaker is the first sister, the survivor of her rejection. Thus the first sister who comes last, who is left behind, also has the last word. She is the authentic consciousness and the authentic voice.

Rivalry, Usurpation, and Authenticity

The poems of rivalry and usurpation are based on the eternal triangle, a closed hierarchical system. In these poems one self, the subject- or speaker-self, is rejected and chastened in the eyes of the world, while another figure triumphs as the "chosen" and often (though not always) obtains social sanction as the lawful wife, the real person. The rejected figure remains authentic, however, by both enduring and witnessing the usurpation; that is, although overtly chastened she displays the survivor's strength and the victim's rebuke.

The structure of rivalry and usurpation can be seen in its purest and most schematic form in an 1856 poem that has nothing to do with female rivalry. In "The Hour and the Ghost" (*Works*, p. 327), the bride is torn between conflicting claims. The ghost says "come," the bridegroom says "stay." The bride feels overwhelmingly compelled by the ghost, who calls her home; the ghost, who has been betrayed by the bride, in fact reproaches her, "taunts her with her past." In his overwhelmingly seductive power the ghost is not unlike the goblin men; indeed, the bridegroom's injunctions to the bride and his innocent reassurances—"Lean on me, hide thine eyes"— suggest a Laura / Lizzie relation between the two. In some way, then, the bride is not innocent; she is "goblin"-ridden by her own past that now pulls her forward into consequences. The poem concludes in the formulation of a new structure of rivalry and usurpation. The bride begs the bridegroom not to forget her as she forgot; the ghost predicts her return as ghost to witness her usurpation; "to see one much more fair/ Fill up the vacant chair." It seems not to matter much who triumphs at any given moment; the structure of exclusion and inclusion, rejection and reproach, always prevails: "While thou and I together, / In the outcast weather, / Toss and howl and spin."

Although the two ballads "Light Love" (*Works*, p. 327, October 28, 1856) and "Cousin Kate" (*Works*, p. 347, November 18, 1859) approach rivalry and rejection from an entirely different narrative base, the underlying structure is the same as in "The Hour and the Ghost": a triangle, with two aligned against one; one who forsakes or betrays, one who is chosen and triumphs, one who is rejected. In "The Hour and the Ghost" the roles remain stable, while the actors shift. The first role is played by the bride and the bridegroom (in the ghost's projection of the future) alternatively; the second by the ghost and the bridegroom; the third by all three. The "one" is always supplanted by "another." In "Light Love" and "Cousin Kate," however, "another" is more precisely "the other," the rival who is everything the "one" is not, and the actors stay in their roles. As the narrative represents the affective life of the rejected one, the rival is more clearly a projection based on Rossetti's fantasies of male expectations concerning desirable women, fantasies that she has every reason to accept as normative. The rival is woman as she is perceived in her acceptable aspects; the rejected woman is woman as she *is*: betrayed, scorned, "illegitimate" either in herself or in the child she bears. In "Light Love" and "Cousin Kate" Rossetti deploys conventional images and diction for didactic effect, with the result that the poems look like conventional Victorian moralizing; yet she elaborates certain images and repeats certain key words in such a way as to subvert conventional attitudes, and criticize conventional literary figures.

Within patriarchal tradition women are frequently spoken of as flowers and consigned to vegetal fates, from Robert Greene's "Fawnia" to Tennyson's "Queen lily and rose" (*Maud*) and Dante Gabriel Rossetti's "Jenny." In "Light Love," however, the language of flowers—as well as birds and fruit—is extended to a whole realm of moral action, as the rejected woman takes up the light lover's metaphor and unfolds it in all its ironic implications. The seducer, who is about to desert the woman who has borne him a child, begins by suggesting that she, his "mateless dove," can find another love, "left from the days of old / To build the nest of silk and gold." That is, she can find another man to keep her. When she silently reproaches him, he turns on her in scorn and invokes his bride-to-be: she is a tangible commodity, a ripe-blooming rose, a ripe-blooming peach that "ripens, reddens, in my sight." In her reaction to this characterization of the rival, the rejected woman seems to respond as much to the false lover's diction as to her betrayal. Moving through a biblical denunciation—"Haste where thy spiced garden blows: / But in bare autumn eves / Wilt thou have store of harvest sheaves?"—she arrives at the true meaning of the language of flowers:

> Pluck up, enjoy; yea trample too.
> Alas for her, poor faded rose,
>   Alas for her like me,
> Cast down and trampled in the snows.—

Her rhetorical sisterhood of the rose is no match for the man's, however. In a cruel sneer, he turns her figure against her: "Like thee? Nay not like thee: / She leans, but from a guarded tree." Against such cruelty there is no defense; in the closest Rossetti comes to attributing a hard fate to divine injustice, the woman raises something like a reproach to Heaven: "Dost Thou forget?"

Although one female figure perceives and the other is perceived, (while the man acts, or announces his action), in these two poems the subject, or "self," experiences herself as primarily "other." She is as much an object as the rival, although the rival is doubly "other";

she is not only the man's acquisition but also the instrument by which he humiliates the first, or rejected, woman, who now becomes decisively "second." Both poems suggest that even if the triumphant rival is publicly authenticated, she and the rejected woman are equally debased. But the rejected woman, although defeated in her attempts to subvert the metaphors that debase her, triumphs to the extent that she perceives the corrupt terms of the contest.

In other poems of woman's fall and exile, even when she does not attempt a critique of the flower/fruit metaphor, by following the metaphor out in all its consequences Rossetti discovers its potential to depersonalize rather than universalize a human situation. In "An Apple-Gathering" (*Works*, p. 335, November 23, 1857), for instance, the rejected woman turns the flower/fruit metaphor masochistically against herself. She is responsible for her own "downfall" because imprudently she plucked the pink apple blossoms of "her" tree to make herself sexually attractive, with the inevitable botanic conse-quences—no apples. Now her rustic lover, Willie, has gone off with plump Gertrude who has a basket full of apples. Whether or not the apples represent sexual consummation, the speaker feels that Willie is wrong to value the part at the expense of the human quality: "I counted rosiest apples on the earth / Of far less worth than love." The speaker chooses her isolation and singularity: she lets her neigh-bors pass her by as she "loiters," like Laura, in the darkness and the cold, excluded from the business of life. She is not only left behind, but she is also the remnant that endures unreconciled, still protest-ing, looking back, desiring. This outsider self is authentic precisely because she chooses her exclusion, however inadvertently, and be-cause she maintains her perspective on "apple" love.

Models of Exploitation:
The Influence of Maturin's *Women*

Four early dramatic monologues, "Eva" (*Works*, p. 12, 1847), "Zara" (*Works*, p. 107, 1847), "Eva" (Hatton, p. 51), and "Look at This Picture and on This"(*Works*, p. 323, July 12, 1856), present a highly charged, melodramatic version of the rivalry situation. The speaker in "Eva" is the renunciatory heroine who struggles to set her thoughts on heaven and reunion with her beloved after death. The first Zara is the "other" woman who in her desertion asserts kinship with her rival—("He shall leave thee also, he who now hath left me")—calls down vengeance on the cruel lover, recants, and asks for the "cup of sorrow." The second Zara's emotional drama parallels the first's: even more intensely haunted by the rival who triumphs over her in a deathbed pose, she vows vengeance on the doubly false lover, and welcomes the "cold cup," dreaming of reunion in death. The speaker in the fourth of the series is the faithless lover himself, who taunts the saintly—and mute—rejected woman (Eva) with his passion for the sensual rival (Zara): the rejected woman triumphs by her transfiguration in death. All four poems, as well as a short unpublished sonnet, are in fact derived from Charles Maturin's novel *Women: Pour et Contre.*[12] William tells us that "Christina, as well as her brothers, was in early youth very fond of Maturin's novels, and more than one of her poems relate to these" (*Works*, p. 477).[13] Maturin's influence is more profound than William's comment suggests. As the following summary should demonstrate, the fantasies of sexual rivalry, betrayal, renunciation, and apotheosis which underly *Women* must have matched closely with Rossetti's own youthful fantasies.

The plot of *Women* is this. On his way to the University of Dublin, De Courcey, the orphaned heir and a passionate and unformed young man, rescues a beautiful young woman from a kidnapping that seems to be engineered by a mad hag, who raves incomprehensibly. The young woman turns out to be Eva Wentworth, the ward of an Evangelical zealot. De Courcey falls ill with desperate love of Eva, joins the sect which centers on the Wentworth household, and is accepted as Eva's fiancé. Eva attracts the hero not only by her beauty and virtue but also by her extreme passivity and helplessness: she is in a dead faint when he first encounters her and feels a strong erotic attraction toward her. But along with her passivity and her single-minded devotion to her religion goes a certain emotional rigidity that baffles De Courcey. It's not that she doesn't feel but that she is markedly unexpressive.

While still attracted to Eva, De Courcey meets the beautiful and intellectually accomplished Zaira, a Continental opera star of myste-

rious origins. Everything that Eva is not, the brilliant Zaira inevit-
ably wins De Courcey's love and is forced to admit her love for him,
despite the difference in their age and education. She becomes a kind
of tutor to him, the older woman who initiates him into the life of
the mind and of the social world beyond provincial Dublin. De
Courcey breaks off with Eva and travels in Europe with Zaira.
Haunted by apparitions of the pale, angelic Eva, De Courcey experi-
ences a revulsion of feeling against Zaira, breaks off with her, and
returns to Dublin, where Eva lies on her deathbed. In their final
confrontation, the transfigured Eva forgives De Courcey but will
have no futher dealings with him because she wants no distractions
from her heavenly love. Zaira follows De Courcey to Dublin, where
she encounters the hag, who reveals to her the truth of her history:
the hag is Zaira's mother, who had been seduced by a libertine
aristocrat, while Eva is Zaira's daughter, spirited away at birth by
Zaira's impresario husband. Zaira rushes to the Wentworth house,
but of course, it is too late. Eva dies and De Courcey dies of a broken
heart shortly thereafter. Zaira lives on in obscurity in Dublin, her
talents abandoned. She is heard to mutter: "My child! I have mur-
dered my child!"

Out of this tangled plot Rossetti reduces her four operatic arias.
All focus on the passion of rejection and renunciation, but it is
helpful to know that the "Zara" poems are written from the perspec-
tive of an erstwhile sexually powerful woman who now is rejected.
Thus pure structure triumphs, for by shifting to another point on
the triangle, by assuming the role of the rejected woman, she sounds
like all other rejected women. Then again, this is the meaning
Rossetti intends; all women are alike in their exploitation: "He shall
leave thee also, he who now hath left me." No less than the self-
abnegating Eva, the self-assertive Zara is reduced to the bitter cup. It
also helps our understanding of "Look on this Picture" to know that
in the novel an incestuous configuration underlies the rivalry; hence
the significance of the title, which otherwise seems to have only the
superficial meaning that the two women are as incomparable as
Claudius and the elder Hamlet. In the context of the Maturin novel,
however, the title indicates violation of the incest taboos comparable
to the violation that occurs in *Hamlet*: here, one rival is the daughter,

the other the mother, the lover a symbolic son or brother. Rossetti seems to be saying that the ravages of ordinary sexual rivalry are as violent and profound as the ravages of incestuous passion. In the courtship game, woman's betrayal of woman can be as deadly as a mother's betrayal of a daughter.

Maturin's influence extends considerably beyond these poems, however, for the basic motifs of *Women* turn up repeatedly in the poems of sexual rivalry. Maturin's rivals are paradigmatically anti-thetical and complementary: the fair, passive, virginal Eva; the dark, aggressive, sexually awakened Zaira. Both are perfect exemplars of de Beauvoir's categories of woman as "other": the Virgin Mary and Beatrice on the one hand, Eve (or Lilith) and Circe on the other. Both are primarily sexual objects, for even the spiritual Eva is tempted into self-display when she is persuaded into a low-cut gown for an opera performance, and Zaira, as an opera star, constantly presents herself theatrically. What Rossetti must have found so compelling in the novel is the romantic posturing of all three main characters, but especially the satisfying combination of erotic self-display and high-minded renunciation that characterizes both heroines. Eva's deathbed triumph is the triumph of all Rossetti's dying heroines: she presents herself to her admiring viewers and mourners as attractive spectacle; she feels passionately; she renounces the world's vanities, including earthly love; she turns her face toward heaven. But Zaira is also important to Rossetti's myth. If Rossetti cannot incorporate Zaira *whole*—the woman at once sexually and intellectually powerful—neither can she exclude her from a female myth. Zaira or, rather, her type appears in the poetry as the divided sisters, as both the sexually powerful rival, the dark lady, and as the remaining consciousness, the witness. In Maturin's scheme Zaira suffers terrible retribution: "When great talents are combined with calamity, their union forms the *tenth wave* of human suffering—grief becomes inexhaustible from the unhappy fertility of genius, and the serpents that devour us, are generated out of our own vitals."[14] But if Zaira's intellectual and sexual force is calamitous, Eva is too passive and unawakened to serve as the perfect model of stoic heroism. Further, in stanzas omitted by William from "Look on This Picture" (Hatton, p. 110) the faithless lover sounds remarkably like a rebellious child, the Eva figure like a cold, judgmental mother:

> Be still, tho' you may writhe you shall hear the
>   branding truth
> You who thought to sit in judgment on our souls forsooth
> To sit in frigid judgment on our ripe luxuriant youth.
>
>   (LI. 194–96)

Although Maturin indicts Eva for her frigidity, there is no confrontation resembling this in *Women*. In elaborating on Maturin's judgment Rossetti expresses her own sense of the inadequacy and destructiveness of Eva's type. This is *mother*-enforced frigidity, and youth rebels flagrantly, only to recant, of course, in the face of the mother Eva's heavenly assumption.

Neither Eva nor Zaira will do as a model of female wholeness because both are equally helpless, both enslaved to their passion for De Courcey, each the other's worst enemy. Significantly, mother and daughter are descended from a mad and degraded woman who has been victimized by a sexually and economically exploitive male. On the one hand, the stone-faced judgmental mother (in this case, actually the daughter, Eva) thwarts youthful luxury, enforces crabbed frugality; on the other, the victimized mother passes on her inheritance of degradation—the sins of the *fathers* are visited on the children. As we shall see, in *The Iniquity of the Fathers upon the Children* Rossetti deals explicitly with this deadly chain: the exploitive father, the frigid and repressive mother (the opposite face of the degraded mother, the mad hag), the subverted daughter whose only role is that of the stoic sufferer. If Rossetti cannot integrate Eva and Zaira as one living, successful woman—any more than Maturin can—she can combine them in the figure of the stoic witness. From Eva she takes the outward posture of martyrdom, the inward gesture of choice, for though rejected in the eyes of the world, Eva in turn rejects De Courcey and the world. From Zaira she takes the capacity for suffering amplified by genius; Zaira survives in order to suffer, but she survives. The two types merge in Rossetti's watcher-personae—the speaker in *The Lowest Room*, the rejected ballad heroines, the passionately renouncing nuns—who present themselves as models of endurance, combining Eva's saintly display with Zaira's Promethean gnawing at the vitals.

Betrayal of Sisters: Strong Speech

Although Rossetti's ballads contain many traditional motifs, they diverge meaningfully from the structures and concerns of ancient ballads, as rendered in Scott and Percy, for instance. Like Rossetti's, Percy's ballads are full of betrayed women, false lovers, and strong speeches of renunciation and reproach, but the theme of rivalry and usurpation is subordinated to the theme of faithless and true love. Volume 3 of Percy's *Reliques of Ancient English Poetry*[15] gives a series of structural variants of this theme that illuminate the nature of Rossetti's poetic choices. "Fair Margaret and Sweet William" (p. 124), "Lord Thomas and Fair Ellinor" (p. 82), "Lord Thomas and Fair Annet" (p. 234), "Sweet William's Ghost" (p. 128), and "Margaret's Ghost" (p. 308) are all versions of the same story. In the first three, which tell the "whole" story, the fair woman is rejected by her lover in favor of a "jolly brown" or "nut browne" bride who has land and money. In "Lord Thomas and Fair Ellinor" and "Lord Thomas and Fair Annet" there is a wedding-day confrontation and a bloody denouement, with the lovers united in death; in "Fair Margaret and Sweet William" the emphasis is on the return of the rejected woman as reproachful ghost with the result that William dies of sorrow, and out of the two graves grow the rose and the briar as testimony of the triumph of true love. In "Sweet William" the story has decayed to the extent that there is no betrayal, only a separation between lovers that must be overcome through a wedding in death, while in "Margaret's Ghost" the story is similarly truncated, with the emphasis on Margaret's reproach, a long disquisition on the decay of her beauty in the grave, and the lover's remorse. Thus in all of these, but in the returning ghost ballads in particular, we see how the motive force behind the story is the breaking and reinstating of vows: true love is defined against faithless love.

Rossetti's ballad plots ostensibly concern the same matter: in "Maude Clare," for instance, the remnants of the "Lord Thomas and

Fair Annet" story show up in the wedding-day confrontation and in the contrast between Maude Clare and her rival. But the conflict does not define true love. Instead, Rossetti seems to be interested in the potential of the traditional ballad situation to render another kind of betrayal, and another kind of commitment. In "Maude Clare," as well as in "Cousin Kate," "Sister Maude," and "Noble Sisters," the focus of interest is not so much the breaking of vows, or the woman's victimization by a fickle lover, as the betrayal of one woman by another. The issue of this betrayal is not violent action but violent speech.

Like her ballad predecessors, Maude Clare, the spurned rival, is tall and queenly, whereas Nell, the sexual and social winner, is like a "village maiden" and short in stature. Here true love does not triumph: Maude Clare haughtily reproaches the faithless lover, the lover attempts to "match her scorn with scorn" but becomes speechless, and the poem ends with a verbal confrontation between the two women. In her pragmatic willingness to take Maude Clare's leavings—the lover as well as the worthless love tokens—Nell proves inwardly low in stature as well, but she, unlike the "nut browne" bride of the ballads, wins: "I'll love him till he loves me best— / Me best of all, Maude Clare."

The poem as printed is considerably shorter than the manuscript original: Rossetti cut down from the original forty-three to twelve stanzas. The tighter narrative and the ballad allusiveness of the printed version support the significance of structure as such. The rivalry is less tied to circumstance, and there is a purer polarization between the one and the other, the high and the low. But the excised stanzas reveal a quite explicit reason for the betrayal. Maude Clare accuses Nell of having bartered for love:

> For you have purchased him with gold,—
> ....
> For its [*sic*] your gold he took you for—[16]

And instead of the bride's childlike taunt in the printed ending, the manuscript version shows a dignified awareness of sisterhood:

> I never guessed you loved my lord,
> I never heard your wrong;

> You should have spoken before the priest
> Had made our tie so strong.
>
> You should have stood up in the Church
> To claim your rights before;
> You should have parted us in the Church
> Or kept silence evermore.[17]

Here the bride recognizes Maude Clare's claims and, herself speaking with dignity, reproaches Maude Clare for failing to speak strongly and directly.

Woman betraying woman is an even stronger motive in the two companion poems "Sister Maude" and "Noble Sisters." The speaker in "Sister Maude" accuses her sister of revealing the speaker's illicit love to their parents, out of her own desires for the lover. Now that the drama has been played out, the lover dead, the focus shifts to the relation between the sisters. The poem is all accusation and vituperation—an extended curse. Although the speaker and her dead lover might gain entry to heaven, not so Sister Maude, who has committed the unforgiveable sin: "But sister Maude, O sister Maude, / Bide *you* with death and sin" (*Works*, p. 348). William Rossetti notes that Christina withdrew this poem in subsequent issues because it resembled Tennyson's "The Sisters" too closely. But the resemblance is not really that close, and it seems more likely that she withdrew it because of the impropriety of such vituperation issuing from a woman's mouth. Only Dante Gabriel's "Sister Helen," who actually performs a curse, can compare in vindictiveness.

In "Noble Sisters" sister again betrays sister. This time a malicious sister has sent away first the lover's messengers—falcon, hound, and page—and finally her sister's lover himself, with a lie that the sister is already married. Responding to the betrayed sister's assertion that she will go seek her lover, the malicious sister speaks a curse:

> Go seek in sorrow, sister,
>   And find in sorrow too:
> If thus you shame our father's name
>   My curse go forth with you.   (*Works*, p. 349)

Thus in both "Noble Sisters" and "Sister Maude" the "accursed" situation—sister betraying sister—is expressed as a linguistic act: the uttering of a vindictive taunt or a curse. Both kinds of utterance are common enough in traditional ballads. Working from within a convention, actually piecing together conventional motifs, Rossetti makes a strong statement about the wages of sexual rivalry and sexual exploitation.

All these ballad poems discussed so far have a similar underlying structure: a triangle with a pair of rivals (usually female) competing for the love of a third figure (usually male). The focus may be on the two rivals or on the betrayed woman and her betrayer. The balance must shift, however, so that the betrayed woman endures as the site of consciousness in the poem. Whether she is highborn or lowborn, pure or impure, the rejected woman is always authentic; conversely, the "other" woman, although outwardly legitimized, is always inwardly unauthentic. Through this structure Rossetti offers a criticism of male-female and female-female relations. Although the man victimizes and exploits, the winning rival is complicit, and guilty of betraying sisterhood: Nell should not have bought love; Maude Clare should have spoken up for her rights; Sister Maude and the other noble sister should not have betrayed their sisters either with the truth or with lies. The only sisterhood is the sisterhood of sorrow, for the rival who apparently triumphs is often threatened with the same fate in a reconstitution of the triangle.

Even if she has been seduced, the betrayed woman retains her purity of motive and a tragic awareness of her situation. Although dominant in the situation, the winning rival is necessarily muted as consciousness. She must remain "other" in order to express woman's otherness as the object of desire. She will ultimately be rejected precisely because desire exceeds its object. The rejected woman endures because she is discarded, undesirable, but also because she remains desirous, an emblem of unfulfilled yearning. From the vantage of the outsider she rejects the system that excludes her. She is the "witness" of her "disgrace" in that she both exemplifies it and testifies to its injustice. In her desperation and her all-embracing consciousness she takes up the language conventions that sanction her exploitation—the language of flowers, for instance—and exploits the conventions, even though, technically, she remains their victim.

The Rebuke: *The Lowest Room* and *The Iniquity of the Fathers Upon the Children*

In two longer poems, *The Lowest Room* and *The Iniquity of the Fathers upon the Children* (*Works*, p.p. 16, 41), Rossetti develops a conflict between rival ideologies. Like the heroines of the ballad poems, these heroines are usurped. They have not found their rightful place because something in "the way things are" does not give them leave to "be." Even more overtly than in the ballad poems, however, these poems represent a self struggling, literally, toward articulation. These heroines dare to speak strongly. In *The Iniquity of the Fathers upon the Children* daughter rebukes mother; in *The Lowest Room* sister rebukes sister. The latter poem mounts a protest against the order that reinforces fragmentation and also offers one of the strongest instances of the sustaining role of the watcher.

In *The Lowest Room* two sisters sit in a room, one idle, the other busily embroidering. One sister is pale and graying; the other has a "comely face" and "golden tresses." The speaker, the pale, graying sister, expresses openly her quarrel with the world, that "Some must be second and not first; / All cannot be first of all." She longs for the golden age when the structure of values was clearer and purposeful action possible. She longs in particular for "Old Homer's sting." Homer's world seemed to allow for the expression of a range of emotions, from rage and hatred to "fuller love." Further, even the princess and her handmaidens had power in this world. We are not told what the golden sister is embroidering, but no doubt it is quite different from the ancient women's needlework: "Beneath their needles grew the field / With warriors armed to strike."

What the speaker appears to want, then, is to be allowed to feel intensely and to articulate, even act on, those feelings. The ability to alternate between one state and another would possibly allow the speaker to feel less self-divided, certainly less depressed. The mild sister is finally stirred to rebuke this troublesome, somewhat "childish" sister who wants all the wrong things. She claims that there is no reason why she and her sister should not attain "heroic strength" within their domestic sphere, and that the lesson to be learned from Homer is this: "Only Achilles in his rage / And sloth is less than man." Rossetti's choice of Achilles is significant, for Achilles' rage stems from his usurpation.

As the golden sister points out, the appropriate model is not the bestially wrathful Achilles but Christ. The speaker feels rebuked in her "secret self," where she nurses "silent envy" and "selfish, souring discontent." She goes on to resolve the problem by a reductive strategy that Rossetti often uses her devotional poetry: all texts, whether world or word, have one meaning only—all is vanity, all shall pass. No need then, to strive, to worry about who is first and who second. The golden sister walks out into the garden, leaving the speaker in what must have been a characteristic pose of Rossetti's, sitting alone with a book, watching somewhat furtively while the more natural and extroverted "sister" collects and arranges flowers "with instinctive taste." Suddenly the golden sister's beloved arrives, there is a break in the poem, and twenty years have passed. The golden sister has married, replicating herself with a daughter and showing a face that has altered very little since the conversation twenty years before. During these years the speaker has remained in one spot, as it were, much like a naughty child compelled to sit in the corner, free only to ruminate on her "lesson" and perhaps lead a secret inner life:

> . . . I sat alone and watched;
>   My lot in life, to live alone
> In mine own world of interests,
>   Much felt but little shown.

> Not to be first: how hard to learn
>   That lifelong lesson of the past;
> Line graven on line and stroke on stroke,
>   But, thank God, learned at last.

Although the "first" sister of *The Lowest Room* does not admit to any rivalry with her sister, she is left with a sense that she has been passed over or passed by. The sisters may not be competing for the same man, but they are competing for legitimacy. The golden sister, both stately and submissive, is authenticated as wife, mother, and Christian; the speaking sister is punished for her curiosity and aggression by forfeiting the joys of wifehood and motherhood, by forever remaining a child.

The substance of the first sister's lesson—not to be first—comes as something of a surprise. The obvious meaning is that the speaker has learned the lesson of Christian humility; but equally obviously she has learned not to be first in love or in the life of the mind. Thus Christian humility seems to require total self-abnegation; or, perhaps, such total self-abnegation can be tolerated only in the context of Christian humility. "Not to be first" remains a somewhat enigmatic, privately coded message, and we are left wondering why the sisters are so polarized and the rivalry, although not sexual, so intense. From William Michael's note to the poem we know that Dante Gabriel had a strong antipathy to *The Lowest Room*, and that Christina, who usually took his advice in poetic matters, firmly refused to withdraw the poem from subsequent editions. Although the primary adversary may be the mother—in the person of the stately sister who administers the rebuke—it is also likely that an implicit adversary is the brother, and the brother-animus within her. If we imagine the first sister's complaints as addressed to a domineering older brother, then we can better understand, perhaps, the querulous tone and the inevitability of the rebuke: the rebuke is administered both to an aspect of herself that would presume against the authority of the brother and to that figure himself as he is incarnated in the first speaker, insofar as she expresses curiosity and aggression. Rossetti plays both the role of the sister who would aggress against the brother/mother and the role of sister/mother who rebukes the destructive brother. The older sister, who is usually the teacher—the younger is usually "Content to listen when I spoke / And reverence what I said"—is rebuked by the younger, who speaks up this once. We know from Eve's example that it is wrong for woman to usurp the teacherly function—she should suffer to learn: "Let woman fear to teach and bear to learn" (*Later Life*, no. 15, *Works*, p. 78). But in this situation the younger sister justifiably administers the rebuke without stepping out of the womanly role, and the older sister bears to learn. Thus Rossetti, by expressing the intellectually and emotionally aggressive component of the self in the first sister, experiences a covert identification with the male; at the same time, by overtly repudiating that component self, she experiences female triumph over the male (the female teaches the "male" a lesson). In an overt identification with the passive female she hands the victory over to the mother.

The rebuked and excluded sister who remains, as if dumb-founded, in the meditative pose, stands, or rather sits, outside of time, watching change but not experiencing it. She maintains an intact, if diminished, self, while the other sister goes about the business of life which, oddly enough, involves repeating herself with a daughter who is exactly like her. The other sister has assumed the "first" or legitimized position because she has played according to the rules. The excluded sister remains an original, alone of her kind. If as a woman she is defined by what she shows, by her surfaces, then she will harden into that woman, assume the pose expected of her with a scrupulosity that borders on impertinence, while drawing on the Christian/Platonic tradition that separates "appearance" and "reality" to preserve her inner mobility. What the rebuked woman gains from assuming the submissive, immobile posture is the free-dom to ruminate, to be herself. Ruminative brooding may turn to depression, for the woman may pine away as many Victorian women did, and as many of Rossetti's heroines do, but it can also deepen into meditation and give rise to meditative poetry.

Further, this speaker, like the captive and confined souls who are about to break the mortal cage in Emily Brontë's poems, inhabits another territory besides the lowest room. She assents to her con-finement not only because she can sustain the feeling life undis-tracted, but because she awaits the apocalyptic redistribution of places, the violent overturning of the established categories:

> Yea, sometimes still I lift my heart
>   To the Archangelic trumpet-burst,
> When all deep secrets shall be shown,
>   And many last be first.

In *The Lowest Room* one speaker in the debate challenges, another replies with a rebuke. In *The Iniquity of the Fathers upon the Children*

(*Works*, p. 41), a solitary persona challenges and rebukes in a confessional dramatic monologue.[18] Like Laura, the heroine challenges by her curiosity about her origins, by her forbidden knowledge. She rebukes by the truth of her parentage that she bears in her face and by her ironic, scornful use of the phrase "sub rosa." This daughter inhabits what looks like a matriarchal system: the mother, an unmarried aristocrat, administers her "kingdom" by herself; the father has abandoned both mother and daughter, who has been conceived and borne "sub rosa." As well as illicit sex, the phrase suggests chthonic birth—the baby found under the cabbage, or the rose. Thus the girl's illegitimacy has deep reverberations: if she was born under the rose then she is only her mother's baby or possibly nobody's baby. At any rate, in this poem true matriarchy is impossible, for the mother must reject her daughter publicly, even while supporting her privately.[19]

This masked mother's stultifying world of convention is represented as literal confinement, but occasionally the girl gets out in the grounds "For a whiff of wholesome air," and she even threatens escape: "Give me a longer tether / Or I may break from it." She cannot really escape, for the system prevails everywhere, so she resolves to offer passive resistance by going to her grave as "nameless"—that is, as autochthonous—as she came. She will endure awaiting the democracy of the grave, and, like the speaker of *The Lowest Room*, whom she resembles temperamentally, feel much and show little. But she will not suffer to learn the hard lesson. Inwardly she will repudiate it, and in her face carried in full view she will show herself as a lesson.

In this self-display she resembles the heroine of *A Royal Princess* (*Works*, p. 35, 1861). The princess acts more strenuously than most Rossetti heroines do: locked into a sterile life, surrounded by mirrors, repining and aging, she repudiates this world of her parents and goes out to the "people," who are demonstrating outside the palace. But her acts are essentially a showing. Like the speakers of *The Iniquity of the Fathers upon the Children* and *The Lowest Room*, she offers herself up as a rebuke. If in Rossetti's myth women cannot escape the restrictions of their social—and literary—roles, they can make an uncompromising stand precisely by taking up a pose: they become icons of resistance and endurance.

Revising the Metaphor: "Brandons Both"

In a much later poem, "Brandons Both" (*Works*, p. 403, B. 1882), Rossetti returns to the theme of unrequited love, the polarization between sister rivals, and the critique of the language conventions of sexual love. This nineteen-stanza ballad summarizes and epitomizes the issues raised by the earlier ballads; and to a certain extent the conflict is more satisfactorily resolved. Like the heroine of *The Lowest Room*, Milly Brandon achieves self-possession by expressing a firm resolve, though less masochistically and obliquely, and like the heroine of *The Iniquity of the Fathers upon the Children* she takes up her strong stance without any hint of querulousness or self-pity.

Milly Brandon is introduced at the point of her decline. Conventionally beautiful, she has been made pale by a "secret care" which the narrator advises her to keep hidden in order to avoid the world's scorn. Her secret torment links her with other heroines: Laura in *Goblin Market* nurses "self-consuming care"; the heroine of *The Lowest Room* nurses "selfish, souring discontent"; the heroine of *The Iniquity of the Fathers upon the Children* must keep the secret of her parentage; the speaker of *An Old-World Thicket* suffers "self stabbing self with keen lack-pity knife." With the exception of the illegitimate daughter of *The Iniquity of the Fathers upon the Children* (though she is her *mother's* secret care), these subjects are indeed guilty of inappropriate feeling that must be hidden. Although not in any way guilty, Milly shares with her sisters a secret passion and a secret worry that produce the same stigmata as moral sins. Intense feeling seems to inevitably turn inward and fester: suffering is the same as guilt.

Milly's secret is that she loves her cousin, Walter Brandon. She knows that his choice is the lowborn Nelly Knollys, whose chief advantage seems to be that she is well nurtured. She has a mother, while Milly, though her father's heiress, has none. While she strolls on her father's "hedged-in" terrace; Milly, like other nineteenth-century heroines, indulges in mental travel;[20] she thinks of her father's lands, the coverts and islands where game and fowl rise startled from their habitat. Like the "golden" sister of *The Lowest Room*, she is distracted by the footfall that makes all romantic heroines' hearts beat faster; it is Walter, come to greet his cousin before his day's "business." As they converse about hawking and hunting, the symbolic identification becomes clear: if Walter is ready for the hunt, we know his true prey. The woman must stay on her hedged-in terrace; the man must not loiter, for "nothing will come of nothing." He must be about "casting a bait toward the shyest daintiest fin."

From the language of heroic predation, the poem shifts to the language of flowers. Milly offers Walter a thorny rose to wear for an hour, "Till the petals drop from the dropping perished flower, / And only the graceless thorns are left of it." Walter refuses her offer; he has a rose sprung in another garden, and he warns her to guard her rose. We are back in the ruthlessly pragmatic world of "Light Love." But Milly turns away with a dignified gesture of renunciation and demarcation:

> Nay, a bud once plucked there is no reviving,
>   Nor is it worth your wearing now, nor worth indeed
>   my own;
> The dead to the dead, and the living to the living.
>   It's time I go within, for it's time now you were gone.

For once the beloved is not cruel. He bids her good-bye with regret, while she wishes her rival well and asserts her own worth:

> Good-bye, Walter. I can guess which thornless rose you
>   covet;
>   Long may it bloom and prolong its sunny morn;
> Yet as for my one thorny rose, I do not cease to love it,
>   And if it is no more a flower I love it as a thorn.

Through this persona Rossetti seems able to relinquish with grace and to accept the "thorniness" that both protects her and isolates her. If the thorns are the given of the feeling and recalcitrant woman's personality, then she will not disavow them: they are at least hers. Similarly, if her domain is limited and tamed, she is its mistress; out in the wild she can only be a prey. Milly and Walter are equally in command of the botanic and zoologic language, but Milly has the last word. She transforms the more or less dead conventions into a living private language.

After engaging in this final dialogue with her cousin-brother-lover, Millie turns inward. The lyric poems can be seen as continuing this dialogue or, rather, this articulation of a self behind closed doors and sealed lips. The passionately feeling woman struggles both to master her feeling and to sustain it as evidence of life. The "thorniness" of her predicament is that to feel is to suffer, but not to feel is to grow soul-less, or to die.

The Lingering Moment and the Poetic Act

If rivalry defines the split between selves, hierarchical subordination is not the only resolution, for as Weathers points out, there is a group of poems which render fragmentation as such. This analytic splitting is an important strategy for Rossetti. By preserving the split, she staves off both the subordination that precipitates the watcher-self, who is defined by standing apart, and the fateful integration that would obliterate that same self. In such poems as the two 1848 "Songs" ("She sat and sang alway," "When I am dead, my dearest"), "Songs in a Cornfield," and "A Triad," Rossetti tries to achieve the balance not of integration but of what may be called "lingering," the pause that allows different selves or opposing states (keeping and losing, remembering and forgetting, for instance) to co-exist without either actualization or reconcilement. In these poems mutually exclusive possibilities are held together, or apart, until the balance collapses.

These poems, as well as the 1863 *Maiden-Song*, which subordinates sisters, link sisterhood with "singing," that is, with making poetry. Weathers sees "singing forth" as a creative act ranging from simple "realization" in "Songs in a Cornfield" to "integration" in *Maiden-Song*. Weathers astutely points out the self-reflexivity of these poems: "The self is not only sung about (as Christina is doing in her poems), but the self is also to sing forth as a part of its sane activity in a threatening world (as Christina's poems are both the action of the self and a commentary upon the self)."[21] Although Weathers sees the poetic act as essentially integrative, as indeed it is in *Maiden-Song*, neither the Orphic song nor the epithalamion is truly characteristic of Rossetti's poetry. Since so much is lost, or "dead," the language as well as the selves, Rossetti's characteristic poetic stance is renunciation, by which she asserts what remains. Her most characteristic poetic mode is elegaic: the lament and the valediction. The lament mourns loss; the valediction says that mourning, too, must end. Both are the expressive outcome of renunciation, and both forms occur both early and late in Rossetti's career. The valediction is the culmination of lyric poems of renunciation; here, the lament seems the logical terminus for the poems of the *un*reconciled self. Although the speaker of the valediction still lingers, she is ready to be gone, turned toward a new future. The lament talks about what might have been but was not: its time is the lingering or threshold moment in which the two unreconcilable conditions—what was, what is not or cannot be—are still sustained.

Thus in the early "Song" (*Works*, p. 290, November 26, 1848), "She," the other, is the singer by day; the speaker is the weeper by night. The two compose a Janus figure: one, as if facing backward, weeps for memory; the other, as if facing forward, sings for hope. These two figures, in their emblematic separateness, represent the lingering self, poised on the threshold. The turn backward (memory) and the turn forward (hope) together constitute an indefinitely prolonged present. The two figures must always remain separate in order to sustain the lingering moment, the moment of the turn, and the lingering must be sustained in order to assure that the two parts of the self, the singer who celebrates and the weeper who laments, remain distinct. There is no larger whole into which they can be integrated. Significantly, neither the singer nor the weeper has any effect on the world: "My tears were swallowed by the sea: / Her songs died on the air." The expiration of both expressions suggests not only that singing and weeping are equally ineffectual, but that neither song nor lament can be fixed as expressions. In the lingering moment, each sings and weeps "alway."

The disjunction between singer and weeper occurs in more muted form in another poem concerned with modes of expression, "Songs in a Cornfield" (*Works*, p. 369, 1864). The sisters are four reapers: Lettice, Rachel, May, and the deserted Marian. The first choric song, rather nonsensical as moral advice, begins to make sense when read in the context of the second song. The first song is about keeping, holding on to what remains and endures: "Take the wheat to your bosom,/ But not a false love"; the second is about losing and letting go, the passing that defines what stays:

> After the swallow
> All good things follow:
> All things go their way,
> Only we must stay,
> Must not follow; good-bye, swallow, good swallow.

These songs of mutually exclusive alternatives break Marian's "listless" trance; a combination of the singer and the weeper in "Song," she sings "like one who hopes and grieves." The song is addressed to "our delight," which Weathers assumes to refer to the absent lover presumed dead, [22] but more likely designates a self that enjoyed the delights of love and is now dead. Death is one possible outcome of the alternation between hope and grief, keeping and losing, one possible resolution of doubleness. So, too, is silence. The singer-weeper's song is a lament not only for lost possibilities but for the inevitable end of the lingering moment. "Songs in a Cornfield" ends with a progressive attenuation that parallels the end of "Song." Not the song or the tears, in this instance, but the singer-weeper herself will melt away: if the lover comes today he will find her "weeping," if the next day, "not . . . at all."

Although Marian combines the two modes of expression—singing and weeping—she is more the weeper who sings than the singer who weeps. Thus, although Rossetti is interested, as "Song" shows us, in the possibilities of the kind of oscillation that achieves perfect balance, one "voice" usually becomes dominant. This is the case in another "singing" poem, *Maiden-Song* (*Works*, p. 38, 1863), which can be read as a pendant to "Songs in a Cornfield." Here the Orphic power of singing brings a world into being and achieves "integration," for the singing is, on the face of it, all celebratory. This poem's resolution depends on a hierarchical alignment of separate figures: the three sisters are not rivals, but one is clearly *first*.

The lesser sisters, Meggan and May, wander out into the countryside and sing themselves a herdsman and a shepherd, respectively. They decide to settle for these rustic mates out of expediency, for they know they are eclipsed by Margaret. Meggan muses:

> Better be *first* with him
> Than dwell where fairer Margaret sits,
>   Who shines my brightness dim,
> For ever second where she sits,
>   However fair I be.   (My emphasis)

Again, as in *The Lowest Room*, the language of exclusivity and usurpation—"'Some must be second and not first; / All cannot be the first of all.'" Marriage, reasonably enough, breaks up the terrible family rivalry whereby one shines while another is eclipsed.

The fair Margaret, who more nearly resembles the ego, stays at home, a watcher, and grows anxious over the sisters who "loiter." While waiting uneasily, she sings a lament, an answer to the nightingale's "old complaining tale." Beautiful women singing sad songs are invariably sexually glamorous, and so the lament is really a mating song. It modulates into an Orphic song of integration as she sings home her sisters, sings birds out of the sky and fishes out of the deep, sings together "friend and foe," and ultimately sings herself a kingly mate.

But if *Maiden-Song* is a poem of integration, then the integration depends on subordination: one voice must dominate. In "Songs in a Cornfield," although there is nothing like sexual rivalry, there is something like expressive rivalry in that Marian's song subsumes the other two songs. The two poems thus offer alternative resolutions to the problem raised in "Song." It does not matter which voice dominates, whether it is the singer who weeps—that is, sings a lament, like the triumphant Margaret—or the weeper who sings, like the defeated Marian. Rather, it is the relation between mutually exclusive possibilities—keeping and losing, hope and grief, marriage and death—that signifies. And what is signified is simply the exclusivity of these possbilities. Thus in these sisterhood poems Rossetti's concerns go beyond the theme of love and courtship. She develops a series of formal variations that constitute a larger set of concerns: how to discover one's place in a scheme that allows only for irresolution or a hierarchical arrangement; how to avoid mismating; how to maintain a stable balance between parts that cannot be integrated.

Rossetti's need to explore fragmentation shows up in two short poems that differ thematically from *Maiden-Song* and "Songs in a Cornfield" but appear to be structural variants. On February 20, 1863, some five months before *Maiden-Song*, Rossetti wrote a short and seemingly inconsequential poem that subtly parodies the latter. The sisters of "A Ring Posy" (*Works*, p. 355) form a more antic triad than Margaret, Meggan, and May. Jess and Jill, the city counterparts of Meggan and May are unmated as yet, though "pretty girls, / Plump and well to do." The speaker, Margaret's antitype, is frankly realistic about her success:

> I'm not pretty, not a bit —
> Thin and sallow-pale;
> When I trudge along the street
>   I don't need a veil:
> Yet I have one fancy hit.

Although the prettier sisters can sing and dance, this plainspeaker wears the ring. Here is a cruder sexual mystery than the mystery of the beautiful woman singing sad songs: for the plainest of women there is always one man at least, and one is enough. As in "Maiden-Song," the sisters are hierarchically aligned. It is not clear, however, whether the married sister is "higher" or "lower" than the other two.

Maiden-Song presents an idealized, romance-pastoral version of the mating and singing sisters; "A Ring Posy" presents the realistic and satiric version; the earlier "A Triad" (*Works*, p. 329, 1856) offers a dénouement bordering on melodrama. In this poem all three sisters are equally mismated and debased. The poem represents them not as singing their love into being or singing to attract a mate but, rather, singing the nature of their desire. Each gets what she sings:

> One shamed herself in love; one temperately
>   Grew gross in soulless love, a sluggish wife;
> One famished died for love. Thus two of three
>   Took death for love and won him after strife.

Although the "sluggish wife" is more successful than the others, on the surface, she clearly does not triumph. All three are lingerers

whose undertakings fail: "All on the threshold, yet all short of life."
Here no resolutions are possible, and marriage does not equal
integration.

The poems discussed above have linked a sexual crisis with a
poetic crisis as metaphors for an identity crisis: Does marriage bring
integration or death of self? Does the song reconcile or separate? Is it
a lament or an epithalamion? The epithalamion that integrates
Maiden-Song is only one possibility; "Songs in a Cornfield," "A Ring
Posy," and "A Triad" represent the alternatives. The visions of these
poems can be seen as at least potentially rivalrous; to choose one is to
exclude the other, and it is difficult to maintain them all. The triad,
after all, has a tendency to assume the form of a triangle, with
internal alignments and shifting focal points. In this group of
"threshold" poems, however, Rossetti attempts to preserve a kind of
irresolution. All of the singers, even Margaret, sing laments. The
singer-weeper laments the inevitable end of the lingering moment in
a resolution that brings the fall of the self: the self will either be
submerged in the "other," and thus expire, or at best remain as the
watchful outsider. The lament preserves the self in the lingering
moment by preserving the split—the distinctions between now and
then, seems and is, keeping and losing, remembering and forgetting,
self and other.

5   From Renunciation to Valediction
The Ongoing Crisis

While in Rossetti's ballad narratives the heroines play out and subvert devaluing images of women as manifested in a recognizable literary tradition, it is in a sequence of lyrics and dramatic monologues extending over her career* that Rossetti develops a more personal symbolism and a more strongly cast female myth. By tracing and retracing the pattern of desire, loss, and renunciation in these poems, Rossetti defines what is essentially an existential female choice and provides a rationale for an imitative rather than an innovative poetic language. As we have seen, change for the Rossettean female figure means insertion within the natural cycle, and hence decline. To counter this entropy, Rossetti adapts the paradoxical reversals of Christian ideology and sets up a symbolic system by which she can determine her own female "progress." In poems like "Memory," "Introspective," and "Endurance," Rossetti evokes a kind of persistence that is strongly linked with repetition and strongly immune to change once the crucial loss has occurred. In Rossetti's canon there is, in fact, only one kind of change: radical loss followed

*Three Nuns, Works, p. 12, 1849–50; "Endurance," Works, p. 297, 1850; "Three Stages," Works, p. 288, 1848–54; "Dead before Death," Works, p. 313, 1854; "Echo," Works, p. 314, 1854; "Introspective," Works, p. 331, 1857; "Memory," Works, p. 334, 1857–65; From House to Home, Works, p. 20, 1858; "The Convent Threshold," Works, p. 340, 1858; "An 'Immurata' Sister," Works, p. 380, ca. 1865; "Love Lies Bleeding," Works, p. 388, ca. 1872; "Soeur Louise de la Miséricorde 1674," Works, p. 411, B. 1882.

by slow decline. The original loss, the "it" that "happens," is often imaged as betrayal by a lover, but this betrayal may well stand for a more radical betrayal of self—the sudden failure or thwarting of potential, as represented in "Symbols." This kind of change can be countered only by reliving or repeating the initial shock and by willing endurance. Underlying this resistance to change is not only the cultural and historical equation between female change and female decline but also the psychological structure of desire. Either by relinquishing the desired object and moving on or by closing the gap between desire and its object, the self would lose the desire that defines the self and motivates language.[1] And underlying this dilemma is a fear of dissolution in an annihilating fusion with the object of desire, a fear which may be particularly acute in women, who have greater difficulty in establishing and maintaining boundaries between the self and the world.[2] Again, it is important to stress that in a very real sense change for the nineteenth-century woman means not only participation in a natural process that involves organic and psychic dissolution but also the assumption of roles which betray or falsify the self. On the other hand, resistance to change may bring on the death-in-life that Laura suffers when she turns stone-cold in her obsession with the goblin fruits. The risk, then, is that the stoically unchanging woman may get stuck with an aborted self—the seed-stone that refuses to germinate. The only solution to this predicament is to keep perpetuating the initial crisis, to keep making the same choice again and again, and thus to rescue the self from slow decline of a living death—and speech from silence—by reviving "hope" and "desire" and reenacting renunciation. This repetitive gesture—or holding pattern—is ultimately superseded by a "real" change, the apocalyptic reversal which redefines all previous assumptions about the subject's role and the normative aspects of language. This psychic structure shapes Rossetti's attitude toward language: to be "original" or "creative," to change language, that is, is not only dangerous but futile, as the only authentic change puts the situation and the speaker beyond speech, while to repeat prior texts is to protect the self and sustain speech. From this standpoint it is possible to make the ready-made language one's "own," and, as I have been arguing all along, to mount various revisions of the very language which deprives the female self of subjectivity. But in the course of her career Rossetti does come to allow a certain kind of change that does not involve either slow decline or violent reversals but, rather, a decision to tolerate ambiguity. From the position of the depleted female figure who is sustained only by unquenched desire and seeks only oblivion, Rossetti moves through the position of the enduring vigil keeper who keeps on enacting renunciation, to the position of the singer-weeper who accepts her losses and makes a graceful farewell. This, as I shall argue, is Rossetti's valedictory mode, an evolution of the lament, and a mode that is present from the beginning of her career. In what follows I shall trace the various stages of this "progress," starting with the most "stuck," or most deeply embedded in repetition, of Rossetti's personae, the repining woman.

Rossetti published the poem *Repining* (*Works*, p. 9, 1847) in the *Germ* in 1850, and chose not to reprint it thereafter. Her choice is easily understandable: the poem is loosely structured and weakly motivated, but more than that, it represents a female figure who is a caricature of transfixed passivity, and it contains traces of the same violence that courses through *Goblin Market* and *From House to Home*. It remains, however, an interesting document of Rossetti's ideas about female action and female creativity. The exhaustion that characterizes "repining" proceeds both from the futility of the persona's attempt to act in the world and from the futility of Rossetti's attempt as a poet to revise existing literary conventions. The repining heroine who is enervated before she begins her quest has no business as either a mental traveler or an actual one. She must die or become a "nun."

At the beginning of the poem the speaker is engaged in an activity that symbolizes both stasis and a deadly tropism. The immured woman is like one of the fates, spinning her own life thread:

> She sat alway through the long day
> Spinning the weary thread away;
> And ever said in undertone,
> "Come, that I be no more alone."
>
> From early dawn to set of sun
> Working, her task was still undone;

> And the long thread seemed to increase
> Even while she spun and did not cease.

The echoes of love-longing from Tennyson's "Mariana" and "The Lady of Shalott" are unmistakable. Not long into this poem, however, the awaited lover does arrive. He speaks like Christ—"Damsel, rise up; be not afraid"; and "Rise and follow me!"—and looks like "a fair young man," with "a dim glory like a veil" about his head. Whether Christ, or bridegroom Death, or the angel Gabriel with a new annunciation, the angelic visitor,[3] like the companion in *From House to Home,* heralds pain. And like Marley's ghost or the angel Raphael, the apparition takes the heroine on a visionary survey of the world outside. At first the excursion promises an end to her isolation through "The noise of life, of human life, / Of dear communion without strife." But as she and her companion look upon a village below them, a terrible noise signifies the approach of an avalanche; the village is destroyed *as if* by her very presence. The pilgrimage becomes increasingly sinister, anticipating the fatal downhill progress of "Amor Mundi":

> The path that lay before them was
> Nigh covered with long grass;
> And many slimy things and slow
> Trailed on between the roots below.

More disasters follow: a shipwreck, a city engulfed in flames, a battlefield with corpses staring in death and wounded men crying in agony. All this explosive force the heroine merely witnesses, and yet as it unfolds before her, it is as if her wish to see brings the horror into being. The poem ends with the speaker's prayer for deliverance:

> Let me return to whence I came.
> Thou who for love's sake didst reprove,
> Forgive me for the sake of love.

The vision has been a chastening for her wish to do anything other than endure: the alternative to isolation and repressed passion is cataclysmic disruption. For Rossetti the polarization is intolerably acute. The solitary self is horribly isolated with itself and might as well die, but the self in the world suffers and inflicts disasters.

The repining figure, like the princess of *The Prince's Progress*, is governed by the conventions of romance narrative. Neither pilgrim nor quester, she merely recoils and waits, finally dwindles. Although she cannot escape the psychic structure of the repining heroine—already the pattern of desire, loss, and endurance is set up in *Repining*—Rossetti will adopt a stronger persona (with the exception of *The Prince's Progress*) in subsequent poems. If the Romantic hero suffers paralysis of will as a consequence of a divided mind, Rossetti's heroines enact the drama of the divided mind that is a consequence of their immobilization. That immobilization is pointedly symbolized in a series of lyrics in which Rossetti adopts the persona of the cloistered nun. In doing so, she chooses a restricted situation for time-honored reasons; by shutting out the world she is freed to make heroic moral gestures and to play out her destiny on a cosmic scale, with a vertical rather than a horizontal axis.

Three Nuns

Each of the female figures in this series of monologues feels passionately while expressing longing not to feel. Although she has experienced a conversion, her crisis is not over, and since she cannot master feeling or translate it into action, she can only endure it, willing the control that almost paralyzes: the painful resurgence of feeling is evidence that she is still alive. While all three nuns share the same predicament, there is a subtle progression from the first nun, who wishes only for relief from her present pain, to the third nun, who is able to envision a new stage in which suffering—and its expression—is no longer necessary. In her representation of the subtle shifts between each figure's situation, Rossetti engages in a process of translating the language of Romantic longing.

The first nun is situated within her cell in a moment when she is free to remember and feel. Full of desire for an end to desire and memory, she implores the "shadow," the only intruder in her cell, to obliterate her:

> Shadow, shadow on the wall,
> Spread thy shelter over me;

Wrap me with a heavy pall,
  With the dark that none may see;
Fold thyself around me, come;
Shut out all the troublesome
Noise of life; I would be dumb.   (*Works*, p. 13)

The woman who feels longs not to feel, to be buried before she is dead; the woman who is nothing but a voice longs to be silent. Outside her cell sings a solitary bird, clearly a descendant of Keats' nightingale. She wishes the "blythe bird that can[st] do no wrong" to sing on to hearten her in her long vigil. Unlike the Keats who addresses the nightingale, she longs for precisely a temporary anodyne. She does not want to be recalled to herself, to her "present sorrow and past sin," though there is little chance that she can get beyond the present sorrow, even for a moment. In the cloister she is both sightless and unseen. She has found refuge from a world in which she was a spectacle, a fair woman with curled yellow hair. Through the bird's song she is transported not to fairy kingdoms but to the childhood world of insatiate pleasure, the green woods where "pleasure grew / Tired, yet so was pleasure too, / Resting with no work to do."

The cloister is the counterpart, then, of the childhood garden, where the speaker thought she could live forever, "Secret, neither found nor sought." Between that "pure" garden and the graveyard garden, the only place for the sinful, lapsed soul is the cell where she endures "aching, worse than pain," which she "must bear and not complain." Or, rather, to the sinful soul who still remembers the childhood garden the world of experience is a cloistered cell. Unlike Keats' "Ode to the Nightingale," Rossetti's poem is dramatic and local, all in the present moment with no sense of other places and times, no continuity between generations. Her moment expands to fill all of time, and hence is timeless, but not in the Keatsian sense of one moment taking its place in a succession. In her cloister, too, the speaker experiences a darkness rather different from Keats' "embalmed darkness." She bids the bird sing, not because she has any choices or hopes to make any discoveries, but because the bird's song is a temporary opiate that helps her endure what is already known, already plotted out. The bird's song offers her access to a regressive vision of childhood which has death in it, as well—the pool at the bottom of the oak tree.

The second nun makes clear that she is a victim of love, but, unlike the first nun who wishes to forget "present sorrow and past sin," she questions whether her suffering is punishment for sin. Like the speaker of the *Monna Innominata* series, she loved selflessly, refusing to participate in the transactions of courtship:

> . . . I pressed forward to no goal,
> There was no prize I strove to win.
> . . . .
> I sacrificed, he never bought;
> He nothing gave, he nothing took;
> We never bartered look for look. (*Works*, pp. 13–14)

This rather casuistical speaker has sinned only in that she prayed "in the sacred choir" for her beloved's happiness and salvation, not even for their meeting after death, Rossetti's usual solace for unrequited love. This nun seems to have arrived at the penultimate crisis when there is nothing left to renounce; she invokes sweet death, the most potent anodyne:

> The draught chilled, but a cordial part
> Lurked at the bottom of the cup;
> And for my patience will my Lord
> Give an exceeding great reward.

For the competition for human love she substitutes the competition for divine Love: "Yea, the reward is almost won, / A crown of glory and a palm." The poem closes with echoes of ballad deathbed instructions: having revised her metaphor she can "rest"; having arranged herself as an icon of renunciation she can instruct those who keep the vigil where to bury her and how to pray. The sleeping/ waking, numbness/pain cycle of her mortal existence will be replaced by the final awakening.

The first nun, wholly isolated, addresses two "accidental" objects, the shadow and the bird, and asks for a temporary anodyne to provide release from the routine of suffering. Her crisis is a parody of a Keatsian crisis, and she returns, as she might have foretold, to "pure" sorrow. The second nun, addressing a gathering of vigil keepers, asks for oblivion and absolution and gives instructions. The past she invokes is more recent, the future more imminent. Under this pressure the language of secular desire and striving is reassigned without modification to divine aims and objects. The third nun addresses the world, articulates the object of her desire, and pleads for grace—appropriately, at the end of her speech: "I yet can plead, and say, / Although my lips are dumb."

At the beginning of the poem, the language she assumes is that of romantic heroism, the language of Emily Brontë's speakers:

> My heart is as a freeborn bird
> Caged in my cruel breast,
> That flutters, flutters evermore,
> Nor sings nor is at rest,
> But beats against the prison bars.

The "cage" is the mortal cage; the exile longs for the home country of paradise in language that needs no qualifications. She longs not for the blushful Hippocrene or Joy's grape but for the grapes "of the True Vine" and waters from "the living Well." The inventory of her paradisal inheritance emboldens the speaker to address the world like an outfaced rival:

> Thou world from which I am come out,
> Keep all thy gems and gold;
> Keep thy delights and previous things,
> Thou that art waxing old.
> My heart shall beat with a new life
> When thine is dead and cold;
> When thou dost fear I shall be bold.

Nor does this speaker set much store by natural phenomena. She does not care to look upon the rose or the sun because the flowers are budding now in paradise for her, and because her destiny is the "untrodden courts" of the New Jerusalem where her crown will outshine the sun.

Having left one world, about to step into another, this speaker occupies only a vantage point from which she can recall her progress. Like the first nun, she gave up her beauty, bartering it for vigils, fasts, prayer, and cross. The terms of this transaction were difficult only at the beginning, when she still felt the call of the world, when she was literally called, that is named, in terms of her relationships:

> While the names still rang in mine ears
> Of daughter, sister, wife,
> The outside world looked so fair.

But these claims subsided; she prayed until she "grew to love what once / Had been so burdensome." Now even when her heart is numbed by "Hope deferred," she can pray silently, in the language of Revelation, for the fulfillment of desire: "The spirit and the Bride say, Come."[4] Now she is free of language, and free of the need to revise it.

Although the three nuns can be differentiated, hierarchical subordination is not as evident as in other "triad" poems. The nuns are truly sister-selves, representing an evolving point of view. The third nun provides the answer to the dialogue set up by the first two nuns, as is borne out by the meaning of the mottoes, "a most exquisite little song which the nuns sing in Italy," which William translates thus: "The heart sighs, and I know not wherefore. It may be sighing for love, but to me it says not so. Answer me, my heart, wherefore sighest thou? It answers: I want God—I sigh for Jesus" (*Works*, p. 460). The poem has progressed from a regressive wish for surcease from sorrow, though a resolution to drink the cup of sorrow and embark on divine transactions (thereby escaping the mortal cycle of sleeping/waking, numbness/pain) to a bolder turning away from earth's "goods" toward the paradisal territory. Along the way several language conventions have been revived only in order to show their inadequacy, their decay into traces, residue. Keatsian language of ecstatic longing, Byronic language of romantic exile, Gothic romance and ballad language of sexual transaction and sexual betrayal, all are replaced (in the third nun's speech) by biblical language. The allusions drop away to reveal the true text; all speech ultimately subsides into silent prayer. The absolute remainder, then, is wordless gesture, for mute inner acts are served best by a "dumb" show. All three nuns assume poses of extremity, presenting themselves as emblems of renunciation indistinguishable from desire frozen at a pitch.

But the poet does not lapse into silence, and the speaker goes on displacing the conventions and exemplifying the authentic language. From this didactic perspective, there is no question of originality. Just as the cycle of desire is endless—if desire cannot be sustained, neither can it subside—so the monologue must start up again, and also the implicit dialectic. The speaker can feel only desire or numbness: when feeling threatens to overwhelm her she can only stifle it. When numbness threatens to obliterate her she can only long to feel. She can speak of her desire only in a language that has been given her by other texts, and by denying that language: she must resist being overpowered by it, while still remaining "inside" it. She finds the narrow margin of language that she can call her own by appropriating a more ancient language that then overlaps perfectly with hers. When she turns to scriptural models she becomes the recorder of the Word of God, the instrument of a divine will and statement.

The speaker of "Endurance," written at about the same time as *Three Nuns* (1850), is another member of the unofficial sisterhood of renunciation. She renounces not the satisfaction of life, however, but the satisfaction of death, and the kind of action that would end the painful cycle of desire. Her renunciation takes the form of a criticism of the rhetoric of heroic renunciation. Implicitly rebuked, this speaker formulates a counterrebuke:

> Yes, I too could face death and never shrink.
>   But it is harder to bear hated life;
>   To strive with hands and knees weary of strife;
> To drag the heavy chain whose every link
> Galls to the bone; to stand upon the brink
>   Of the deep grave, nor drowse tho' it be rife
>   With sleep; to hold with steady hand the knife
> Nor strike home:—this is courage, as I think.
> Surely to suffer is more than to do.
>   To do is quickly done: to suffer is
>   Longer and fuller of heart-sicknesses.
>   Each day's experience testifies of this.
> Good deeds are many, but good lives are few:
>   Thousands taste the full cup; who drains the lees?
>
>   (*Works*, p. 297, ca. 1850)

This speaker is a prisoner—like Byron's, like Emily Brontë's—but heroic action did not get her in, nor will it get her out. Nor can she allow herself the luxury of rage, despair, or contempt for her captors. There is no enemy here, not even the enemy within. It is almost as though Rossetti has asked the Sartrean question, and come up with the Sartrean alternative to suicide. The metaphorical prison is life itself; stoic endurance is the only heroism. Unlike Hamlet, who can debate "Whether 'tis nobler in the mind to suffer / The slings and arrows of outrageous fortune / Or to take arms against a sea of troubles" (III.i), this speaker is confident that "to suffer is more than to do." She knows that "doing" is always ambiguous, for "To do is quickly done"; that is, action can be murderous, like Macbeth's: "If it were done, when 'tis done, then 'twere well / It were done quickly" (I.vi). Unlike Hamlet and Macbeth, bearers of the knife, whether against themselves or others, this speaker is not undone by conscience or thought, for in her world courage consists precisely of thinking, feeling, remembering, and refraining from action. And unlike Hamlet and Macbeth, who live by their imaginations, anticipating future consequences, this speaker lives by the testimony of "each day's experience," in which act and consequence are immediately present.

In the closing couplet, a moral apothegm that issues from "experience," the speaker asserts the elitism of the righteous, and invokes the authoritative text. Behind the final metaphor stands, as always, Christ's cup at Gethsemane, with all its implications.[5] Christ's cup is both the same as and different from the fortifying draught the hero drinks before his last encounter; it is both the same as and different from the fatal potion that drugs the hero to death. Christ's cup is the full cup of mortality: its significance lies in the human pathos of his request that it pass, and in the Christian heroism of his acceptance of the Father's will—that is, the consequences of mortality. Following Christ's example, then, the speaker of "Endurance" asks the parabolic question that contains its own answer. The resolution offers a system of values that can be defined by its opposition to the values of romantic heroism.

In "Three Stages" (*Works*, p. 288), a three-part poem written in the years 1848, 1849, and 1854, we see Rossetti dealing with the same

emotional and expressive crisis as in *Three Nuns* and "Endurance."
The speaker narrates a private history that has by now a familiar
pattern: the singular catastrophe is followed by stoic endurance that
tends toward deathlike insensibility, punctuated by resurgences of
the crisis, and ongoing acts of renunciation. By a repeated process of
reduction, the speaker finds what is irreducible. In the first part, "A
Pause of Thought," the speaker "looked for that which is not, nor
can be," and "watched and waited" persistently even "though the
object seemed to flee away / That I so longed for." This receding
object of desire is never designated in the poem, and yet it becomes a
"name" which still compels the speaker's desire:

> Sometimes I said: 'It is an empty name
> I long for; to a name why should I give
> The peace of all the days I have to live?
> Yet gave it all the same.'

This is the anatomy of pure desire, without object or end. The
speaker ends with a rebuke to this allegorized self:

> Alas thou foolish one! alike unfit
> For healthy joy and salutary pain:
> Thou knowest the chase useless, and again
> Turnest to follow it.

This "foolish" quester is a parody of the heroic quester, and obses-
sional desire begins to seem indistinguishable from single-minded
renunciation. While the speaker in part I of "Three Stages" describes
the attenuation of the quest, the speaker of part II, entitled "The End
of the First Part," narrates the catastrophic reversal that is the
outcome of the quest. She is as forlorn as the speaker at the end of
Keats' "Ode to the Nightingale," except that the distinction between
dream and waking is unambiguous, and the dream is unambigu-
ously false:

> Oh weary wakening from a life-true dream!
> Oh pleasant dream from which I wake in pain!
> I rested all my trust on things that seem,
> And all my trust is vain.

The speaker has awakened to an antiworld—call it the world of experience— where "laughter" becomes "sad tears for guilt"; where "freedom" changes to "control," and, disturbingly, "hidden hope" and "cherished secrets" are known as "sin." Her rude awakening entails drastic deconstruction and relocation. Like Tennyson's "Soul" in "The Palace of Art" she must find a new "home"; "I must pull down my palace that I built, / Dig up the pleasure-gardens of my soul." In the place of the palace, she will "uprear a shady hermitage," where her spirit shall "keep house alone"; the pleasure-gardens will be replaced by beds of "sweet-briar and incense-bearing thyme," a modest and salutary garden where she will sit listening for "the sound / Of the last lingering chime." Unlike Tennyson's "Soul," however, this speaker goes from isolation to deeper isolation, for the hermitage is not a cottage, and the palace, unlike Tennyson's, must be razed—and by the speaker's own hand. In this way the hermitage, like the cloister, becomes a stage for the passions.

For the speaker of part III (1854) has not found peace in the hermitage; like the speaker of part II she has had an awakening as yet another illusion has dropped away: "I thought to deal the death-stroke at a blow: / To give all, once for all, but never more." Her aim had been the same as the first nun's (*Three Nuns*), to find the numbness that would allow her to endure without hope: "Gone dead alike to pulses of quick pain / And pleasure's counterpoise." But this hope, that she could live without hope—"and so I thought / My life would lapse, a tedious monotone"—becomes a vain hope also. She cannot sustain the concentration, she tires and grows "slack" and sets to dreaming again. The "full pulse of life" starts up again, and it is as though she is wholly governed by the need to sustain desire, even to the extent of making the renunciation that reorients desire. Although she cannot enjoy gratification ("Alas I cannot build myself a nest, / I cannot crown my head / With royal purple blossoms for the feast") she cannot relinquish desire, only let it play itself out, shift, and reshift:

> These joys may drift, as time now drifts along;
> And cease, as once they ceased.

> I may pursue, and yet may not attain,
> Athirst and panting all the days I live;
> Or seem to hold, yet nerve myself to give
> What once I gave, again.

She may return to her original Tantalus state, or reactivate the cycle by dealing the death stroke again. The result is the same: the deadly numbness gives way to the pulsing life which surges toward its goal for a while; then when the steady distance between desire and its object can no longer be maintained, the death stroke brings about numbness again.

But although the pattern of feeling—desire, radical loss, renunciation, numbness, desire, renunciation, and so on—is clear, its expression remains problematic. In the poems of renunciation Rossetti repeatedly comes up against a difficulty in sustaining expression. How does one keep on making renunciations and revising one's position without also constantly revising one's language? Or, how does one articulate resolution and enact endurance without maintaining or reinstating the original forms? Rossetti characteristically does both. The final stanza of "Three Stages" announces dedication to a life of frustrated longing and renunciation in terms of romantic pursuit of an ideal. The speaker is the quester once more— "I may pursue, and yet may not attain, / Athirst and panting all the days I live," but this time embarked on a "pure" motiveless quest. She is also prepared for some kind of total recommitment: "Or seem to hold, yet nerve myself to give / What once I gave, again." "Endurance" claims that courage consists in holding the knife steady and not striking home; these lines suggest the same kind of steely restraint. "Giving" usually involves bestowing oneself or one's properties on someone, but here it is impossible to read "give / What once I gave" except as restatement of the opening lines of part III: "I hoped to give once for all," that is, to give up, renounce. Both direct and indirect object are unstated; the emphasis is on the gesture in and of itself. Just as the cycle of desire is inescapable, so is the language of romantic passion and heroism. Rossetti can, however, impose her will on this given language, forcing it into a position where desire and renunciation, giving and giving up are equivalent.

In the 1858 poem *From House to Home* (*Works*, p. 30) Rossetti is able to use the framework of allegorical narrative and romance dream-vision to express the familiar pattern of desire and renunciation without the constant struggle to revise and reinstate language conventions. The visionary mode allows her to say what she means without ironic crosscuttings and to move more naturally toward a didactic resolution. This speaker is the spiritual heir of the speaker of "Three Stages," who feels, renounces, and feels again, and a secular sister of the nuns of *Three Nuns,* who retreat to the cloister in order to obliterate, but also refine—by containing—the feeling life. Like all the subjects and speakers of the poems under discussion, she is dispossessed, shut out from her rightful inheritance.

This speaker, like the Ancient Mariner a chastened survivor and a narrator, tells her story to a "friend." She recounts two experiences, one like a "dream," the second like a "swoon." Although these are causally related, the speaker treats them as merely contiguous—first this, then this, before and after—stressing her passivity and the catastrophic nature of the fall. The first experience, denounced as "a tissue of hugged lies," was her life in a "pleasure-place" within her soul, containing castle of "white transparent glass" and an Edenic "pleasaunce," teeming with "curious" goblin life: frogs, lizards, toads, mushrooms. There she has an angelic companion who without reason or reproach turns into the angel of banishment. He leaves, like the cooling suitor who must be about his business, receding into the distance, calling for her to follow him "home." So this is not her home and must be destroyed, like the palace and pleasure gardens of "Three Stages," yet the speaker cannot follow her angelic spirit to his home. Having relinquished her epipsyche and the garden of self, this speaker, like the third nun, has only a vantage point for witnessing and enduring. Only questers and anchorites have visions. This speaker, an anchorite by default, a quester who has been nowhere, is granted a fortifying vision of a sister self, the suffering woman who drinks the bitter cup made sweet. This is followed by a vision of the paradisal territory where the tormented woman is transfigured and united with her companion. This dream transformation allows the speaker to endure in patience, as the radical discontinuity between past and present is replaced by the contiguity between present and future. The speaker at the end of the poem has evolved to the position of the third nun whose joy is muted but intense. Where the third nun finds her authentication finally in the language of Revelation, the speaker of *From House to Home* finds hers in the intonations of Psalms (xxiii.4):

> Although to-day He prunes my twigs with pain,
>   Yet doth His blood nourish and warm my root:
> To-morrow I shall put forth buds again
>   And clothe myself with fruit.
>
> Although to-day I walk in tedious ways,
>   To-day His staff is turned into a rod,
> Yet will I wait for Him the appointed days
>   And stay upon my God.   (*Works*, p. 25)

As a narrative of passion—the suffering as well as the desire—and as dream vision, "The Convent Threshold" (*Works*, p. 340, July 9, 1858) belongs with *From House to Home*. Thematically, of course, it belongs with *Three Nuns* and the other renunciation poems. Unlike these, however, it is relatively unrestrained in its treatment of erotic and aggressive feelings: its tone is far more florid, its imagery more sensuous. Here Rossetti explores the "operatic" and Gothic possibilities of the nun's situation. The nun, chaste and chastened, sings an aria of sexual passion, all the more powerful because it is controlled, all the more titillating because the sexuality is expressed as masochistic fantasy. This persona is far removed from the refined Anglican sister; she is more the seventeenth- or eighteenth-century young woman of the world who has been committed—or has committed herself—to the convent because she needs to be saved from her own turbulence and sensuality. She chooses the convent not because she has been exhausted by life but because she has exhausted it.

The poem is a dramatic monologue, or an epistle, as William points out, the nun an Héloïse addressing an Abélard (*Works*, p. 482). The beloved is more intimately related to the speaker than in any previous poem. He is kin in flesh and in spirit, he is lover, "brother," epipsyche, and, rather than a stern spirit who announces, judges, and departs, a companion in suffering. He inhabits her dream, and her consciousness determines the limits of his experience.

The opening is, as Packer says, "sensational":[6]

> There's blood between us, love, my love,
> There's father's blood, there's brother's blood;
> And blood's a bar I cannot pass.
> I choose the stairs that mount above,
> Stair after golden sky-ward stair,
> To city and to sea of glass.
> My lily feet are soiled with mud,
> With scarlet mud which tells a tale
> Of hope that was, of guilt that was,
> Of love that shall not yet avail;
> Alas, my heart, this selfsame stain is there:
> I seek the sea of glass and fire
> To wash the spot, to burn the snare;
> Lo, stairs are meant to lift us higher:
> Mount with me, mount the kindled stair.

The blood is blood spilled in an ancestral feud, presumably, but it is also the blood relation: "And blood's a bar I cannot pass." If an incestuous passion is implied, it is done so only inadvertently. But the poem does mean to suggest, I think, desire for a "brother" soul, a complementary aspect of the self,[7] and to demonstrate the impossibility of such a union by a prohibition that is ambiguously exogamous and endogamous. That is, he is outside the family and thus she can not mate with him, but neither can she mate with him if he is inside. The prohibition is reinforced by the "scarlet mud," which is a striking image of ritual defilement.

The rest of the monologue is a long exhortation urging the earthbound lover, who sinned with her "a pleasant sin," to repent, so that he can join her in paradise. Like Dante Gabriel's blessed damozel, she cannot disavow her earthly love: "How should I rest in Paradise / Or sit on steps of heaven alone?" Through the woman's traditional role as mediatrix, then, she becomes the dominant figure: she leads, he follows. In order to press home her point, she tells him her dream:

> I tell you what I dreamed last night.
> A spirit with transfigured face
> Fire-footed clomb an infinite space.
> . . . .

Worlds spun upon their rushing cars:
He mounted shrieking "Give me light!"
Still light was poured on him, more light;
Angels, Archangels he outstripped,
Exultant in exceeding might,
And trod the skirts of Cherubim.
Still "Give me light," he shrieked; and dipped
His thirsty face, and drank a sea,
Athirst with thirst it could not slake.

Overtly the beloved, this Faustian spirit stands for the speaker's own
aspirations. At one pole are the blood and mire that pull downward,
at the other, pure energy, cosmic power that expands through the
universe to stop short at the moral limit:

He left his throne to grovel down
And lick the dust of Seraph's feet:
. . . .
Yea all the progress he had made
Was but to learn that all is small
Save love, for love is all in all.

Having dared so much, the speaker falls back on her own torment;
the rest of the dream is what Packer calls "mortuary imagery."[8]

Cold dews had drenched my plenteous hair
Through clay; . . .
. . . .
My heart was dust that used to leap
To you; I answered half asleep:
"My pillow is damp, my sheets are red,
There's a leaden tester to my bed:
. . . .
You wrung your hands: while I, like lead,
Crushed downwards through the sodden earth.

This leaden woman is the stone-woman once more, burdened with
the dead weight of self, laboring at her dream-work. All night she
dreamt, woke, struggled in a Gethsemane passion:

I cannot write the words I said,
My words were slow, my tears were few;

> But through the dark my silence spoke
> Like thunder . . .

When she wakes she is like someone who has struggled with the demonic: "My face was pinched, my hair was grey, / And frozen blood was on the sill." In fact, her face is so transformed that the beloved would not recognize her; her true face "tarries veiled in Paradise." Having split herself in this way—the actual woman pinched and gray, the symbolic double with the veiled face ensconced in paradise—she simply relocates the relation with the beloved: "There we shall meet as once we met, / And love with old familiar love."

Given the nature of the old familiar love, rooted in blood and mire, the ending is singularly unconvincing. Yet the division between "real" and "ideal," between "now" and "then," does make the proposition tenable. Although this splitting of the self is a familiar strategy in Rossetti's poetry, this nun is not quite as passive as, say, the speakers of *From House to Home* and *Three Nuns*. She dreams strongly, even violently; she follows out a certain logic. And in her suffering she projects a phantasmagoria which she alone directs.

Rossetti uses the nun persona twice more: once at the end of the period 1849–65, in "An 'Immurata' Sister" (*Works*, p. 380, ca. 1865) and once later in her career, in "Soeur Louise de la Miséricorde 1674" (*Works*, p. 411, B. 1882). The four-stanza "An 'Immurata' Sister" attains the perfection of the didactic mode Rossetti had been developing all along. The poem as a whole looks like another operatic burst, on the order of "The Convent Threshold," but each stanza works as a separate text, a moral epistle. Beyond resignation, this nun is the fervid exemplar of Christian paradoxes and apothegms which she strings together to justify her self-immolation. Stanza one begins with the premise that "Life flows down to death, as rivers find / The inevitable sea." Stanza two takes off on another tack, at least on the surface:

> Men work and think, but women feel;
> And so (for I'm a woman, I)
> And so I should be glad to die,
> And cease from impotence of zeal.

The suppressed connection between this premise and its conclusion is that men's and women's roles are as inescapable as the flow toward death described in the first stanza; in drifting toward death a woman merely succumbs to the general drift. In this context, "But women feel" implies self-consuming feeling without any outlet in action; feeling's only issue is not-feeling, death. But Christian paradox, in the third stanza, allows the speaker to find justification for what has begun to look like despair: "Hearts that die, by death renew their youth." She is transported beyond the world where men work and think and women only feel to a world where dead and reborn hearts contemplate "unveiled" Truth. From this perspective the speaker can denounce the world's values including, presumably, the distinction between men's and women's roles: both world and speaker have been foolish seekers, whose time has run out. This world view is the basis for the final self-definition:

> Sparks fly upward toward their fount of fire,
>   Kindling, flashing, hovering:—
> Kindle, flash, my soul; mount higher and higher,
>   Thou whole burnt-offering.

This nun does not need the beloved; she sees Truth unveiled, she mounts by herself. Although her progress parallels that of the angelic spirit in "The Convent Threshold" she transgresses no bounds. She is totally self-contained, indeed self-consumed, and about to be absorbed by the divine fire.

By the time the nun makes her last appearance in "Soeur Louise de la Miséricorde," renunciation is perfectly stylized, if not perfunctory. This poem is a litany of the language of desire. A limited number of phrases and images are distributed over the three stanzas in a predictable design, each stanza ending with a didactic refrain: "Oh vanity of vanities, desire." The poem echoes the polarities of "The Convent Threshold": desire is a "disenkindled fire," memory a "bottomless gulf of mire," and desire turned her garden-lot to "barren mire." This nun does not mount in the spirit's fire for fire-drops of life's "dross" trickle from her heart. She is being burnt out, refined to what is really irreducible: the few words that count and that can be repeated endlessly—desire, fire, mire, vanity of vanities.

"Introspective" and "Memory": Original Symbolism

In the poems dealing with loss, with something that has happened, Rossetti frequently responds by taking apart the "old" structure of feeling and reconstituting it in a "new" structure. She does so thematically, as we saw in "Three Stages" and *From House to Home*, in the destruction of the pleasure palaces and the reorientation of desire; and formally in the simultaneous exemplification and disassembling of literary conventions, from which she proceeds usually not to a "new" construction but to a reassembling of fragments of scripture in a more democratic and public, yet at once private, language. In two lyric poems, "Introspective" (*Works*, p. 331, June 20, 1857) and "Memory" (*Works*, p. 334, November 8, 1857; February 27, 1865), Rossetti goes over the same territory yet again, but in a language that comes as close as she ever gets to a private and original symbolism. In their uncompromising confrontation with pain and loss, these poems mark the limits of the lyric exploration of the cycle of desire and renunciation.

"Introspective" deals with the same aftermath as the second and third parts of "Three Stages" and "Endurance":

> I wish it were over the terrible pain,
> Pang after pang again and again:
> First the shattering ruining blow,
> Then the probing steady and slow.

The speaker recalls the trauma as if to master it, and discovers that she is alive, though "blasted," and stuck in a present moment framed by a "short" past and a "long" future. This speaker derives strength from her silence. She did not utter her pain when the blows came, though she lets these words fall like blows: "Dumb I was when the ruin fell, / Dumb I remain and will never tell." This speaker takes her place with all the silently suffering heroines who hide their shame/ sin/suffering (all equivalent) and converse only with themselves: "O my soul, I talk with thee, / But I will not groan when I bite the dust." The speaker in "Endurance" had to nerve herself to *not* strike the blow, and the speaker of "Three Stages" needed to be prepared to deal the blow again. Putting these poems together, it is clear that the agent and the receiver are a single self, that it does not matter whether the blow is dealt or received or refrained from, that there is simply an inevitable sequence: the crisis of once for all, followed by endurance, followed by repetition of the crisis and the start of a new cycle.

The interconnections among these poems also underline Rossetti's power to revive dead forms. The blow, the "nerved" awaiting, the steady probing or the endless monotone, the resurgence of feeling, and, as we shall see in "Memory," the irreducible residue of self, make up a myth of suffering and female endurance. That endurance is not won at the cost of feeling but, rather, sustains and is sustained by feeling. In "Introspective" the familiarity of the image of the blasted tree and the proverbial echoes of "But I will not groan when I bite the dust" do not detract from the poem's power; the monosyllables, the regular beat, the strong rhymes, all contribute to the poem's ritual effect: it measures out and contains suffering.

In "Memory" written only five months after "Introspective," Rossetti seems to have found the perfect symbolic expression for the ritual of suffering. Here the temporal sequence is elaborate spatially. The crises and the renunciation take place in a private, enclosed space at the center of which sits something that shifts in character, but remains irreducible. This is *it*, the speaker seems to say, the final truth, the one thing I am left with. "It" is the inert entity in relation to which the speaker makes a series of ritual gestures. Out of her endurance of being done to, or not done to, she contrives an object, lodges it in an inner space, and acts in relation to it. "It" can be neither integrated nor shaken off: the "I" has to discover a way to deal with the "it" that both "once was" and "still is." The speaker in the first stanza of part I is a mother to it: "I nursed it in my bosom while it lived, / I hid it in my heart when it was dead." She shared it with no one: "In joy I sat alone; even so I grieved / Alone, and nothing said." So what she had she gave birth to and mothered parthenogenetically. A reading that equates "it" with a human love and a specific biographical circumstance does not really account for the details of the poem. If "it" began as a specific love it has been so transformed as to be unrecognizable. "It" has been detached from, and yet made part of, the "I" in such a way as to suggest a foreign object or a fetus in the womb. It underwent a strange reverse gestation, for first it lived outside the body and then was reincorporated in a burial. Although the death-dealing blow is technically an infanticide, it sounds strangely like a miscarriage or an abortion: as in "Symbols," a self that failed.

In the next stanza Rossetti marks out the private space where she confronts the "truth" and ritually incorporates it:

> I shut the door to face the naked truth,
> I stood alone—I faced the truth alone,
> Stripped bare of self-regard or forms of ruth
> Till first and last were shown.

This is the woman as she "is," for not only is the truth naked,[9] but the speaker is "stripped bare." The naked truth is the monster-child generated in the first stanza. As it is dead, she, like God, judges it as a soul, and finds it wanting. The judging, a silent ritual, is followed by an inarticulate inner gesture, the "choice," and its concrete correlative:

> None know the choice I made; I make it still.
> None know the choice I made and broke my heart,
> Breaking mine idol: I have braced my will
> Once, chosen for once my part.

Again, words fall like blows, as "None . . . None" echoes "Dumb . . . Dumb" of "Introspective." Uncovered truth mandates choice, and choice leads to action: a death blow to the heart and to the idol nesting within it. The monster-baby has become a totem, a rigid and breakable object of the speaker's own making. This idol is the "ideal" become the "illusion." Whether it is the best self or the false self, however, the speaker must give up the attempt at integration in the hopes of salvaging a durable self. "Once, chosen for once my part" recalls the speaker of "Endurance," who hoped to give "once for all, but never more," and who nerves herself to give "what once I gave, again." As we know from "Endurance," "once for all" is an heroic illusion, for the monotone of suffering extends indefinitely. Thus although the speaker acts decisively—"I broke it at a blow, I laid it cold"—we know that the process is not over. The crushed fragments seed the speaker's slow death: "My heart dies inch by inch; the time grows old, / Grows old in which I grieve."

Part two, written some eight years later, depicts a symbolist scene of arrested ritual gesture:

> I have a room where into no one enters
>   Save I myself alone:
> There sits a blessed memory on a throne,
>   There my life centres.

This room is the epitome of all Rossetti's rooms and enclosures: the cloister and the lowest room—a room of her own. Because the broken idol has been driven so deeply inward it can be salvaged as remains, as a "blessed memory." Although she no longer worships, she keeps vigil:

> If any should force entrance he might see there
>   One buried yet not dead,
> Before whose face I no more bow my head
>   Or bend my knee there;
>
> But often in my worn life's autumn weather
>   I watch there with clear eyes,
> And think how it will be in Paradise
>   When we're together.

In "Memory" Rossetti fuses private vision and public symbol. The struggle to discover a self has been expressed in the language of the religion of love, a tradition that stretches from Plato through courtly love to Shelleyean Romanticism. But the difference for Christina Rossetti is that the "other" that she longed for was a self that she already possessed and had to deny and treat as a false self. What she wanted and needed—to live more fully, to speak strongly—could only be expressed as longing for the unattainable beloved. And indeed what she lacked and mourned was an impossible ideal in the context of her culture. Because she cannot give up this ideal that she has given birth to and murdered—without giving up too much of herself—and because she cannot move on to new sources of self-love, she must become the stone-woman watching over the buried—but not dead—self, itself a stone, death-in-life incarnated.

The watcher and the buried idol are the final stage of the split between self and other. Although Rossetti will go on writing poems about desire, loss, and renunciation, the kind of confrontation represented in "Memory" is neither possible nor necessary. The disillusionment Rossetti experiences—the realization that to be yourself is dangerous, that in fact a part of the self must live always behind closed doors, never see light—calls for a death blow of the kind described in "Memory." Rossetti will translate one kind of discontinuity—between "seems" and "is," between the woman as she is seen and as she feels herself to be —into another: between "then" or "once"and "now," and between "now" and a future "then." In the meantime, in the now, she makes the ritual gesture of demarcation over and over again. In the 1860 "Mirage" (*Works*, p. 350) she extends the gesture of renunciation explicitly to poetic language:

> I hang my harp upon a tree,
> A weeping willow in a lake;
> I hang my silenced harp there, wrung and snapt
> For a dream's sake.

Although the act is less violent than in "Memory," it is no less radical, for it is as though the singer-weeper of "Song" has exchanged "alway" for "once for all." The speaker who has awakened from the "dream" enjoins silence and motionlessness to that part of her that has felt, and still feels, the blow; "Lie still, lie still, my breaking heart; / My silent heart, lie still and break." But just as the idol-self will not die, and the choice has to be made "still," so the poet does not remain silent. She will return to the same loss and employ the same strategies over and over again. Increasingly, however, she will adopt the persona of the exemplar, the model who has learned and who teaches the hard lesson. Having found her authentication in didacticism, she will claim as hers the officially sacred language, the only mode of expression adequate to her unutterable predicament.

The Final State: "Dead before Death" and the Return of the Dead

The various nuns and the speakers of *From House to Home*, "Endurance," "Introspective," and "Memory," all maintaining inner mobility while playing "dumb," demonstrate female stoicism. Because they feel but cannot act, they must suffer, all the while longing for the numbness—and completion—of death:

> I wish I were dead, my foe,
> My friend, I wish I were dead,
> With a stone at my tired feet
> And a stone at my tired head.
>
> ("To-day and To-morrow," *Works*, p. 339, June 29, 1858)

But the immobilized woman who has achieved that numbness while still alive is, as we have seen in chapter 3, a horrifying figure. "Dead before Death" represents the woman of "Memory" as seen from the outside:

> Ah changed and cold, how changed and very cold,
> With stiffened smiling lips and cold calm eyes!
> Changed, yet the same; much knowing, little wise,—
> *This* was the promise of the days of old!   (*Works*, p. 313)

Changed yet the same, this woman is an emblem both of unfulfillment and finality, the last stage of a monstrous evolution. She is not only dead but damned: "So lost till death shut-to the opened door, / . . . / So cold and lost for ever evermore." She does not need to rebuke the restive heart, stifle the cry, or brace herself to endure repeated shocks; everything has happened "once for all." But it is perhaps preferable to remain forever deadlocked in this way, because to become any one thing, to take up any position, is to "die" in the sense of forfeiting other possibilities. Rossetti, for cultural and psychological reasons finding it impossible to "move," has a particular horror of losing herself, and a vivid sense of what it means to retain a continuing self. As we have seen in "Symbols," the natural development of the rosebud, the birds' eggs, and the bough is aborted, as if any fruition is premature. For Rossetti maturity seems always premature—producing a stillborn self. Thus the woman dead before death is a step removed from the woman of "Memory" who tends her broken idol. She is more nearly the monstrous birth, the idol itself.

If she refuses to be born, she also refuses to die. She is a spectacle of disenchantment, yet also a captive of her previous enchantment;

she cannot change, and so she must preserve the remaining shell. She is also culpable in her "self-respect." Like the speaker of "Symbols" she is both guilty and victimized. What she is guilty of is self-murder, and her cold stare is the result of an awful vision: she has become what she has witnessed, and she witnesses what she has become. "Dead before Death" thus offers a crucial symbolic conception of the self on the order of "Memory." Around it can be grouped a number of poems belonging to the 1850–66 period in which Rossetti once more exploits conventional modes to embody her private vision. In lyrics lamenting dead love and in "ghost" ballads Rossetti expresses her longing for, and fear of, the return of the dead self. In a poem written only sixteen days after "Dead before Death" Rossetti invokes her night visitor:

> Come to me in the silence of the night;
>   Come in the speaking silence of a dream;
> . . . .
> Yet come to me in dreams, that I may live
>   My very life again though cold in death.
>
> (*Works*, "Echo," p. 314, 1854)

To live authentically, it seems, the self must integrate the lost "love," or lost self, but only in the symbiosis of dreamer and dream: in order to sustain her "very life" the dreamer must remain in a deathlike sleep.

In "Dream-Love" (*Works*, p. 312, May 19, 1854), the dreamer is "Young Love" itself, and the state is even more deathlike: "Young Love lies drowsing / Away to poppied death." Although this speaker withdraws in the hopes that there will be a seasonal rebirth, dream-love—dead-love—revives rather differently in a poem written almost twenty years later:

> Love, that is dead and buried, yesterday
>   Out of his grave rose up before my face;
>   No recognition in his look, no trace
> Of memory in his eyes dust-rimmed and grey.
>
> (*Works*, "Love Lies Bleeding," p. 388, ca. 1872)

This return parallels the persisting life of the memory idol, buried but not dead, and also suggests the living death of the woman dead before death. A part of the self is entombed but alive; it has no real connection with the self that sees and knows, and returns as the demonic double signifying death.

Like the resuscitation of love's body, the return of the ghost is a metaphor for the return of the dead self, forcing the speaker to confront the murder once more. Again, we see, "once for all" is an illusion. The speaker who is visited by the ghost endures a horrifying reproach on the order of the voices of the eggs and branch that haunt their pathetic murderer in "Symbols." Whether the visitation is sought or unsought, human and ghost are drawn together for the moment of terrified recognition and lack of recognition.[10] Thus, in a "A Chilly Night" (*Works*, p. 321, February 11, 1856) the ghost is the most pitiful and fearful apparition that a woman could imagine. The dead mother, sought out by the lonely and friendless daughter, is as blank as the revived Love in "Love Lies Bleeding":

> My mother raised her eyes,
> They were blank and could not see;
> Yet they held me with their stare
> While they seemed to look at me.

The chief horror seems to be the failure to fit two kinds of incompleteness together: the daughter sees but cannot hear her mother; the mother cannot see, and speaks but cannot be heard.

Yet even if the living and the dead can communicate, they are at cross-purposes. In "The Poor Ghost" (*Works*, p. 359, July 25, 1863) the sleeper is visited by his pale, golden–haired "friend" who reproaches him for his failure to recognize her: "Am I so changed in a day and a night / That mine own only love shrinks from me with fright?" The lover affirms his fidelity: he loved her for life, but now that death has set the term, she must stay in her bed, he in his. As the ghost leaves, she reproaches him for his failure to observe the boundary by refusing to leave off mourning. The importance of the final severance between the living and the dead is borne out in "The Ghost's Petition" (*Works*, p. 364, April 7, 1864) in which the returning husband reassures his wife about the "rest" of the dead and urges her to go on with life.

For looking upon the dead is, after all, a witnessing of one kind of primal scene. The one who has seen has penetrated a mystery and seen "Truth" unveiled. In an early poem Rossetti, released and focused by the exigencies of form, writes starkly:

> She turned round to me with her steadfast eyes.
> "I tell you I have looked upon the dead;
> Have kissed the brow and the cold lips," she said;
> "Have called upon the sleeper to arise."[11]
>
> (*Works*, "The Last Answer" p. 113, December 2, 1847)

The speaker, full of doubt and fear, kneels and prays, while the woman who has looked remains standing, a statue-woman, and an early version of the woman dead before death, or of the custodian of the memory idol. As we have seen in chapter 3, one kind of visionary arising may be the woman clothed in the sun: this is the vindication of the repining woman and the release of the statue-woman. But as was also suggested in chapter 3, there are other, more petrifying confrontations between the gazer and the seen. If she is to go on at all, it seems that the poet must move away from these confrontations with "idols," with dead selves. In the poems discussed above, the dead body struggling up to life or the returning wraith represents the last traces, the final lingering of those dead selves. By relinquishing the confrontation Rossetti learns how to lay to rest as well as conjure. She finds the mode that is most characteristically hers, and that comes closest to solving her expressive crisis: the valediction allows her to hold and let go, to weep and to sing.

Monna Innominata

It is in this central sonnet sequence that Rossetti, once again addressing herself to the crucial theme of renunciation, works through to the valedictory mode. *Monna Innominata*, (*Works*, p. 58) was written, Rossetti tells us in a brief preface, in order to give voice to unnamed but real women—as opposed to the idealized names, Laura and Beatrice—the lady troubadors who might have shared their lovers' poetic talent. In a self-conscious nod to her precursor, Rossetti hypothesizes that Elizabeth Barrett Browning, had her love story been unhappy rather than happy, might have created a "'donna innominata' drawn not from fancy but from feeling." The opposition between fancy and feeling is peculiarly ambiguous in reference. Clearly Laura and Beatrice are creatures of fancy, but is Elizabeth Barrett Browning's love story in the *Sonnets from the Portuguese* also in some way fanciful? With this careful but equivocating introduction Rossetti acknowledges that she is challenging both a complex masculine tradition and a contemporary poetic "rival" because she wants to correct their partial vision with the underlying truth. Male poets idealize the beloved out of existence, without any concern for the actual woman's feelings, Rossetti implies, while Barrett Browning draws upon an anomalous situation, or at least one that is not poetically fruitful. Like the male poet, the female poet draws inspiration from loss and absence; her innovation is that she tells the woman's side, the "tender part," the "hidden world below" that Landon talked about, the discoveries that Rossetti's Sappho would have made "had her leap not killed but cured her." Again the woman's story mimics the man's story—life is meaningless without the beloved but only the woman knows the true meaning of renunciation: the total abdication of self, the inexhaustibility of both desire and the capacity for suffering, and the adamantine resolve to break connections with this vain world altogether. And, significantly, only she knows what it is to live for another.

Rossetti's unnamed lady says and sees—sets her sights on, watches and waits for—only what Rossetti can, of course. Passionate without eroticism, she is obsessed with the original loss and with apocalyptic endings as the subjects of *From House to Home* and "The Convent Threshold," the rejected ballad heroines, and the speaker of the devotional lyrics. Unrequited love is a particular instance of the human condition, one of its most powerful symbols, but for Rossetti it is only one stage in a female progress in which this world is translated into the next, conceptually and verbally: love into Love, breath into spirit, dream into reality. In the *Monna Innominata* series Rossetti is concerned not so much to render a hitherto untold love story as to demonstrate that the same old story is transcended by its incorporation into the "new" story of Christian scripture.

The first sonnet begins with an imperative, "Come back to me, who wait and watch for you," which the speaker addresses to her unnamed and absent lover. So far we have the repining woman, the exhausted and unflagging Mariana, who longs for an end to her solitude and her reverie. But the next line, "Or come not yet, for it is over then," executes an abrupt reversal which introduces a metaphysical conceit, a turn that allows the speaker to value recurrence more than occurrence and renunciatory yearning more than consummation. Since she is somehow critically deprived, "in want" as well as wanting, because some change has already happened, as it has always happened in the world of Rossetti's poems, this speaker seeks to fill her emptiness with inexhaustible desire. And the only way she can keep to this pitch is to play with recurrence. Although the beloved is her "world," his coming brings the pain of parting, and so she can draw little comfort from his longed-for presence. What she can do, however, is maintain recurrent, alternating feeling states: "My hope hangs waning, waxing, like a moon / Between the heavenly days on which we meet." It is the alternation of feeling, always at a peak of intensity, that sustains her, just as it is his perpetual coming, not his arrival, that is the source of her pleasure. The closing couplet seals off the perpetual cycle with a reference to the prelapsarian state in which there was no need for the speaker to avert change and occurrence by alternation and recurrence: "Ah, me, but where are now the songs I sang / When life was sweet because you called them sweet?" This begins to sound like an aesthetic question, an attempt to discover the origins of the aesthetic of renunciation.

But once having raised the issue of a point of origin, the speaker is impelled to impose a sequential time frame on what appears to be a perpetual present. While in the first sonnet the beloved comes and goes repeatedly, without a clear beginning or a future destiny, the speaker in the second sonnet struggles to remember the precise moment of their meeting, which slipped by "unrecorded": the issue here is that the reality of the experience resides in its being recorded, transformed into poetry. If she could recover the originary point in that time scheme in which there is a beginning, a middle, and an end, she could perhaps escape this ceaseless alternation, this constant beginning and ending. But if sequential time brings only loss, then it is better to sustain a never-ending present that waxes and wanes— until the ultimate end. By sustaining this recurrence, the lady troubador sustains her writing, her lament, and by writing she sustains the recurrence—until the need for this kind of writing, at least, is no more.

The third sonnet proposes another kind of perpetual alternation: "I dream of you, to wake." What she wakes to is his absence and her deprivation; what she finds in dreams is his perpetual and sufficient presence. Since their union is possible only in dreams, the speaker makes the hyperbolic claim that "If thus to sleep is sweeter than to wake, / To die were surely sweeter than to live." What is manifested here is once again a resistance to change, to beginnings and endings, and a search instead for a perpetuity that is out of this world, far beyond mutability. If in sonnets one and two the speaker postulates an eternal present in which her lover is always leaving her and always coming to her, and in sonnet two declares the impossibility of recovering the originary moment that would unfold the end, in sonnet three she invokes another timeless world in which her lover is always present to her, in dream or in death.

As well as sequence in time, Rossetti is concerned to deny differentiation altogether. What she asserts instead, as well as endless recurrence, is a process in which separate identities are continually merged. While the quality of the lovers' feeling at first appears to differ—she loved first and more steadfastly, but he once "seemed to wax more strong"—such differences are cancelled by love, which makes each take on the qualities of the other. Love makes the two one, a denial of difference that Rossetti will take up again in the *Later Life* sonnet sequence.

And yet, in the following sonnet, Rossetti reinstates difference, indeed hierarchical difference, which culminates in the infamous assertion that "woman is the helpmeet made for man." The only alternatives, then, seem to be fusion in which individual identity and, by implication, female identity are canceled, or hierarchical subordination in which female identity can be defined only in relation to male identity. For her lover—her "heart's heart" and "more than myself myself"—she suggests a pattern of perfect behavior modeled on obedience to God. For herself, she again devises an escape from time and mutability, her task being "To love you without stint and all I can, / To-day, to-morrow, world without end." Again Rossetti transcends the pain of loss and differentiation by drawing upon her inexhaustibility, her capacity to love without limit. It is this limitlessness, then, that defines and sustains the meekly subordinate helpmeet. Because her limitless love is modeled on God's infinite love, it empowers the helpmeet who, instead of being swallowed up herself, swallows up—and outlasts—the beloved.

But in the following sonnet (six), ostensibly in answer to her lover's rebuke for making an idol of her love, the donna innominata affirms the context of all her loving, the framework that not only endorses her selflessness but also effaces the lover as a separate ego and cancels their mortal bond. She loves God "the most," "Would not lose Him, but you, must one be lost." Where hierarchy and difference were, Rossetti again asserts identity, sameness: "Yea, as I apprehend it, love is such / I cannot love Him if I love not you."

By this point the speaker seems to have arrived at the point of being able to tolerate living without a memory idol, without an unrealized love or an unrealized self that needs to be both retained and transcended. Having risked such radical assertions in sonnet six—I love you but I love God more; my love for you and my love for God are interdependent—Rossetti envisions a declaration of mutual feeling and the establishment of a daring equality in love: "so shall we stand / As happy equals in the flowering land / Of love, that knows not a dividing sea." But after a series of bravado assertions of love's power in the midst of beleaguerment, the speaker declares her weakness: "My heart's a coward though my words are brave." She feels their love waning as the recurrences, the meetings and partings, are succeeded by movement toward an inevitable end. In the last line of sonnet seven Rossetti turns to her usual consolation, scripture, which defines love absolutely: "And death be strong, yet love is as strong as death." Not that she hopes for a renewal of their love, but that she knows the full extent of endurance: her love will outlast even the death of love.

Having invoked scripture, in sonnet eight Rossetti turns to a biblical heroine, not a slave of love or a rejected maiden but a heroic queen who saves her people: Queen Esther. A variation of the fatal woman, she "spread abroad her beauty for a snare, / Harmless as doves and subtle as a snake." Like Fanny Cornforth, perhaps, "she trapped him with one mesh of silken hair"; but also like Christina Rossetti, "she vanquished him by wisdom of her wit." What the speaker identifies with is not the fatal beauty but the heroism of great risk and the altruism of a woman who would save a nation; so would *she* pray to Love for her love's sake. Yet the heroic identification with Esther fails, and in sonnet nine, the speaker represents herself as overcome by spiritual dread, suffering from loss of faith and hope, but enabled by love and grace to venture herself still in a metaphor of Love's transactions: "Ready to spend and be spent for your sake." By sonnet ten the tone is one of great strain and attenuation, as if the speaker had run out of analogies and transforming paradoxes. How many ways, after all, can this speaker restate her selflessness and the wholly internal—and so obsessional—nature of her love affair? The lover, whose presence was evanescent from the start, ceases to have any presence whatsoever, and the poem's progress stiffens into an allegorical pageant where "Time flies, hope flags, life plies a wearied wing; / Death following hard on life gains ground apace;—" and all of time is telescoped into "a little while," until "life reborn annuls / Loss and decay and death, and all is love." From this point on, the poem's concerns become increasingly linguistic, or rhetorical.

Thus in sonnet twelve the speaker projects a rival only to rise above the rivalry in an extravagant rhetorical gesture by giving the beloved what amounts to a dying wife's blessing. She gives him leave to love another—nobler, prettier, and wittier—should there be such a one. For herself she projects a ghostly symbiosis. Since her heart is now his, she shares all his experiences: "Your honourable freedom makes me free, / And you companioned I am not alone." She sets aside both occurrence—the radical loss—and recurrence: the persistence, in stasis, of the lost love, the lost self, the memory idol. It seems unlikely that this speaker would need to become the cloistered nun, forever caught in an expressive crisis. Rather, the donna innominata's untiring pursuit of ultimate paradoxes, radical undoings of meanings, has empowered her, so that she is finally delivered pure and whole, like the death-white Cleopatra of "A Soul," as the woman in the last stage before her apocalyptic transformation.

Now, at last, she is able to let go, both of the beloved and her obsessive concerns, and to move into a valedictory mode that retrieves the possibilities of language. Having commended the beloved again to God, in sonnet fourteen she makes her declaration of abdication. As her own elegist, she expresses herself in the language of flowers—Ophelia-like, though neither mad nor suicidal: "I will not bind fresh roses in my hair, / . . . / I will not seek for blossoms anywhere, / Except such common flowers as blow with corn." Having sung her lament, the lady troubador, like the exile from the country of love and youth in "Mirage," hangs up her harp. "Youth gone and beauty," she chooses "Silence of love that cannot sing again." Although Rossetti herself will continue to oscillate between the "common flowers" of devotional poetry and the faded roses of love laments, in *Monna Innominata* she does bid farewell to lost possibility with something like serenity and grace.

Valediction: From "Song" to "Sleeping at Last"

But she had said it all years before in two of her most powerful early poems, long before youth and beauty could have gone. In "Song" (*Works*, p. 290, 1848) and "Remember" (*Works*, p. 294, 1849), the young poet has already grasped the possibilities of the valediction for holding opposites in balance, for keeping and letting go. Together, the poems show what death and memory have to do with imagining a self. Both poems present an "I" speaking to a "you" and issuing commands. "Song" begins with the famous injunction: "When I am dead, my dearest, / Sing no sad songs for me." The speaker not only commands, however; she gracefully and playfully gives her auditor permission to be of two minds: "And if thou wilt, remember, / And if thou wilt, forget." If opposites cannot be reconciled, if self-division cannot be healed, then at least one can imagine the perfect equipoise. In the second stanza the "I" in effect dismisses the "you," as the speaker withdraws to the balance of her own mind. Like Wordsworth's Lucy, she does not see but knows. Unlike Wordsworth's Lucy, she possesses her own voice and makes her own choices:

> I shall not see the shadows,
>   I shall not feel the rain;
> I shall not hear the nightingale
>   Sing on as if in pain:
> And dreaming through the twilight
>   That doth not rise nor set,
> Haply I may remember,
>   And haply may forget.

Everything is achieved, and yet no possibilities are closed. The same perfect balance is realized in the sonnet "Remember," which begins with the command:

> Remember me when I am gone away,
>   Gone far away into the silent land;
>   When you can no more hold me by the hand,
> Nor I half turn to go yet turning stay.

The turn to go and the turn to stay are paralleled by the sonnet structure: the octave turns toward memory, the sestet toward forgetfulness. Again the speaker conveys permission, even forgiveness:

> Yet if you should forget me for a while
>   And afterwards remember, do not grieve:
>   For if the darkness and corruption leave
> A vestige of the thoughts that once I had,
> Better by far you should forget and smile
> Than that you should remember and be sad.

Even at the beginning of her career, then, Rossetti commemorates the buried, but not dead, self. In these poems, however, like the threshold poems of chapter 4 in which opposites are preserved unreconciled, the self does not harden like a stone, but lingers as a vestige, a memory trace that freely comes and goes.

But in the mid-life poems of renunciation, in "Memory," for instance, the speaker continually encounters a core of paralysis that can only be converted into an inward pose of stoic endurance. The confrontations with dead or buried selves may be immobilizing, but they give rise to powerful poems, as firmly incised as stone markers. Yet, over the course of her career, Rossetti was able to activate a more mobile persona. If the dominant figure in her poetry is something like Florence Nightingale's stone-angel, her sisterhood of self also includes the Englishwomen who are "deep at their deepest, strong and free," the rising woman clothed in the sun, the walker in white in the country of paradise. And in opposition to the petrifying confrontations between gazer and seen in the secular poems, there are the reciprocities of the religious poems, in which the vigil keeper discovers the changeful reality of Christ's suffering face and the expressiveness of His look of compassion. For Rossetti, an alternative, then, to the renunciatory mode—and the poetry of endurance—is the valedictory mode, as in the *Monna Innominata* series, as in "Song" and "Remember." In what is taken to be her last poem, "Sleeping At Last," she returns to the scene of "Dream-Land" and to the Wordsworthian figure of the woman dead in nature. Here, however, there is no hint of an apocalyptic rising, but neither is there a sense of the deadly spectacle, the woman trapped in her body. Finally beyond the cycle of natural womanhood, "out of sight of friend and lover," she gives her own valediction:

> Fast asleep. Singing birds in their leafy cover
> Cannot wake her, nor shake her the gusty blast.
> Under the purple thyme and the purple clover
> Sleeping at last.   (*Works*, p. 417, 1893)

Conclusion

In chapter 1 of *A Room of One's Own*, Virginia Woolf, expressing her sense of the dissonance that obtrudes on a comfortable "Oxbridge" luncheon party, suddenly recalls the "humming noise" that accompanied luncheon parties before the war. Put to words, that faint music becomes the verse of Tennyson and Christina Rossetti, in particular lines from *Maud* and "A Birthday" that express Romantic passion, or, as Woolf sees it, Romantic illusion. That has all disappeared, Woolf claims, changed by the war, which has stripped away a whole range of illusions that have kept us from seeing—now it is impossible not to see—the disparity between the conditions that foster men's intellectual life and the conditions that foster women's.[1]

Woolf's use of Rossetti in this context, as an example of a music that has been lost—and is perhaps well lost—reminds us that Rossetti is in no way a premodernist but, rather, a poet in a tradition which, by the end of the century, is literally exhausted. This is not to say that the poetry of loss, renunciation, and endurance that is based on an "illusion" concerning women's fictive and cultural roles, and in which women and men cooperate, disappears. Its persistence can be seen in the poetry of female and male poets who are both contemporaneous with and follow Rossetti: Philip Marston, for instance, displays an exaggerated female sensibility, as evidenced in his "Not Thou But I," in which the lover asserts such identity with the beloved that "It must have been for one of us, my own, / To drink this cup and eat this bitter bread. / Had not my tears upon Thy face been shed, / Thy tears had dropped on mine."[2] His is not only the "bitter bread" but, as in numerous poems by Rossetti, the dregs of the bitter cup, whose only alleviating sweetness is the thought that "Thou hadst the peace and I the undying pain."[3] In a similar vein, the heritage of L. E. L. is obvious in these lines from Mary M. Singleton ("Violet Fane," 1843–1905) in which she asks how a poet may "sing" and yet know that "Blood and roses alike bloom red— / Pleasure in pain, and pain in pleasure," and claims of the female singer that "all her songs are sad—of withered leaves / And blighted hopes, and echoes of the past, / And early death; and yet she cannot die, / But lives and sings, as he, too, lives and climbs."[4] Again, if we entertain the proposition that the conscious "I," the lyric voice and the narrative persona of much of Victorian literature is female, whether authored by a woman or a man, then the lack of a clear demarcation between Rossetti's and Singleton's voices, and, say, Marston's, is not surprising. It is not that Rossetti, Singleton, and Marston belong to a larger, nongendered tradition, but that literature may be always dialectically gendered, and at this point in cultural history, "female-ness" is critically positioned. Poets like Rossetti and Marston, and Tennyson before them, are haunted by displays of female renuncia-tion and passivity, by the powers of powerlessness—except to en-dure—and by the feminization of desire. I would still argue, how-ever, that the gender of the author matters: that is, that female experience makes a significant difference in how poetic language is generated. Marston is able to write those lines not only because he has read certain other poems but also because he had been able to match something within his interior self with something that he has intimations of in female experience, as rendered by female language. Those images then resonate for him in a particular way, as a man writing a particular kind of poem.

Nevertheless, if this mode—the cup of renunciation, the cult of suffering—can be seen to extend and persist among nineteenth-century poets, it is still a literary mode that both signifies exhaustion and, as a literary mode, gets played out. In Rossetti's own movement from the personal secular lyrics to the relative impersonality of the religious poems, she acknowledges that literary exhaustion: she goes on writing in a mode that is inexhaustible because it is extraliterary, and because its mainspring is not creative originality. All religious poetry supposes the proximateness of language, and is constituted by a rewriting of an "original" text. Its test is sincerity, but not the Romantic sincerity which would establish authenticity by a graph of feeling uniquely experienced. Rather, by going through the motions, by repeating the words only, and by willing the meaning or by wagering that meaning will come, the speaker makes the poem or the prayer mean. It may be said, of course, that this kind of lip service is precisely what Romantic poetry is in revolt against, establishing instead the rites of feeling as a new religion. But the Romantic poets are always in the process of discovering, as well, the limits of language, if not before the ultimate realities, then in the face of the chaotic multiplicities of experience. The transition from the subjective assurance of the Romantic poets, their confidence in the power of language to constitute a subject which shapes the world and achieves transcendence, to the dissolution of the subject and the self-referentiality of language that marks the direction of post-Romantic literary practice and theory, is too complex and ambiguous a process to trace here. In fact, recent critical theory, which sees all literary language as depersonalized and decentering, would put this kind of literary historicizing into question entirely. But if we are to posit, however tentatively, that there is some kind of change between Tennyson and Swinburne, it is surely in the direction of what Jerome McGann has described as Swinburne's "impersonalism," his aim to divest his poetry of personal qualities in a protest not only against conventional ethics but also against Romantic sincerity.[5]

No poet would at first seem more different from Rossetti, in both ideology and forms, and yet each admired the other, Swinburne to the extent of writing dedicatory verses to her. Viewed another way, the mutual admiration is less surprising. It is not only Rossetti's Pre-Raphaelite effects, her concentration on the liminal moment and trancelike states, as well as the cultivation of suffering that Swinburne must have been drawn to, but also her echoing structures and the paradoxes and contradictions that disturb the normal order of things. Although it cannot be my purpose here to examine how Swinburne's aesthetic is a response to a complex cultural breakdown, it is my task as a feminist critic to explore the ways in which Rossetti's aesthetic is a response to her cultural situation as a woman poet. Just as Swinburne translates and rewrites traditional texts in order to release his mythic energies, so Rossetti translates traditional texts in order to shape her own female myth. In retreat from her problematic selfhood as a woman and poet, she takes refuge, for instance, in the impersonality of art in the service of religion. And within the religious tradition she is able to find a context for reframing certain existential predicaments—how to "see" and be "seen," how to give all and receive enough, how to tolerate the pain of isolation and separation—and for breaking out of the cycle of natural womanhood which links female change to organic decline.

If at the heart of the Romantic vision there is silence and absence, then one way to be a poet is Swinburne's: to generate a language full of contradictions and shifting transformations that, as McGann points out, almost, but not quite, deconstruct the ineffable. Another way is Rossetti's, which involves a paring down and stripping away of language that reinforces limits, and so deliberately demarcates the ineffable—that which not only never can be said but never has been said. As McGann has so eloquently put it, Swinburne's derangements of language lead not to "a view of a better world but a better view of the only world there is."[6] Rossetti's revisionary language, on the other hand, suggests that there has to be a better world than this one, both beyond this one and perhaps hidden within it, because so much of this world's experience, as shaped by language, is repressive and falsifying.

It would seem that from this perspective Swinburne is epistemologically superior to Rossetti, a modernist who sees things as they "really" are. McGann comments interestingly on Swinburne's "sapphic position," which he defines as a conviction that "no gain, however great, will compensate loss," and that "life is a process of perpetual loss."[7] While Swinburne responds to this loss by embracing the process, in a sense mastering it, Rossetti, as a woman at her particular cultural moment, cannot afford to give herself up to process and must with great difficulty maintain her "sapphic position" as a tight binary structure: if nothing, then all, if perpetual loss, then endless gain. Both are alike, perhaps, in denying the possibility of mediation, although Rossetti comes closest to mediation—or, perhaps, to Swinburne's abandonment to process—in what I have described as her valedictory mode.

Without denying the obvious ideological base—Christian, Romantic—for Rossetti's attitude toward language, I want to suggest that her sense that language stands for an undisclosed reality, and that she must somehow reinscribe the given—that is, patriarchal—language, has also a base in concerns of gender. Rossetti cannot choose the kind of impersonalization that is modernist or premodernist because she operates within a language system that has already *de*personalized women, precisely by inscribing them as signs, and devaluing them as originators of meaning. On one level, then, the silence at the center of her language is the divine All; on another, the silence is within the language, unbordered, present at every interstice, and it may well be what Irigaray has called the "undisclosed feminine," or what Alice Meynell, Rossetti's contemporary, termed the "unpublished blood."[8]

I want to turn now to a brief consideration of the career and works of Alice Meynell, the poet who is not only Rossetti's contemporary but her heir, in order to see what shape the aesthetic of renunciation and the poetry of endurance might take for other women poets. The inescapable conclusion is, as I have pointed out, that the aesthetic and the practice do not outlast the century by much, that they are not only swept up in the wave of modernism but also inherently constituted to conclude in silence: the lute and the harp permanently hung up, the withered leaves crumbled to dust, the song and the lament vanished on the air.

As Meynell's most recent critic, Beverly Ann Schlack, has neatly summarized it, both Meynell's life and career were demanding and outgoing: "Born in London in 1847, she was a converted Roman Catholic and a Socialist, a feminist, essayist, journalist, poet, translator, literary critic, and mother of eight children. She was active in humanitarian causes (the prevention of cruelty to animals); involved in social issues both general (the war and pacifism) and particular (the amelioration of conditions in the London slums); president and vice-president of suffrage societies, writer for suffrage papers and marcher in the processions."[9] Moreover, she was a literary figure: she played an important role not only in the art but also in the lives of Coventry Patmore, George Merideth, and Francis Thomas, finding it easy, apparently, to play muse, mother, angel of the house, and *femme fatale* to their woman worship. No woman would seem, on the surface, to be more unlike Rossetti, except for the interest in the prevention of cruelty to animals. Even more striking, Alice Meynell spent the happiest years of her childhood in Italy, the mother country from which Rossetti was exiled. Both poets were aware of each other, and Meynell wrote a tribute to Rossetti upon her death, but the relation between them was certainly cautious: they never met, and the difference in religion must have been a formidable barrier. Still, the similarity of their aesthetic concerns and their poetic practices is strong. Witness this early poem of Meynell's, "Renouncement":

> I must not think of thee; and, tired yet strong,
>   I shun the thought that lurks in all delight—
>   The thought of thee—and in the blue Heaven's height,
> And in the sweetest passage of a song.
> Oh, just beyond the fairest thoughts that throng
>   This breast, the thought of thee waits hidden yet bright;
>   But it must never, never come in sight;
> I must stop short of thee the whole day long.
> But when sleep comes to close each difficult day,
>   When night gives pause to the long watch I keep,
>   And all my bonds I needs must loose apart,
> Must doff my will as raiment laid away—
>   With the first dream that comes with the first sleep
>   I run, I run, I am gathered to thy heart.[10]

Here is the loss, the desire, the renunciation, the vigilant endurance, the return in dream—and above all—the hidden interiority, the secrecy which Rossetti discloses in poems like "Memory," "Endurance," and "Introspective." Like Rossetti, too, Meynell's renouncement is traditionally linked to a disappointment involving a man, in her case a priest who was her mentor and then moved away.[11]

Meynell's output, in contrast to Rossetti's, is very small: some one hundred forty poems, thirteen of which were not reprinted when she issued her *Collected Poems* in 1913, and five of which were never printed in her lifetime. That her output over the course of a long life

(1847–1923) is small is not surprising, considering the fact that she mothered eight children and was so active in social causes; she would, in fact, serve as a memorable example for Tillie Olsen's thesis in *Silences*. Of the one hundred forty poems, a high proportion—twenty-two—are specifically about the nature and purpose of poetry.[12] The overriding theme of all her poetry is that which *is not*, absent or silent: a future that has not yet come, an experience that is unarticulated, "sealed in silence," or articulated differently, in some *unvoiced* way. In the poems about poetry she is concerned specifically with *a*) the problem of precursors, the language that inhabits her without her knowledge or her will, an "immortality" that presses "heavily on this little head," and *b*) the poets "unborn and unrevealed," in relation to whom she is like the maid who found Orpheus' lyre, an instrument that she does not know how to play, and that signifies the death of one tradition and the birth of another. That tradition might very well have to do with previously unvoiced subjects that Meynell herself ventures: the complexity of motherhood, the unique horrors of world war and how it consternates parentage. There is much, then, that has been said, that has not been said, and that remains to be said, and Meynell sees herself as someone on the outposts, marking out the undiscovered territory.

While Meynell is more forward-looking than Rossetti in this respect, there are important ways in which their views of the unvoiced in poetry converge. In "The Courts," for instance, Meynell articulates a traditional Christian view of the limits of language, claiming that while similes are "golden doors," on the other side of language lies the "ultimate poetry," which is "plain, behind oracles," and "past / All symbols, simple," the song "some loaded poets reach at last" (p. 58). To renounce, then, to seek the minimal, is to approach closer to the ultimate poetry. In a similar vein, Meynell writes about language in "The Lord's Prayer" in a way that strongly recalls Rossetti's attitude toward language in her devotional poetry. Meynell justifies the reiteration of the words of the prayer—"forgive," "give," "lead us not"—because merely by speaking them we give voice to an unknown meaning that will come "shuddering through the paradox of prayer" (p. 76). But Meynell's ultimate poetry is not simply the unvoiced divine All; it is also linked deeply to the "unpublished blood," to the secrets of the body, even—that interiority which she calls "Thou inmost, ultimate / Council of judgement," that which the phenomena of the world seek out ("To the Body," p. 60). It is also the secret of the quotidian, the hidden poetry that is the undisclosed feminine. In "Unlinked," for instance, she is Tillie Olsen's quintessential woman writer who, if she gives up writing, will still be a poet, though poignantly unaware of her articulations: "Through my indifferent words of every day, / Scattered and all unlinked the rhymes shall ring, / And make my poem; and I shall not know" (p. 17). The "indifferent words" and the "unlinked" rhymes which make up her life-poem are like the words of the Lord's Prayer that, even stripped down to unlinked verbs— "forgive," "give," "lead us not"—let the meaning "shudder" through them.

Meynell does not remain mute, but she writes few poems, and poems which celebrate silence, absence, and negation. All of these, it seems, are one way of conveying the undisclosed feminine. Another way, more obvious, of course, of disclosing the undisclosed is to say it: to take on new subjects, as Meynell did in her poems of motherhood and of how mothers and children suffer in war. So, too, do other women poets of the nineteenth century who, while writing lyrics of ritualized renunciation and endurance, look beyond their own interior lives. Augusta Webster (1840–94), for instance, can turn out both lyric laments and dramatic monologues in which she challenges oppressive conventions: "that round / Of treadmill ceremonies, mimic tasks / We make our women's lives."[13] Another, less well known, contemporary, Emily Pfeiffer (1840–90), like Rossetti, chooses the "barbed blossom of the gorse" rather than the rose as her emblematic flower but also sees a kind of social and aesthetic progress, as she portrays the odalisque, with her parasitic dependence on men, fading as an artistic subject, while in her place "a dull-robed figure stands, / With wistful eyes, and earnest, grappling hands, / The working woman."[14] This kind of awareness of the possibilities for regrouping poetic energies is evident in the work of a later poet, Annie Matheson (1853–?), who in her "A Song of Women," juxtaposes the narrative voice with the lyric:

And if she be alive or dead,
That weary woman scarcely knows;
But back and forth her needle goes
In tune with throbbing heart and head.
Lo, where the leaning alders part,
White-bosomed swallows, blithe of heart,
Above still waters skim and dart.[15]

Here two kinds of music are juxtaposed: the woman's painful body rhythms and the kind of "humming noise" that Woolf characterizes. Here, also, what has been previously unvoiced in poetry—the changing experience of women in their culture—is set, without comment, against what has always been voiced in poetry, the unchanging beauties of nature that traditionally resolve and negate human suffering. This is what becomes of lyric rapture, then, when female experience is contextualized. But neither the wider inclusiveness nor the contextualization is Rossetti's primary mode; for her, the lyric voice, essentially without irony (although, as I have argued, in her case fundamentally parodic), is sufficient to render both female alienation and female transcendence. Occasionally, as in "In an Artist's Studio," she does bring previously unvoiced female experience into the poem; more usually, she allows glimpses of the hidden interiority of female experiences within the transparencies of her poetic language.

It is remarkable, surely, that Meynell's tribute to Rossetti says less about Rossetti's themes and images than about her forms—her technical achievement. In particular, Meynell chooses to talk about Rossetti's use of the mid-line rest, as in a line like "Is the night chilly and dark?"[16] What Meynell focuses on, then, is that which is unvoiced and unarticulated in Rossetti's poetry, that which inhabits the silence of a mid-line rest, that which is gathered in linked rhymes and words that are as charged and as transparent as "give," "forgive," "lead us not": the undisclosed feminine, the unpublished blood. In these practices Rossetti provides a model for women poets: how to renounce everything, including language, and still to persist in remaking that language into a female language, even to the extent of pausing for the silence that lets the meaning come "shuddering" through.

Notes
Select Bibliography
Index

Notes

Introduction

1. Quoted in Marya Zaturenska, *Christina Rossetti: A Portrait with Background* (New York: Macmillan, 1949), p. 294.

2. Arthur Waugh, "Christina Rossetti," *Reticence in Literature and Other Papers* (New York: E. P. Dutton, 1915), p. 152.

3. Virginia Woolf, "I Am Christina Rossetti," in *The Common Reader: Second Series* (London: Hogarth Press, 1932), pp. 237–44.

4. Janet Camp Troxell, ed., *Three Rossettis: Unpublished Letters to and from Dante Gabriel, Christina, William* (Cambridge, Mass.: Harvard University Press, 1937), p. 138.

5. William Michael Rossetti, ed., *The Poetical Works of Christina Georgina Rossetti* (1904; rpt. London: Macmillan, 1911), p. lxix.

6. Rossetti, *Works*, p. lvi.

7. A previously unpublished letter cited by Lona Mosk Packer in *Christina Rossetti* (Berkeley and Los Angeles: University of California Press, 1963), p. 394.

8. Sandra Gilbert and Susan Gubar, *The Madwoman in the Attic: The Woman Writer and Nineteenth-Century Literary Imagination* (New Haven: Yale University Press, 1979), pp. 539–80.

9. Luce Irigaray, *This Sex Which Is Not One*, trans. Catherine Porter with Carolyn Burke (Ithaca, N.Y.: Cornell University Press, 1985), p. 76 (originally published in French under the title *Ce Sexe qui n'en est pas un*, 1977, by Éditions de Minuit). Irigaray claims that by a playful or parodic repetition of masculine discourse, it is possible to uncover the hidden feminine operations within language.

There is, in an initial phase, perhaps only one "path," the one historically assigned to the feminine: that of *mimicry*. One must assume the feminine role deliberately. Which means already to convert a form of subordination into an affirmation, and thus to begin to thwart it. Whereas a direct feminine challenge to this condition means demanding to speak as a (masculine) "subject," that is, it means to postulate a relation to the intelligible that would maintain sexual indifference.

To play with mimesis is thus, for a woman, to try to recover the place of her exploitation by discourse, without allowing herself to be simply reduced to it. It means to resubmit herself—inasmuch as she is on the side of the "perceptible," of "matter"—to "ideas," in particular to ideas about herself, that are elaborated in/by a masculine logic, but so as to make "visible," by an effect of playful repetition, what was supposed to remain invisible: the cover-up of a possible operation of the feminine in language.

10. For an extended and brilliant discussion of the power of the female icon in Victorian culture, see Nina Auerbach's *Woman and the Demon: The Life of a Victorian Myth* (Cambridge, Mass.: Harvard University Press, 1982). While I agree with Auerbach's thesis that certain images of women in the nineteenth century were subversive images of power, I think that there is a significant difference between male-authored and female-authored representations of women. The status of women as signs or images has a long cultural history of denial of actual power in favor of symbolic power as manipulated by male subjects. I would argue that female writing, painting, and sculpture create images of women from a double consciousness, grounding the power of the image in a parodic mimetism. It is not so much the content of the image—whether it projects power or weakness, for instance—but the attitudes conveyed by discourse that has been shaped by female usage and female consciousness which determines whether or not it is an authentic image of female power. Such images can, in fact, be projected by male writers who are aware of what the image might signify for the female—and for the female within themselves.

11. Myra Jehlen, "Archimedes and the Paradox of Feminist Criticism," *Feminist Theory: A Critique of Ideology*, ed. Nannerl O. Keohane, Michele Z. Rosaldo, and Barbara C. Gelpi (Chicago: University of Chicago Press, 1982), pp. 210–14.

12. Simone de Beauvoir, *The Second Sex*, trans. and ed. H. M. Parshley (New York: Knopf, 1952), p. 210.

13. Frederic G. Kenyon, ed., *The Letters of Elizabeth Barrett Browning* (New York: Macmillan, 1897), I, 231–32.

14. Donald H. Reiman, in his introduction to Hemans' *Records of Woman* (New York: Garland Publishing, 1978), points out that although L. E. L. might have had a greater readership during the heyday of the literary annuals between 1824 and 1835, Hemans' number of editions outnumber that of all rival women poets in the nineteenth century (p. v.)

15. This characteristic has been pointed out to me by Donald H. Gray of Indiana University.

16. Rossetti, *Works*, p. xlix.

17. *Poetical Works of Letitia Elizabeth Landon* (London: Longman,

Brown, Green, and Longmans, 1855), I, 19. Subsequent citations are to this edition, and page numbers are given in the text.

18. *Miscellaneous Poems* in *The Poets and the Poetry of the Nineteenth Century*, ed. Alfred H. Miles (1907; rpt. New York: AMS Press, 1967), VIII, 109.

19. Landon, *Works*, pp. ix–x.

20. Gwynneth Hatton, "An Edition of the Unpublished Poems of Christina Rossetti, with a Critical Introduction and Interpretive Notes to All the Posthumous Poems," Master's thesis, Oxford University, 1955, p. 80. Subsequent citations are to this edition and are given in the text.

21. Dora Greenwell, *Selected Poems* (London: H. R. Allenson, 1906), p. 68.

22. Rossetti, *Works*, p. 377. Subsequent citations are to this edition, and page numbers are given in the text.

23. D. E. Enfield, *L. E. L.: A Mystery of the Thirties* (London: Hogarth Press, 1928), p. 67.

24. Enfield, p. 67.

25. Enfield, p. 42.

26. Enfield, p. 55.

27. Reginald Heber, *Poetical Works* (London: John Murray, 1841), p. 57.

28. Heber, p. 124.

29. Miles, VIII, 37.

30. Miles, VIII, 37.

31. Miles, VIII, 51.

32. Margaret Homans, *Women Writers and Poetic Identity: Dorothy Wordsworth, Emily Brontë, and Emily Dickinson* (Princeton, N.J.: Princeton University Press, 1980).

1. *An Exemplary Life*

1. *Time Flies: A Reading Diary* (London: Society for Promoting Christian Knowledge, 1885), p. 137.

2. *Time Flies*, p. 45.

3. Sigmund Freud, *The Complete Psychological Works: Standard Edition*, ed. and trans. James Strachey (London: Hogarth Press and the Institute of Psycho-Analysis, 1976), XXII, 121.

4. Lona Mosk Packer, *Christina Rossetti* (Berkeley and Los Angeles: University of California Press, 1963) p. 10.

5. Oswald Doughty, *A Victorian Romantic: Dante Gabriel Rossetti*, 2d ed. (London, 1960), p. 29.

6. Brian and Judy Dobbs, *Dante Gabriel Rossetti: An Alien Victorian* (London: Macdonald and Jane's, 1977), p. 8.

7. Dobbs, p. 7.

8. R. D. Waller, *The Rossetti Family: 1824–1854* (Manchester: Manchester University Press, 1932), p. 41.

9. William Holman Hunt, *Pre-Raphaelitism and the Pre-Raphaelite Brotherhood* (London, 1905), I, 154–55.

10. Packer, p. 1.

11. Waller, p. 152.

12. Stanley Weintraub, *Four Rossettis: A Victorian Biography* (New York: Weybright and Talley, 1977), p. 4.

13. Waller, p. 172.

14. Waller, pp. 50–51.

15. Packer, p. 1.

16. Packer, p. 2.

17. Packer, p. 2.

18. William Michael Rossetti, *Some Reminiscences*, (New York: Scribner's, 1906), I, 16.

19. This is the line taken most recently by Georgina Battiscombe in *Christina Rossetti: A Divided Life* (London: Constable, 1981).

20. The chief exponent of this view is R. D. Waller.

21. Rossetti, *Some Reminiscences*, I, 31.

22. Rossetti, *Some Reminiscences*, I, 25.

23. Weintraub, p. 7.

24. Packer, p. 23.

25. Packer, pp. 18–23.

26. Rossetti, *Some Reminiscences*, I, 35.

27. Rossetti, *Some Reminiscences*, I, 39.

28. Packer, p. 20.

29. Mackenzie Bell, *Christina Rossetti: A Biographical and Critical Study* (1898; rpt. New York: Haskell House, 1971), p. 20.

30. Battiscombe, p. 31.

31. Battiscombe, p. 56.

32. Battiscombe, p. 56.

33. Gilbert and Gubar, pp. 249–54.

34. Battiscombe, p. 92.

35. *The Family Letters of Christina Georgina Rossetti*, ed. William Michael Rossetti (New York: Scribner's, 1908), p. 29.

36. W. Bell Scott, *Autobiographical Notes*, ed. W. Minto (London: Osgood, 1892), I, 245.

37. The most important of these is David Sonstroem's *Rossetti and the Dark Lady* (Middletown, Conn.: Wesleyan University Press, 1970).

38. William remarked that for all that he and she lived in the same house together until 1876, he never saw her in the act of composing (Bell, p. 146).

39. Bell, p. 146.

40. In 1875, Macmillan was to write, "She is a true artist and will live" (*The*

Rossetti-Macmillan Letters, ed. Lona Mosk Packer [Berkeley and Los Angeles: University of California Press, 1963], p. 116).
41. William Michael Rossetti ed., *Rossetti Papers, 1862–1870* (London: Sands and Co., 1903), p. 88.
42. Troxell, p. 143.
43. Rossetti, *Some Reminiscences* II, 343–57.
44. Sandra Gilbert, "From *Patria* to *Matria*: Elizabeth Barrett Browning's Risorgimento," *PMLA,* 99, No. 2 (1984).
45. *The Diary of William Michael Rossetti: 1870–1873* ed. Odette Bornand (Oxford and New York: Oxford University Press, 1977), p. 127.
46. *Time Flies,* p. 213.
47. *Rossetti-Macmillan Letters,* p. 123.
48. *Rossetti-Macmillan Letters,* p. 123, n. 2.
49. *Family Letters,* p. 103.
50. *Family Letters,* p. 106.
51. *Family Letters,* p. 168.
52. *Rossetti-Macmillan Letters,* p. 113.
53. *Rossetti-Macmillan Letters,* p. 114.
54. *Rossetti-Macmillan Letters,* p. 133–35.
55. *Rossetti-Macmillan Letters,* p. 137.
56. *Rossetti-Macmillan Letters,* p. 135.
57. *Rossetti-Macmillan Letters,* p. 154.
58. *Family Letters,* p. 65.
59. *Family Letters,* p. 60.
60. Adrienne Rich, "Vesuvius at Home: The Power of Emily Dickinson," *Shakespeare's Sisters: Feminist Essays on Women Poets,* ed. Sandra M. Gilbert and Susan Gubar (Bloomington: Indiana University Press, 1979), p. 101.

2. Goblin Market: *Dearth and Sufficiency*

1. W. M. Rossetti, ed., *Ruskin: Rossetti: Preraphaelitism* (London: George Allen, 1899), p. 258.
2. David H. Richter, in *Fable's End: Completeness and Closure in Rhetorical Fiction* (Chicago: University of Chicago Press, 1974), discusses two types of "apologue," the fable and the allegory: the allegorical parable contains one-to-one correspondences between the fiction and the external world; the fable, like the parable of the Good Samaritan, is a "rhetorical fiction" in which "each detail is chosen to make us understand something in the external world," but the individual details cannot be detached from the fiction and given one-to-one correspondences with the external world (pp. 13–16). By this definition, a useful one, *Goblin Market* would belong to the category of "rhetorical fiction," or fable, thus requiring no allegorical exegesis of details.

3. Stephen Prickett, *Victorian Fantasy* (Bloomington: Indiana University Press, 1979), p. 72.

4. Prickett, p. 106.

5. Maureen Duffy provides the most extensive treatment of the poem's erotic dynamics in *The Erotic World of Faery* (London: Hodder and Stoughton, 1972), pp. 285–98.

6. See headnote to poem, Rossetti, *Works*, p. 459.

7. *The Poems of Tennyson*, ed. Christopher Ricks, (London and Harlow: Longmans, Green, 1969), p. 1463.

8. Packer, p. 145.

9. Ellen Moers, *Literary Women* (Garden City, N.Y.: Doubleday, 1976), pp. 164–72.

10. Moers, p. 105.

11. Moers, p. 102.

12. *Goblin Market*, introduction by Germaine Greer (New York: Stonehill Publishing, 1975), pp. xxx–xxxiii.

13. Gilbert and Gubar, *Madwoman*, p. 567.

14. Gilbert and Gubar, *Madwoman*, p. 571.

15. Gilbert and Gubar, *Madwoman*, p. 573.

16. "Paradise," p. 180; "The Heart Knoweth Its Own Bitterness," p. 192; "Whatsoever is right, that shall ye receive," p. 194.

17. Freud. In *The Complete Psychological Works*, xv, 160, Freud makes the philological point that in several languages there is a connection between "wood" and "raw material," with the Latin "materia" being derived from "mater," or mother. Freud says, "the material out of which anything is made is, as it were, a mother to it." In this view, there is a good case for regarding the tree as a female symbol.

18. Gilbert and Gubar, *Madwoman*, p. 567.

19. See Isaiah xxxv.1 for the flowering of the wilderness: "and the desert shall rejoice and blossom as a rose."

20. Rossetti's interest in the theme is borne out by the fact that she wrote two poems on the Babylonian exile, one in 1861, and one in 1864.

21. "The longing of my heart cries out to Thee, / The hungering thirsting longing of my heart" (*Works*, p. 269); "Hungering and thirsting for that blessed hour" (*Works*, p. 260); "Upward I look with eyes that fail to see, / Athirst for future light and present grace" (*Works*, p. 227).

22. The self who is "athirst" longs for God as an "unreturning torrent to Thy sea," and God is the "gulf and fountain of my love," "the measureless ocean for my rill" (*Works*, p. 227). We humans are like rivers that seek a sea "they cannot fill / But are themselves filled full in its embraces, / Absorbed, at rest" (*Works*, p. 276).

23. See G. B. Tennyson, *Victorian Devotional Poetry: The Tractarian Mode* (Cambridge, Mass.: Harvard University Press, 1981), pp. 198–203, for

an account of the doctrine of Reserve, and for an analysis of the ways in which Rossetti was and was not a Tractarian poet.

24. The fruit tree, especially, in its capacity to re-create itself through the fruit "whose seed is in itself," is a natural symbol for the self that would generate its own integrity (Genesis i.12).

3. The Female Pose: Model and Artist, Spectacle and Witness

1. *In Memoriam*, LXX.

2. Elizabeth Barrett Browning, *Sonnets from the Portuguese*, XXXIX, *The Complete Works*, ed. Charlotte Porter and Helen A. Clarke, III (1900; rpt. New York: AMS Press, 1973).

3. The alienated experience of self can be intensified by the actual experience of being looked at. The art critic John Berger, echoing Simone de Beauvoir's distinctions, describes woman as split between the surveyor and the surveyed; the surveyor part watches the surveyed in order to exemplify how the whole self is to be treated. In so exemplifying herself, woman "turns herself into an object—and most particularly an object of vision: a sight" (*Ways of Seeing* [New York: Penguin, 1977], pp. 46–47).

4. Alexander Welsh, *The City of Dickens* (Oxford: Clarendon Press, 1971), pp. 182–85.

5. "Tintern Abbey" l. 120, *The Poetical Works of Wordsworth*, ed. Thomas Hutchinson, rev. Ernest de Selincourt (Oxford: Oxford University Press, 1936, 1950).

6. The examples are obvious and many, ranging from Sidney's, Spenser's and Shakespeare's sonnet sequences to light "songs" by poets like Waller, Dryden, and Matthew Prior, addressed to countless Phillises, Chlorises, Delias, and Chloës. The tradition also generates its own parodies, by poets like Sackville and Gay, for instance, and more serious diatribes against the folly and artifice of female beauty by Pope and Swift. I do not mean to suggest that there is a uniform and continuous tradition but, rather, to emphasize that there are many available models for apostrophizing female beauty in general, the female face in particular. By the nineteenth century, the mode has become both highly stylized and cloyingly sentimental, as in Tennyson's early portraits of "Lillian," "Isabel," "Adeline," "Claribel," etc.

7. Gilbert and Gubar, *Madwoman* p. 564.

8. In *Aurora Leigh*, the heroine's authentication of her poetic vocation is bound up with a crucial encounter in which Aurora recognizes the face and speaking voice of the "lost" and "fallen" Marian Erle.

9. See Katherine Jordan Lochnan, "Images of Confinement," *Victorian Studies Bulletin*, 2 (December 1978), 1–4, for a discussion of how Pre-Raphaelite paintings represent their subjects as "imprisoned in a tower, cramped by a frame, or confined within a two-dimensional space."

10. Bell, p. 53.

11. *Maude: Prose and Verse*, ed. R. W. Crump (Hamden, Conn: Archon, 1976), pp. 30–31.

12. Bell, p. 19.

13. Bell, p. 20.

14. Edmund Gosse, *Critical Kit-Kats* (London: W. Heinemann, 1896), p. 156.

15. For a riveting image of female horror see Dante Gabriel's "The Orchard Pit": "Life's eyes are gleaming from her forehead fair, / And from her breasts the ravishing eyes of Death" (*The Works of Dante Gabriel Rossetti*, ed. William M. Rossetti [London: Ellis, 1911], p. 239).

16. Packer, p. 222.

4. Self-Sisters: The Rhetorical Crisis

1. Winston Weathers, "Christina Rossetti: The Sisterhood of Self," *Victorian Poetry*, 3 (Spring 1965), 81–89.

2. Weathers, pp. 81, 84.

3. For an overview of nineteenth-century divided consciousness, see Masao Miyoshi, *The Divided Self* (New York: New York University Press, 1969), pp. i–xix.

4. Brian and Judy Dobbs discuss Mrs. Rossetti's stern and dominating personality in *Dante Gabriel Rossetti*, pp. 1–15.

5. *The Poetical Works* are dedicated to her mother, her "first Love . . . on whose knee / I learnt love lore." In the decade 1876 to 1886 she wrote a series of valentines to her mother, the first of which contains an indication of Mrs. Rossetti's family role as judge: "Endearing rectitude to those who watch / The verdict of your face" (Rossetti, *Works*, p. 391).

6. In carrying out these sisterly functions, Christina Rossetti performs an erotic role for Dante Gabriel. See Alexander Welsh's discussion of the crucial importance of the conjugal family in the emotional life of the individual in the Victorian age and the conflation of roles of sister and wife (pp. 156–63).

7. Bell cites a Mr. Clayton, who was convinced that it was from "'the fascinating mystery and soft melancholy of his sister's face,' that Dante Gabriel gained that impulse towards the sad female face so noticeable in the pictorial work of his whole career" (p. 20).

8. Weintraub, p. 5.

9. Otto Rank, *The Double*, ed. Harry Tucker, Jr. (Chapel Hill: University of North Carolina Press, 1971), p. 86.

10. Weintraub comments that Dante Gabriel "almost ended the Brotherhood before it had even begun by also nominating Christina" (p. 29).

11. Freud, *The Complete Psychological Works*, XIV, 85.

12. Charles Maturin, *Women: Pour et Contre* (Edinburgh: Constable, 1818).

13. As Diane D'Amico illustrates, Maturin's influence extends to at least

three other dramatic monologues, and Rossetti's use of his themes illuminates basic dilemmas of conflict and choice in her own work. See "Christina Rossetti: the Maturin Poems," *Victorian Poetry*, 19, No. 2 (Summer 1981).

14. Maturin, p. 408.

15. Thomas Percy, *Reliques of Ancient English Poetry* (Edinburgh, 1864).

16. Packer, p. 117.

17. Packer, p. 118.

18. From a letter of Christina Rossetti's it appears that Dante Gabriel objected to the "realism" of "The Iniquity . . . ," its "coarse" subject, incredible as that judgment may seem to modern readers. See Troxell, pp. 142–43.

19. The mother-child relation here bears comparison with the mother-child relation in Elizabeth Barrett Browning's *Aurora Leigh*, where Marian Erle, the "lowborn" woman, welcomes her illegitimate child (a son) and gladly forms a little community comprising herself, Aurora, and the child. See also Rossetti's "Cousin Kate," in which the "lowborn" mother boasts of her "gift," the child that is her "shame" and her "pride." It is significant that in these instances the children who are acknowledged by their mothers are boys: they constitute a claim on the father. Girls are not "useful" in this way.

20. Ellen Moers, in a seminar presented at SUNY Albany in the spring of 1977, pointed out this capacity in female heroines, notably Jane Eyre, to transcend their cramped environs.

21. Weathers, p. 88.

22. Weathers, p. 88.

5. From Renunciation to Valediction: The Ongoing Crisis

1. It is Jacques Lacan's theory that the discovery of absence or lack motivates speech. Lacan bases this hypothesis on Freud's interpretation of the child's game of "Fort/Da" in which the child makes a symbolic object appear and disappear. In Lacan's view, the lack of this object stimulates the desire to reunite with it, and language flows from the effort to fill the gap. See Lacan's *Écrits: A Selection*, trans. Alan Sheridan (London: Tavistock, 1977), pp. 103–12.

2. This is the theory advanced by Nancy Chodorow in *The Reproduction of Mothering* (Berkeley: University of California Press, 1978).

3. Ellen Moers points out the usefulness of angelic lovers for woman poets. The angel figure is "at once sexy, of no particular sex, and independent of gravity" (p. 169).

4. "And let the Spirit and the bride say Come" (Revelation xxi.17).

5. As well as Matthew xxvi.39, Mark xiv.36, Luke xxii.42, and John xviii.11, see also Isaiah ii. 17: "Awake, awake, stand up, O Jerusalem, which hast drunk at the hand of the Lord the cup of his fury; thou hast drunken the dregs of the cup of trembling and wrung them out."

6. Packer, p. 127.

7. Miyoshi discusses the meaning of the incest theme in Romantic literature as a metaphor for "dual and undecided identity." "Given the time-honored sense of the family as an extension of self, a larger self in a sense, the incestuous act becomes the moment for the self meeting with itself" (p. 11).

8. Packer, p. 129.

9. Packer considers "the naked truth" to be Rossetti's realization that Scott either did not love her at all or did in his "own way." In Packer's view, the transition in mood between "Memory" and "A Birthday" can only be accounted for if the poems are considered items in an "emotional autobiography" (pp. 113–14).

10. Freud mentions this close connection between the unfamiliar and the familiar in manifestations of the "uncanny" (*Complete Psychological Works*, XVII, 224.

11. This particular "look" is similar to the look of "Might-have-been," the dead self who returns to regard the speaker with "cold commemorative eyes" in Dante Gabriel's "A Superscription" (*Works*, p. 107).

Conclusion

1. Virginia Woolf, *A Room of One's Own* (New York: Harcourt, Brace, 1929), pp. 19–41.

2. *The Collected Poems of Philip Bourke Marston* (Boston: Roberts Brothers, 1892; rpt. New York: AMS Press, 1973), p. 118.

3. Marston, p. 118.

4. Miles, p. 203.

5. Jerome McGann, *Swinburne: An Experiment in Criticism* (Chicago: University of Chicago Press, 1972), pp. 63–91.

6. McGann, p. 181.

7. McGann, p. 176.

8. Alice Meynell, *Essays* (1947; Westport, Conn: Greenwood Press, 1970), p. 171.

9. "The 'Poetess of Poets': Alice Meynell Rediscovered," *Women's Studies*, 7 (1980), 111–26.

10. *The Poems of Alice Meynell* (London: Hollis and Carter, 1947), p. 13. All citations are to this edition, and subsequent references are given in the text.

11. June Badeni, *The Slender Tree: A Life of Alice Meynell* (Padstow, Cornwall: Tabb House, 1981), pp. 40–41.

12. These are: "Singers to Come," "The Moon to the Sun," "Unlinked," "A Song of Derivations," "West Wind in Winter," "The Two Poets," "Two Boyhood," (Dante and Wordsworth), "A Poet's Wife," "The Courts," "The Lord's Prayer," "The Poet and his Book," "The Laws of Verse," "The Question," "The Return to Nature in Poetry," "To Silence," "The English

Metres," "To Antiquity," "The Poet to the Birds," "To Any Poet," "A Shattered Lute," "The Day to the Night: The Poet sings to His Poet."

13. Miles, p. 137.
14. Miles, p. 175.
15. Miles, p. 334.
16. "Christina Rossetti," *New Review*, 12 (February 1895), 205.

Select Bibliography

The following is a select bibliography with emphasis on recent criticism and criticism with a feminist slant. The interested reader is referred to Rebecca W. Crump's *Christina Rossetti: A Reference Guide* (Boston: G. K. Hall, 1976), which contains references up to 1973.

Barr, Alan P. "Sensuality Survived: Christina Rossetti's *Goblin Market*." *English Miscellany*, 28–29 (1979–80), 267–82.

Battiscombe, Georgina. *Christina Rossetti: A Divided Life*. London: Constable, 1981.

Brownley, Martine Watson. "Love and Sensuality in Christina Rossetti's *Goblin Market*." *Essays in Literature*, 6 (1979), 179–86.

Connor, Stephen, "'Speaking Likenesses': Language and Repetition in Christina Rossetti's *Goblin Market*." *Victorian Poetry*, 22, No. 4 (Winter 1984), 439–48.

D'Amico, Diane. "Christina Rossetti: The Maturin Poems." *Victorian Poetry*, 19, No. 2 (Summer 1981), 117–37.

De Vitas, A. A. "*Goblin Market*: Fairy Tale and Reality." *Journal of Popular Culture*, 1 (Spring 1968), 418–26.

Diehl, Joanne Feit, "'Come Slowly—Eden': An Exploration of Women Poets and Their Muse." *Signs*, 3 (1978), 572–87.

Duffy, Maureen. *The Erotic World of Faery*. London: Hodder and Stoughton, 1972.

Fass, Barbara. "Christina Rossetti and St. Agnes' Eve." *Victorian Poetry*, 14 (1976), 33–46.

Gilbert, Sandra M., and Susan Gubar. *The Madwoman in the Attic: The Woman Writer and the Nineteenth-Century Literary Imagination*. New Haven: Yale University Press, 1979.

Goldberg, Gail Lynn. "Dante Gabriel Rossetti's 'Revising Hand': His Illustrations for Christina Rossetti's Poems." *Victorian Poetry*, 20, Nos. 3–4 (Autumn–Winter 1982), 145–59.

Greer, Germaine, introd. *Goblin Market.* By Christina Rossetti. New York: Stonehill Publishing, 1975.

Jiminez, Nilda, comp. *The Bible and the Poetry of Christina Rossetti: A Concordance.* Westport, Conn.: Greenwood Press, 1979.

Kaplan, Cora. "The Indefinite Disclosed: Christina Rossetti and Emily Dickinson." In *Women Writing and Writing about Women.* Ed. Mary Jacobus. New York: Barnes and Noble, 1979.

Kent, David. "Sequence and Meaning in Christina Rossetti's *Verses* (1893)." *Victorian Poetry,* 17 (1979), 259–64.

Leavy, Barbara Fass. "Christina Rossetti, Anglo-Italian Woman." *Italian Americana,* 3 (1977), 205–25.

McGann, Jerome J. "Christina Rossetti's Poems: A New Edition and a Revaluation." *Victorian Studies,* 23 (1980), 237–54.

————. "The Religious Poetry of Christina Rossetti." *Critical Inquiry,* 10, No. 1 (September 1983), 127–44.

Mermin, Dorothy. "Heroic Sisterhood in *Goblin Market.*" *Victorian Poetry,* 21, No. 2 (Summer 1983), 107–18.

Michie, Helena. "The Battle for Sisterhood: Christina Rossetti's Strategies for Control in Her Sisters Poems." *Journal of Pre-Raphaelite Studies,* 13, No. 2 (May 1983), 38–55.

Moers, Ellen. *Literary Women.* Garden City, N.Y.: Doubleday, 1976.

Packer, Lona Mosk. *Christina Rossetti.* Berkeley and Los Angeles: University of California Press, 1963.

Prickett, Stephen. *Victorian Fantasy.* Bloomington: Indiana University Press, 1979.

Rosenblum, Dolores. "Christina Rossetti: The Inward Pose." In *Shakespeare's Sisters: Feminist Essays on Women Poets.* Ed., with an introd. by Sandra M. Gilbert and Susan Gubar. Bloomington: Indiana University Press, 1979.

————. "Christina Rossetti's Religious Poetry: Watching, Looking, Keeping Vigil." *Victorian Poetry,* 20, No. 1 (1982), 33–50.

Tennyson, G. B. *Victorian Devotional Poetry: The Tractarian Mode.* Cambridge, Mass.: Harvard University Press, 1981.

Walsh, Eve. "A Reading of Christina Rossetti's 'Three Stages.'" *Journal of Pre-Raphaelite Studies,* 2, No. 1 (1978), 27–35.

Weathers, Winston. "Christina Rossetti: The Sisterhood of Self." *Victorian Poetry,* 3 (Spring 1965), 81–89.

Index

Burne-Jones, Sir Edward, 4
"By the Waters of Babylon"
    (1861), 79
"By Way of Remembrance"
    (1870), 98

*Called to be Saints: The Minor Fes-
    tivals Devotionally Studied* (1881),
    57, 58
"Cannot Sweeten" (1866), 94, 95,
    99, 100
Cayley, Charles B., 40, 41–42
"Charlie is my Darling"
    (Oliphant), 17
"Chilly Night, A" (1856), 202
Chodorow, Nancy, 233n.2
Christian symbolism: and ana-
    logue for isolation of self, 137;
    in *Goblin Market*, 66, 76, 87,
    96, 104, 109; stoicism in, 6; of
    suffering, 13
Clayton, Mr., 232n.7
Coleridge, Samuel Taylor, 129
Collected Poems (Meynell, 1913),
    218
Collinson, James, 40–41, 43
Commonplace (1870), 53, 55
"Consider the Lilies of the Field"
    (1853), 78
"Convent Threshold, The" (1858),
    11, 175n, 190–93, 194
Cornforth, Fanny, 44
"Courts, The" (Meynell), 219
"Cousin Kate" (1859), 56–57, 151,
    159, 233n.19
Crump, Rebecca, 58

D'Amico, Diane, 232–33n.13
Daydream, The (D. G. Rossetti),
    116, 120, 123
"Day-Dreams" (1857), 120–22, 123,
    124–25, 133
"Dead before Death" (1854), 111,
    134, 175n, 200–201

De Beauvoir, Simone, 7, 8, 148,
    156, 231n.3
"Descent from the Cross" (B.
    1882), 138
Dickinson, Emily: compared to
    C. Rossetti, 3, 4, 45, 100, 130;
    as contemporary of C. Ros-
    setti, 3, 61
"Dirge, A" (1852), 101, 127
Divided consciousness, 146,
    232n.3
Dobbs, Brian, 29, 232n.4
Dobbs, Judy, 29, 232n.4
Dodsworth, William, 39
Donna Della Finestra, La (D. G.
    Rossetti), 120
"Dream-Land" (1850), 45, 127, 128,
    129, 211
"Dream Love" (1854), 201
"Dumb Friend, A" (1863), 102

"Easter Day" (1886), 98
Ecce Ancilla Domini (D. G. Ros-
    setti), 117
"Echo" (1854), 19, 175n, 201
Ellis, F. S., as publisher of C.
    Rossetti, 52–53
"End, An" (1850), 45
"Endurance" (ca. 1850), 175, 184–
    85, 195
Endurance, poetry of: in C. Ros-
    setti's poetry, 15; defined, 5; ex-
    cesses of, 10; and female sym-
    bolism, 6–7; in *Goblin Market*,
    70; in nineteenth century, 5–6;
    of Oliphant, 17–18; as response
    to patriarchal literary tradition,
    7–8
Enfield, D. E., 13–14
"Enrica, 1865" (1865), 50, 134
"En Route," 50
"Erinna" (Landon), 10, 12–13
"Eva" (1847), 153–54, 155
"Eye Hath Not Seen" 74–75